Contents

A LEVEL COMPUTING for AQA

Bob Reeves and Dave Fogg

Hodder & Stoughton

A MEMBER OF THE HODDER HEADLINE GROUP

Dedicated to:

Wendy, Jack and Harry Reeves.

Karen, Alice, Barnaby and Christopher Fogg.

Acknowledgements

The publishers would like to thank the following individuals, institutions and companies for permission to reproduce screenshots or photographs in this book. Every effort has been made to trace ownership of copyright. The publishers would be happy to make arrangements with any copyright holder whom it has not been possible to contact:

Bob Battersby/BDI Images (pages 4, 92 'courtesy of Yamaha', 99, 104, 105, 112, 181, 230 bottom 'courtesy of Access Keyboards', 243), Corbis (pages 113 both, 120, 218), Hewlett Packard (page 231), Hodder and Stoughton (pages 100, 230), Mike Bull (pages 119), Science Photo Library (pages 2, 3, 229).

Orders: please contact Bookpoint Ltd, 130 Milton Park, Abingdon, Oxon OX14 4SB. Telephone: (44) 01235 827720. Fax: (44) 01235 400454. Lines are open from 9.00–6.00, Monday to Saturday, with a 24 hour message answering service. You can also order through our website www.hodderheadline.co.uk.

British Library Cataloguing in Publication Data
A catalogue record for this title is available from the British Library

ISBN 0 340 816554

First Published 2004
Impression number   10 9 8 7 6 5 4 3 2 1
Year   2007 2006 2005 2004

Copyright © 2004 Bob Reeves, Dave Fogg

Typeset by Pantek Arts Ltd, Maidstone, Kent
Printed in Great Britain for Hodder & Stoughton Educational, a division of Hodder Headline Plc, 338 Euston Road, London NW1 3BH by Arrowsmiths Ltd

CONTENTS

Introduction

This book is designed to cover the AQA GCE Computing specification for Advanced Subsidiary (AS) and Advanced (A2) modules. It includes explanations, diagrams, summary questions, study questions, past exam questions, case studies, a glossary and coursework advice. It assumes no prior study of Computing or ICT.

Section One is designed as a general introduction for all students. Thereafter the sections follow the topics covered by the four main theory modules in the specification:

Module 1 – Computer systems, programming and network concepts

> Computer systems
> Programming
> Information and data representation
> Communication and networking

Module 2 – Principles of hardware, software and applications

> Applications and effects
> Files and databases
> Operating systems
> Hardware devices

Module 4 – Processing and programming techniques

> Machine level architecture
> Programming concepts
> Machine operation and assembly language
> Operating systems

Module 5 – Advanced system development

> Applications and effects
> Files and databases
> Systems development
> Hardware devices
> Networking

There are also chapters that specifically cover the requirements of project work (Modules 3 and 6) including advice on selecting and documenting a project.

HOW TO USE THIS BOOK

Several topics are covered at AS and again in more depth at A2. Where this is the case, all of the chapters are in the same section of the book for easy reference. A2 chapters are identifiable by the word 'advanced' in the title of the chapter. AS students may skip these in the first year or may choose to extend their understanding by reading the A2 chapters as well. A2 students may benefit from a refresher by re-reading the AS chapters.

CODE EXAMPLES

This book is *not* intended to be a guide to any particular programming or query language. Examples of code are included to demonstrate specific theoretical points and are not designed to be copied and pasted into any particular application. The examples are based on Visual Basic, Prolog and SQL but have been edited or written in pseudo-code for clarity.

COMMUNICATIONS AND NETWORKING

This book includes a major section on the latest developments in a constantly changing world. Topics have been grouped under five main headings: Communication methods, Local Area Networks, Wide Area Networks, the Internet and the World Wide Web. You should note that some concepts fall under more than one heading. For example, 'broadband' is explained in Chapter 22 (Communication methods) although it is also related to Wide Area Networks and the Internet. Appendix 1 is a look-up table of all concepts covered in this section identifying which other topics they are also related to.

QUESTIONS

Three types of questions have been used:

Summary questions: these are to test your knowledge of the chapter. All of these questions can be answered directly from the text.

Study questions: the answers to these questions are not necessarily in the text and may require further research or discussion. Some of these questions may go outside the knowledge required for A level.

Examination questions: Extensive use has been made of many of the AQA and AEB past papers currently available. Year and paper references have been included for all questions. Mark schemes are available from the exam board.

CHAPTER:1
Computer hardware

Definition of a computer

A computer is any machine or device that controls and processes information. The word computer also implies that the 'machine' is electronic or digital. In simple terms this means that it will contain a microprocessor that can be programmed to control the device. Microprocessors are made up of microscopic electronic circuits and belong to a group of devices commonly referred to as 'chips'.

This definition is deliberately broad. It is important as A Level students that you realise that your PC (Personal Computer) is only one type of computer and that there are other types in common use. For example, you could look at any number of devices and describe them as computers – a burglar alarm, a microwave oven and a mobile phone all fit this definition. Computers used in this context are referred to as 'embedded systems' as the chip is embedded within another device.

The microcomputer

The correct term for a PC is the microcomputer. The 'micro' refers to the fact that it contains a microprocessor. There are now dozens of manufacturers producing PCs in a variety of formats. The most common are the 'desktop' or 'tower unit'. Laptops are increasingly popular as they are portable and lightweight yet are just as powerful as desktop systems. The palmtop or personal digital assistant (PDA) is also becoming popular due to its small size. Although they can't do everything they still contain many of the features of a larger PC including the ability to word-process and e-mail.

Another common definition of a PC is a 'system'. This refers to the fact that your PC will be made up of a number of devices and software packages. A basic PC will have a mouse, keyboard, monitor, floppy disk drive, printer and an operating system such as Windows or Linux. More advanced systems will also include peripherals such as a scanner, speakers, hard disk drive, CD drive, DVD drive, modem, digital camera, and a range of application software. Buying a new system has become a complicated process as the manufacturers will put different combinations of systems together at different prices. The system you buy will depend on what you want to use it for.

Mainframes, minicomputers and supercomputers

A mainframe is a large computer system only found in organisations which have large numbers of users. A mainframe computer comprises one very large computer which has a vast amount of processing power and storage capacity. Physically this will be much larger than a PC. In fact, mainframe computers are usually located in their own climate-controlled rooms. Such a computer will

Summary Question

1 What is a computer?

Photograph 1.1 **Mainframe computer**

contain all of the applications and data needed by an organisation.

Using cables, connections are made between the mainframe computer and hundreds of terminals. A terminal is usually made up of a keyboard, mouse and monitor which the user can use to access the mainframe computer. They are often referred to as 'dumb terminals' as they have no processing power of their own. They are simply a connection to the mainframe which provides all the processing power and storage capacity. In many cases, PCs are used as terminals to link to the mainframe.

Mainframes are costly to install and maintain but do provide an efficient way of providing computer access to hundreds of users at the same time. If you have studied computing prior to this course you will be familiar with networks. In many ways, a mainframe is similar to a PC network, the main difference being that a mainframe distributes computing resources from a central source whereas network users have local resources on their workstations.

The minicomputer is a smaller version of a mainframe. Whereas a mainframe can service hundreds of users, a minicomputer will be used in smaller organisations. Minicomputers are much more powerful than PCs though less powerful than full mainframes. Typically, a minicomputer will be used to service up to 50 users. Students often confuse minicomputers and micro-computers. A minicomputer is a mini version of a mainframe. A microcomputer is a PC. Minicomputers are becoming increasingly rare these days as most medium-sized organisations tend to use a network instead.

As the name implies, a supercomputer is not an ordinary computer. In fact, supercomputers have much more processing power than standard PCs. They use thousands of microprocessors so that complex processing can be carried out in less time.

Whereas PCs are built for general use, a supercomputer will probably be built for a specific application. These applications require enormous processing capability. For example, weather prediction requires masses of data to be analysed and graphically displayed very quickly; NASA needs information processed very quickly and in real time when they send missions into space.

Computer 'systems'

The term 'system' is often used to refer to the various physical components of your computer – the monitor, keyboard, etc. A computer system has two main elements: hardware and software. It is only when the two are combined that you create a fully working system. There is no point in having one without the other. Some definitions of a computer system add in a third vital element – the user.

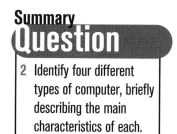

Summary
Question

2 Identify four different types of computer, briefly describing the main characteristics of each.

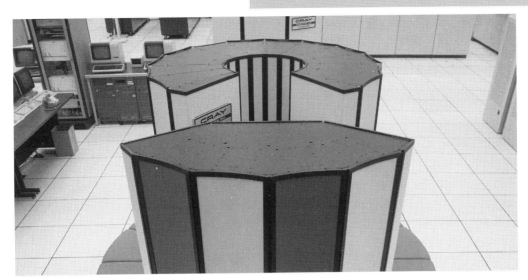

Photograph 1.2 **Supercomputer**

Hardware

Computer hardware is the physical components of the computer. Sometimes this is described as 'the parts you can touch'. This is not particularly helpful as many elements of hardware are contained inside your computer and can only be seen (or touched) by taking off the case. Therefore, it is important to distinguish between the internal components, which are the processing and storage devices, and external components, normally referred to as peripherals.

EXTERNAL COMPONENTS (PERIPHERALS)

The external components of hardware are the parts that you can touch, for example the monitor, mouse, keyboard, and printer. The external components are used either to get data into or out of the system. Consequently, they are referred to as input and output (I/O) devices. Some storage devices are also external, for example CD and DVD drives may be added as peripherals.

Input devices include the keyboard, mouse, scanner, digital camera and microphone. Output devices include the monitor, printer and speakers. There are other input and output devices and these are discussed in more detail with explanations as to how they work in Chapter 47.

INTERNAL COMPONENTS (PROCESSING AND STORAGE)

The internal hardware components are housed within the casing of the desktop or tower unit. The box itself is often referred to as the CPU or Central Processing Unit. This is not strictly correct as CPU really only refers to the processor. In fact, there are a number of hardware devices inside the casing including the processor, the hard disk, memory chips, sound cards, graphics cards and the circuitry required to connect all of these devices to each other and to the I/O devices. Additional storage devices such as floppy disks, and CD and DVD drives are usually housed within the computer case.

The capacity of storage devices and memory is an important factor when selecting and comparing components. The base unit of measurement is the byte, which, in simple terms, represents one keyboard character. Modern computers require measurements to be made in larger units as shown in the table below:

Unit	Abbreviation	Approximate size
Kilobyte	Kb	1000 bytes
Megabyte	Mb	1 million bytes
Gigabyte	Gb	1000 million bytes (1 billion bytes)
Terabyte	Tb	1000 billion bytes (1000 gigabytes)

It is very important to realise that these sizes are only approximate. The exact measurement is made in terms of the binary number system which is explained in Chapter 3.

Processor

The processor is the 'brains' of the computer. It handles all of the instructions that it receives from the user and from the hardware and software. For example, you may press 'A' on the keyboard in which case an electrical signal is sent through the cable into the 'port' at the back of the computer. This signal is routed through the processor which recognises the signal as an 'A'. It then sends a signal to the monitor which displays the letter.

Obviously, it is more complicated than this and the process of displaying a letter on a monitor would require the processor to carry out a number of processes which will be invisible to the user. The processor will also be receiving instructions from other programs and other devices at the same time. Your computer has only one processor so it must handle them all one after the other.

Physically, the processor is made up of a thin slice of silicon approximately 2 cm square. Using microscopic manufacturing techniques, the silicon is implanted with millions of transistors. Microscopic wires called buses connect groups of transistors together. The transistors are used to control the flow of electrical pulses that are timed via the computer's

Photograph 1.3 a micro-processor

clock. The pulses of electricity represent different parts of the instruction that the processor is carrying out. Each of these pulses is routed around the circuitry of these transistors at very high speeds. In theory a 3 GHz processor could process 3000 million instructions per second.

Consequently, the higher the clock speed of the processor, the faster it will carry out instructions and the faster your computer will work. Manufacturers of processors such as Intel and AMD bring out newer, faster chips each year. On average, processors double in clock speed every 18 months.

Memory

Memory is used to store data and instructions. It is connected to the processor which will *fetch* the data and instructions it needs from memory, *decode* the instructions and then *execute* them. Any new data created will be stored back into memory. Put simply, memory is a method of storage. There are two main types: RAM and ROM.

RAM – RANDOM ACCESS MEMORY

RAM is also known as the immediate access store (IAS), main memory or primary storage. It is temporary storage space that can be accessed very quickly. This means that applications such as word processors and spreadsheets will run at high speed. Speed of operation becomes more apparent when you use your computer for games or videos as these require more memory in order to refresh the graphics. Physically, RAM is a chip or series of chips on which the data is stored electronically. It is made up of millions of cells each of which has its own unique address. Each cell can contain either an instruction or some data. The cells can be accessed as they are needed by the processor, by referencing the address. That is they can be accessed randomly, hence the name. Because they are electronic they are able to be accessed quickly. However, RAM is volatile, which means that when you turn your computer off, all of the contents of RAM are lost.

Whenever a program is run on your computer, the entire program, or parts of it are loaded into RAM. For example, if you load a spreadsheet file, both the file and the spreadsheet application are stored in RAM. When you are creating formulae, these are stored temporarily in RAM. If you turn the computer off without saving it will close down the spreadsheet and your work will be lost.

The more memory you have, the more applications you can have loaded at any one time. However, memory chips are relatively expensive to manufacture compared to other forms of storage. Therefore, most PCs will have either 256 Mb or 512 Mb of RAM.

Like processors, manufacturers are always bringing out more powerful memory chips and the price of memory has actually fallen over the years. In 1997, 32 Mb was standard. By 2003, 512 Mb was standard. By the time you read this book, it will probably be at least double this amount. Software manufacturers are also bringing out new products all the time that take advantage of the larger memory available. You may have noticed this yourself as certain programs will not run on machines that do not have enough memory.

ROM – READ ONLY MEMORY

ROM is also a method of storing data and instructions. However, it is not volatile which means that the contents of ROM are not lost when you switch off. Unlike RAM, the user cannot alter the contents of ROM as it is read-only. ROM is used to store a limited number of instructions relating to the set-up of the computer. These settings are stored in the BIOS which stands for Basic Input/Output System.

When you switch on your computer it carries out a number of instructions. For example, it checks the hardware devices are plugged in and it loads parts of the operating system. All of these instructions are stored in ROM. The instructions are programmed into ROM by the manufacturer of the PC.

Hard disk

As we have seen, the user can use RAM to store programs and data. It gives the user high-speed access to their applications, but it is only temporary.

To get round this problem there needs to be some form of permanent storage. There are a number of devices, known as secondary storage devices, that will permanently store data. Internally, computers use a hard disk.

Hard disks work in a similar way to a CD in that they are flat disks that spin round while data is written to or read from them. The similarity ends there though. A hard disk is usually made up of a series of flat metallic disks stacked on top of each other. The surface of the disks stores the data magnetically. The disks spin at speed of approximately 12 000 rpm while a 'head' floats across the surface either writing to or reading data from different areas of the disk.

All applications and all data are stored on the hard disk. They are transferred from the hard disk into RAM when you need to use them. Accessing the data directly from the hard disk would make the computer too slow so the programs and files are transferred to RAM. When you close a program it simply removes it from memory.

When you save a file, it is saved on the hard disk. As you install more applications and save more files, you will fill up your hard disk. Manufacturers of hard disks bring out faster, larger capacity disks every year. The bigger the disk, the more data it can store. As multimedia applications and PC gaming have become more popular, the demand for higher capacity hard disks has grown. A typical hard disk at the time of writing would be around 40 Gb for a home PC. Hard disks are relatively cheap to manufacture which is why most computers will have several gigabytes of hard disk and only several megabytes of memory.

Summary Questions

3 Identify the three other terms that are commonly used to mean RAM.
4 Identify one advantage of increasing the amount of RAM on a PC.

Case study

Games consoles

Summary Questions

5 Describe the purpose of the following components:
(a) Processor;
(b) Memory;
(c) Hard disk.

6 Explain why it is necessary to have ROM, RAM and a hard disk within a computer system.

7 Identify one advantage of increasing the size of the hard disk.

You might be wondering why you need memory and a hard disk as they both appear to do the same thing – store data. Memory is very fast but expensive – also, it is only temporary. Hard disks are relatively slow to access, but cheap and permanent.

When you play on a CD-based games console you can see how it works.

When you buy a game it is all stored on the CD. When you run the game you will have to wait while the game loads. What it is doing is copying the appropriate parts of the game (usually the level you are on) from the CD onto the RAM chips in your console. You then play the game which operates at a suitable speed for realistic game-play. When you finish the level, it will unload the current level from RAM and load the next level from the CD into RAM and so on. This way you have the data permanently stored on the CD so it cannot be lost.

So why not run it straight off the CD and miss out RAM completely? Simply because the CD cannot spin fast enough to allow the game to be played at a reasonable speed. Exactly the same thing happens when you run any application on your PC – data is passed from the hard disk, in this case, into RAM and back again.

Study Questions

1. Identify six examples of embedded computers.

2. Identify the main characteristics of each of the following types of computer. For each, identify a suitable application:

(a) Mainframe;
(b) Embedded;
(c) Personal;
(d) Super.

3. Look at the advert on page 7 which shows a PC package which was considered to be reasonably high specification at the time this book was written.

Explain the following terms:

(a) 2 Ghz processor;
(b) 256Mb RAM;
(c) 40 Gb hard drive.

Using a magazine or the Internet, find the latest high specification PC system. Compare the price and the specification.

Product Description

IBM NetVista A30p 8310 – Pentium 4 2 GHz

£1040 inc VAT

Processor: 1 × Intel Pentium 4 2 GHz

RAM: 256 MB (installed) / 1 GB (max) – DDR SDRAM – non-parity – 133 MHz – DDR266/PC2100

Storage Hard Drive: 1 × 40 GB – standard – DMA/ATA-100 (Ultra)

Optical Storage: 1 × DVD-ROM – 48x (CD) / 16× (DVD) (read) – internal

Optical Storage (2nd): 1 × CD-RW – 40× (read) / 40× (write) / 12× (rewrite) – 5.25" × 1/2H

4. At one time it was common to supply application software on ROM. Explain the benefits of buying software this way to:

[a] the customer;

[b] the software manufacturer;

[c] What are the drawbacks to using software in this way?

[d] Why is software no longer supplied on ROM?

5. On a games console, explain why it can take over a minute to load a game.

Examination Questions

1.　(a)　A computer system is made up of hardware and software.
　　　　What is meant by:
　　　　(i) hardware;　　　　　　　　　　　　　　　　　　　　[1]
　　　　(ii) software?　　　　　　　　　　　　　　　　　　　　[1]

　　(b)　A home user wants to link up a stand-alone personal computer to the Internet.
　　　　(i) What computer hardware is required?　　　　　　　　[1]
　　　　(ii) What is the function of this hardware?　　　　　　　[2]

AQA June 2001 Module 1

CHAPTER: 2
Software

In the previous chapter we considered all of the physical components that go into making a computer. We also identified that the hardware was useless on its own unless we have some programs to run on it. Software is the general term used to describe all of the programs that we run on our computer. These programs contain instructions that the processor will carry out in order to complete various tasks.

This covers an enormous range of possibilities from standard applications, such as word processors, spreadsheets and databases, to more specific applications, such as web-authoring software and games. It also includes programs that the computer needs in order to manage all of its resources, such as file management and virus checking software. As users, we tend to be aware of the software that we use on a regular basis, yet this is only one part of the software that is on our computers.

The range of software is so great now that some classification is needed in order to make sense of it all. A first level of distinction is made between Application Software and System Software.

Summary
Question

1   What is software?

Application software

Application software refers to all of the programs that the user uses in order to complete a particular task. In effect, it is what users use their computers for. People do not buy computers for the sake of it, they buy them because they have a need to do something: write essays, e-mail, manage a business, create web pages, etc. To carry out any of these, application software is needed that has the necessary features.

There is a wide range of application software available and, in most cases, a number of different applications to choose from that complete the same task. For example, you need application software to access web pages on the Internet – it is called a browser. There are two main ones to choose from: Internet Explorer and Netscape Navigator. Both do the same thing although there are subtle differences between the two. When choosing application software, users must ensure that it has the features they need. If there are a number of choices (which there usually are), the selection depends on a number of factors which will be discussed in more detail in Chapter 30.

Application software can be subdivided into three categories: general purpose, special purpose and bespoke (custom).

GENERAL PURPOSE SOFTWARE

General purpose, or 'generic' software refers to applications that have a number of common uses among a range of different users. For example, a student may need an application in order to write essays while a secretary in a business needs to write business letters. The two users have different needs but they can both be met with a piece of general purpose software – in this case, a word processor.

The most common general purpose applications are:

- **Word-processing: used to create text-based documents of all kinds including letters, essays, legal documents, contracts, etc;**

- **Spreadsheets: used to handle numbers and calculations, for example, company accounts, sales figures, etc;**

- **Databases: used to store and search information for a particular purpose, for example, customer records, criminal records, dental records;**

- **Desktop publishing: used to create a variety of publications, for example, magazines, newspapers and brochures;**

- **Presentation software: used to create multimedia presentations usually to be displayed as a slide show;**

- **Graphics: used to create and display any kind of pictorial information, for example, line drawings, paint packages and animations.**

These six standard applications (or permutations of these six) are often supplied together either as an 'integrated package', or as a 'software suite'. They are known better by their brand names, for example, Microsoft Office and Lotus SmartSuite. However, as A Level students you should always refer to software by its generic name rather than its brand name.

In addition to the above there are numerous other general purpose applications, for example, web browsers, e-mail software, web page design software and CAD/CAM software.

SPECIAL PURPOSE SOFTWARE

Special purpose software is designed to carry out a specific task rather than providing the range of features available in a general purpose application.

Many users have more specific requirements for their computers than the general programs mentioned above. In many cases, this need will be so specific that an application written solely for this one task is needed. For example, many businesses will need a payroll system to calculate wages and generate pay slips. The business could attempt to use a spreadsheet package, or they could buy a piece of special purpose software designed specifically for payrolls. Obviously a payroll application would not have the same flexibility as a spreadsheet package, but it will handle payrolls much better.

Business users in particular will use special purpose applications for tasks such as financial accounting, cash flow forecasting and stock control. There are also an increasing number of special purpose applications now being used by home users, for example, software for writing music, photograph editing or money management.

BESPOKE SOFTWARE (CUSTOM)

Bespoke means customised or tailor-made. There will be some occasions when even special purpose software is not specific enough for a user's needs. In this case, the user will need to have the application made especially for them. This is normally only undertaken by businesses as the cost will be much higher than buying an 'off-the-shelf' package. Some larger businesses may have their own in-house programmers who can do this for them. Alternatively, there are businesses known as 'software houses' who will write a program to the user's specification.

The advantage of this is that the users get an application that does exactly what they need it to do and it can be written to integrate with the current system. However, it will take some time to write and software houses usually charge several hundred pounds a day per programmer. You will also know from writing your own programs that 100 per cent error-free software does not exist and bespoke software is more likely to suffer from bugs than software that is more widely available. This is because it has fewer users and some bugs only surface after extensive use.

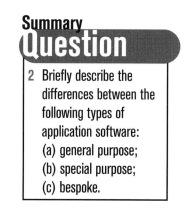

Summary Question

2 Briefly describe the differences between the following types of application software:
(a) general purpose;
(b) special purpose;
(c) bespoke.

The decision to have bespoke software written is one that the user will need to consider carefully. It may be that a general or special purpose package could be adapted to provide a working solution. This would certainly be a quicker and cheaper alternative. Bespoke software also needs to be maintained which adds another cost.

System software

Whereas application software is what we use our computers for, system software covers a range of programs that are concerned with the more technical aspects of setting up and running the computer. Many aspects of system software are invisible to the user which means that they will not even realise that they have system software on their computer. System software exists to support the applications software.

There are four main types: operating system software; utility programs; library programs; and compilers, assemblers and interpreters.

OPERATING SYSTEM SOFTWARE

The operating system is critical. Without it you would not be able to use any of the other software on your computer. It performs a number of tasks which are covered in more detail in Section 7. In brief, the operating system provides an interface between the user, the hardware and the applications software. Effectively, it controls everything that happens on your computer. If you select 'Print' from one of your applications, it is the operating system software that handles this request. If your printer runs out of paper, it is the operating system that generates the error message.

Most PCs have an operating system pre-installed when you buy them. There are a number of systems available though some are specific to certain types of computer. For example, Apple Macs use Mac OS. PCs mainly use Windows or Linux. Mainframe systems tend to use Unix. As with applications software, the brand names are less important than an understanding of the purpose of the operating system.

Summary Question

3 Briefly describe the characteristics of the following types of system software:
(a) operating system software;
(b) utility programs;
(c) library programs.

UTILITY PROGRAMS

This covers software that is written to carry out certain housekeeping tasks on your computer. They are normally supplied with the operating system though they can be purchased separately. Utility programs are often supplied on the cover disks of computing magazines. Utility programs are designed to enhance the use of your current computer and programs though your computer will still work without them.

Common file functions such as renaming, copying, deleting and sorting are all features of utility programs. Another common utility program is compression software which allows you to compress files making them much smaller. This is useful if you are short of space on your hard disk or if you wish to transport a file using a floppy disk and it won't fit. It is also used to compress files that are sent as attachments to e-mails, in order to reduce transmission times.

Other examples include formatting routines and spell-checkers. A lot of mainstream software therefore uses utility routines, for example, graph drawing in spreadsheets and wizards in desktop publishing packages.

LIBRARY PROGRAMS

Library programs are similar to utility programs in that they are written to carry out common tasks. The difference is that they are created for systems with multiple users where those users have common tasks specific to the work that they do.

Whereas some utility programs are non-essential, library programs tend to be critical for the applications for which they were built. For example, a large science department within a university may have a number of library programs designed to help scientists carry out routine tasks related to mathematical or data-handling problems. The word 'library' indicates that there will be a number of software tools available to the users of the system.

COMPILERS, ASSEMBLERS AND INTERPRETERS

These three types of software are used by programmers to convert the code that they write into a form that can be understood by the processor in the computer.

At some point, every piece of software, whether it is application software or system software, has to be written by a programmer. A program is simply a

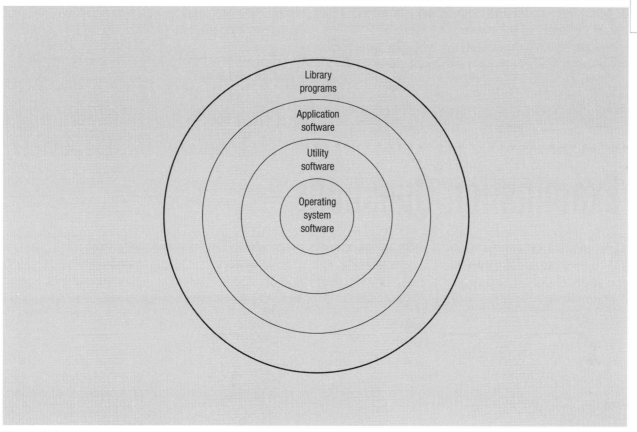

Figure 2.1 **Layers of software**

series of instructions written by a programmer that the computer's processor must carry out.

In order to write software, programmers use programming languages which allow them to write code in a way that is user-friendly for the programmer. However, the processor will not understand the programmers'

code, so it has to be translated into machine code. Compilers, assemblers and interpreters are used to carry out this translation process. This is explained in more detail in Chapter 5.

Summary Question

4 Briefly describe the characteristics of:
(a) application software;
(b) system software.

Study Questions

1. Describe three distinctive features of each of the following types of general purpose application software:

(a) word processor;
(b) spreadsheet;
(c) database;
(d) desktop publisher;
(e) presentation package.

2. Describe three features that are common to all general purpose packages.

3. Use the Internet to find an example of:

(a) a utility program;
(b) a library program.

4. Use the Internet to compare the price and features of Microsoft Office and Lotus SmartSuite. Give two reasons why a user would choose one in preference to the other.

5. Many individuals and organisations are choosing Linux as their operating system software. Identify three reasons why you think this is the case. Identify three reasons why you think other users are staying with the Windows operating system.

6. What software would you choose to create a web site and why?

Examination Questions

1.   (a)   Two classifications of software are **system software** and **application software**.

          What is meant by:

          (i) system software;   [1]

          (ii) application software?   [1]

   (b)   Give an example of:

          (i) system software;   [1]

          (ii) application software.   [1]

AQA January 2001 Module 1

CHAPTER:3
Generation of bit patterns

The bit

Computers process data in digital form. Essentially this means that they use microprocessors, also referred to as 'chips', to control them. A chip is a small piece of silicon implanted with millions of electronic circuits. The chip receives pulses of electricity that are passed around these microscopic circuits in a way that allows computers to create text, numbers, sounds and graphics. But how?

It all comes down to the 'bit'. A bit is a **Bi**nary Dig**it**. The chip can only handle electricity in a relatively simple way – either electricity is flowing, or it is not, that is, it is either on or off. This is often referred to as two states. The processor can recognise whether it is receiving an 'on' signal or an 'off' signal. This is handled as a zero (0) for off and a one (1) for on. A binary digit therefore is either a 0 or a 1.

The processor now needs to convert these 0s and 1s into something useful for the user. Although it might be difficult to comprehend, everything you use your computer for is made up of zeros and ones. To help you understand this, think of the Morse code.

Morse code only uses two signals – a dot and a dash. These two states can be used to create every letter in the alphabet. It achieves this by stringing dots and dashes together in different combinations. Perhaps the most well-known piece of Morse code is 'dot dot dot – dash dash dash – dot dot dot'. 'Dot dot dot' is S and 'dash dash dash' is O. Therefore we get SOS which stands for Save Our Souls – the standard distress call for ships in trouble.

Computers string zeros and ones together in a similar way to represent text, and in addition they also store numbers, sound, video and everything else we use our computers for. The really clever thing about computers is their ability to string zeros and ones together at very high speed. The 'clock speed' of your computer indicates the speed at which the signals are sent around the processor. A clock speed of 2 GHz means that it will receive 2000 million pulses per second.

The byte (and the nibble)

The first hint most students get of the nature of the byte is when they begin to measure the size of memory or disk space in terms of megabytes and gigabytes.

A single byte is a string of eight bits. Eight is a useful number of bits as it creates enough permutations (or combinations) of zeros and ones to represent every character on your keyboard. Follow this through:

● **With one bit we have two permutations: 0 and 1.**

- With two bits we have four permutations: 00, 01, 10 and 11. This could be represented as 2^2 or 2×2. As we increase the number of bits, we increase the number of permutations by the power of two.

- Three bits would give us 2^3 which is $2 \times 2 \times 2 = 8$ permutations.

- Four bits would give us 2^4 permutations which is $2 \times 2 \times 2 \times 2 = 16$ permutations.

Summary Questions

1 How many different permutations of numbers can you represent with:
   (a) 4 bits;
   (b) 8 bits;
   (c) 16 bits;
   (d) 20 bits;
   (e) 24 bits.

2 What is the biggest denary number you can represent with:
   (a) 4 bits
   (b) 8 bits
   (c) 16 bits

3 What is the range of numbers that can be represented with 8 bits?

If we stop at four you can see that 4 bits would give us enough permutations to represent 16 different letters of the alphabet, 16 different numbers, or 16 different colours. 4 bits is half a byte. It is commonly referred to as a 'nibble'. In fact a nibble can be any number of bits less than eight, so you could break a byte up into four nibbles each with 2 bits if you wanted to. When computer memory (RAM) was expensive, nibbles were often used, but now memory is so much cheaper there is much less need for this technique.

If we move onto 8 bits, we get 2^8 permutations. This represents 256 permutations. Therefore, 8 bits is enough to represent every letter in the alphabet and every keyboard character with a few to spare.

Case study

Games consoles

It might help you to think about games consoles at this point. You will be familiar with the PlayStation 2, which is a 128-bit system which provides high quality graphics and sound, and fast game-play.

Think back to the earlier models. One of the first games consoles was the Sega Mastersystem which was an 8-bit system. At the time, the main advantage of the 8 bits was that it allowed 256 different colours to be used in the games. As they developed there was a 16-bit version. 16 bits is the word length – in this case, two bytes. 2^{16} gives 65 356 colours.

Then came the Nintendo 64. The 64 here represents the number of bits. Get your calculator out and work out 2^{64} – there won't be enough digits to represent the number in full.

Therefore, 8 bits is equal to 1 byte which represents one character.

Larger combinations of bytes are used to measure the capacity of memory and storage devices. In Chapter 1, these were described in approximate terms using denary equivalents. For example, the kilobyte (Kb) was shown as approximately 1000 bytes. In fact, the nearest binary equivalent is 1024 which means that 1 Kb is actually 1024 bytes.

Unit	Abbreviation	Exact size in bytes
Kilobyte	Kb	1024
Megabyte	Mb	$1024 \times 1024 = 1048576$
Gigabyte	Gb	$1024 \times 1024 \times 1024 = 1073741824$
Terabyte	Tb	$1024 \times 1024 \times 1024 \times 1024 = 1099511627776$

The word

A word is formed by adding bytes together. You will probably have realised by now that the more bits we use, the more data we can store. For example, using one byte allows us to store up to 256 different numbers. A modern computer system that worked on 8 bits would not be powerful enough for the types of applications that we use these days.

As a consequence, bytes are often grouped together to form words. Therefore the length of a word must be a multiple of 8 as there are 8 bits in a byte. Typically a word is two bytes added together to produce a 16-bit word. The 'word length' refers to the size of word that the processor can handle in one operation.

ASCII code

In the early days of computing, programmers would combine groups (sequences) of zeros and ones to represent different things. For example, they might decide that 00000000 could be used to represent an A and 00000001 could be used to represent a B and

so on. The problem was that different programmers used their own coding systems so the sequences meant different things to different people.

As a result of the confusion this caused, a standard was agreed upon for the representation of all the keyboard characters and other commonly used functions. This standard is ASCII or the American Standard Code for Information Interchange. In fact, a 7-bit code was agreed upon as 7 bits gives 2^7 permutations (128) which is enough for the most commonly used characters. Below is an extract of the keyboard characters and the string of bits that represent them. You don't need to remember any of these but it is useful to understand the principle behind them.

You will notice that all the keyboard characters have a code covering upper and lower case letters, numbers on the keypad, special characters (%, @, /, #, etc.) and non-printing characters (ACK, BS, etc.). Non-printing codes mainly cover the communication codes that are used to allow devices such as the keyboard and mouse to be understood by the processor.

Character	ASCII	Character	ASCII	Character	ASCII	Character	ASCII
NUL	0000000	Space	0100000	@	1000000	'	1100000
SOH	0000001	!	0100001	A	1000001	a	1100001
STX	0000010	"	0100010	B	1000010	b	1100010
ETX	0000011	#	0100011	C	1000011	c	1100011
EOT	0000100	$	0100100	D	1000100	d	1100100
ENQ	0000101	%	0100101	E	1000101	e	1100100
ACK	0000110	&	0100110	F	1000110	f	1100110
BEL	0000111	(	0101000	G	1000111	g	1100111
BS	0001000	)	0101001	H	1001000	h	1101000
HT	0001001	*	0101010	I	1001001	i	1101001
LF	0001010	+	0101011	J	1001010	j	1101010
VT	0001011	,	0101100	K	1001011	k	1101011
FF	0001100	.	0101110	L	1001100	l	1101100
CR	0001101	/	0101111	M	1001101	m	1101101
SO	0001110	0	0110000	N	1001110	n	1101110
SI	0001111	1	0110001	O	1001111	o	1101111

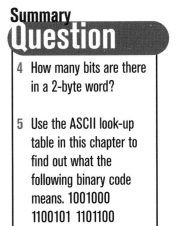

Summary Question

4 How many bits are there in a 2-byte word?

5 Use the ASCII look-up table in this chapter to find out what the following binary code means. 1001000 1100101 1101100 1101100 1101111.

Representing numbers

This is covered in more detail in Chapter 16, but at this stage it is worth understanding how sequences of zeros and ones can be turned into numbers. From the ASCII table you can see that there is a 7-bit code for each of the numbers on your keyboard. However, these are only used to display the numbers on the monitor or printer. Therefore, we cannot use the ASCII codes to perform mathematical operations.

This may seem odd, but think about this like a telephone number. Obviously a telephone number is made up of numbers, but we are not using these numbers in order to carry out any calculations, we are simply using them as a code. Phone numbers do not really need to be numbers – they could just as easily be made up of letters.

Numbers in the mathematical sense are stored differently. If you have studied any maths you will know that there are different classifications of numbers, for example, integers, which are whole numbers, and real numbers, which includes decimals.

An introduction to binary and denary

When performing any maths, humans use number base 10 probably because we have ten digits on our hands. Commonly this system is known as decimal though in computing terms, base 10 is called denary. Denary uses 10 different digits 0, 1, 2, 3, 4, 5, 6, 7, 8 and 9. When we get to 9 we add an extra digit and start again. When we get to 99, we add a further digit and so on. Each digit we add is worth ten times the previous digit. This is easier to understand if you think back to how you were taught maths at primary school.

Thousands (1000)	Hundreds (100)	Tens (10)	Units (1)
2	0	9	8

Clearly the number is 2098, which is easy to understand in denary terms. To state the obvious, it is made up of $(2 \times 1000) + (0 \times 100) + (9 \times 10) + (8 \times 1)$. When creating a number, we start with the units and add the further digits as needed to create the number we want. Each extra digit is ten times the previous one because we are using number base 10.

Binary is number base 2 and works on exactly the same principle. This time we only have two digits, 0 and 1. It has to be binary because computers only work by receiving a zero or one (off and on). So, 1 is the biggest number we can have with one bit. To increase the size of the number, we add more bits. Each bit is worth two times the previous bit because we are using number base 2. The table below shows an 8-bit binary number 10000111.

128	64	32	16	8	4	2	1
1	0	0	0	0	1	1	1

Again, using the same principle to work out the number we have:

$(1 \times 128) + (1 \times 4) + (1 \times 2) + (1 \times 1)$. This adds up to 135.

Summary Question

6 Work out the denary equivalent of the following 8-bit binary numbers. You might find it useful to write it out in the format shown.
(a) 00011100;
(b) 10110011;
(c) 11000011;
(d) 00000000;
(e) 11111111.

Examination Questions

1. Bit patterns can be interpreted in a number of different ways.
    A computer word contains the bit pattern 0101 1001. What is
    the decimal value as a pure binary integer?   [1]

    AQA January 2001 Module 1

2. Some personal computers are referred to as 32-bit machines.
    This means their word length is 32 bits.
    (a)   What is a word in this context?   [1]
    (b)   State the different values for one bit.   [1]
    (c)   Give three different interpretations which can be associated with a pattern of
          bits in a 32-bit word.   [3]

    AQA January 2002 Module 1

CHAPTER:4
Functional characteristics of a processor

Introduction

The modern definition of the computer arose following the invention of the chip. However, computing existed for many years before this. Early computers used valves to represent the on and off states. Computer programming involved setting switches into different positions. It was time consuming and an error-prone occupation. Worse than this, nothing could be saved permanently so performing the same task again involved programming it all over again from the beginning. It was a major breakthrough therefore, when the ability to store programs and data became possible.

The stored program concept

In Chapter 2 we identified that a program is a series of instructions that the processor will carry out. Programs also require the data on which these instructions will be carried out. As we have seen, a program is loaded into main memory when it is run. The stored program concept means that the instructions and data that comprise a program are both stored in main memory. The early computers that used this concept were known as von Neumann machines after the man who first invented the technique in the 1940s. By definition, all computers nowadays are von Neumann machines.

Memory is made up of millions of addressable cells and the various instructions and data that make up a program will be stored across a number of these addresses. Each address can be uniquely identified – usually by a hexadecimal number. It is the job of the processor to retrieve each instruction and data item and to carry out instructions in a sequential manner.

Memory is organised in a systematic way. Using the addresses, different programs can be stored in different parts of memory. For example, a block of memory addresses will be allocated for the operating system, another block for the application software and so on. This way, the processor is able to find the data and instructions it needs much more quickly than if the programs were stored completely randomly.

A memory map can be produced which shows which programs are stored at which addresses. You will see that memory addresses are normally stored in hexadecimal format. Hexadecimal is explained in Chapter 17.

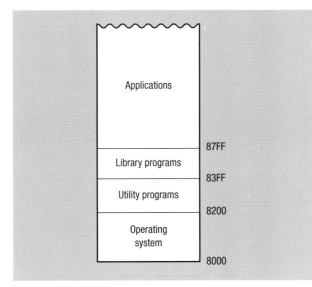

Figure 4.1 **A basic memory map**

The 'Fetch-Decode-Execute' Cycle

When a program is run, the processor runs through the 'fetch-decode-execute' cycle. This means that the processor will fetch an instruction from memory, decode it and then carry out the instructions on the data. Therefore, all the processor is doing is running through this cycle over and over again, millions of times every second. The computer's clock times the electrical pulses into the processor. Each pulse of the clock represents one stage of the 'fetch-decode-execute' cycle.

- **Fetch – the processor fetches the program's next instruction from memory. The instruction will be stored at a memory address and will contain the instruction in binary code.**

- **Decode – the processor works out what the binary code at that address means.**

- **Execute – the processor carries out the instruction which may involve reading an item of data from memory, performing a calculation or writing data back into memory.**

It is worth pointing out that a simple instruction for a user, for example, adding two numbers together, would actually involve a number of cycles for the

processor. There is also an unanswered question in terms of **how** the processor fetches, decodes and executes each instruction. To understand this fully, you need to understand the use of registers in the processor. A basic definition is provided here and a fuller explanation can be found in Chapter 53.

Registers

If you imagine a microprocessor as a series of microscopic circuits, a register is one specific part of the circuitry. Effectively, it is a small area of temporary memory used by the processor to store instructions or data as they are being handled by the processor. Different registers are set up to perform different functions within the 'fetch-decode-execute' cycle.

Buses

Connecting all of the registers to each other and to memory are microscopic parallel wires called 'buses'. Buses are also used to connect the processor to the various input and output controllers being used by the computer. There are three types of bus: data, address and control.

DATA BUS

The instructions and data that comprise a computer program pass back and forth between the processor and memory as the program is run. The data bus carries the data both to and from memory and to and from the I/O controllers, that is, they are bi-directional or two-way. The instructions and data

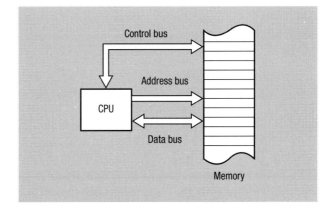

Figure 4.2 **Buses connecting the CPU to memory**

held in memory will vary in size. Each memory 'cell' will have a width measured in bits. For example, it may have a width of 8 bits.

The data bus connects the registers to each other and to memory. The amount of data that can be passed along the bus depends on how many parallel wires are in the bus. An 8-bit data bus has eight wires. There are only two things that can pass down each wire, that is a zero or a one. Therefore, by using eight wires on the data bus, we can transmit any item of data that can be represented using 2^8 combinations which is 256. As we saw in Chapter 3, these patterns can be used to represent text, numbers, sound and graphics or instructions.

Therefore, when large data items are transmitted, the data will have to be split into smaller parts and sent one after the other. The greater the width of the data bus, in terms of wires, the more data can be transmitted in one pulse of the clock. Consequently, the size of the data bus is a key factor in determining the overall speed and performance of the computer. 32-bit buses are the norm at the time of writing. The data bus width is usually the same as the word length of the processor and the same as the memory word length. Most microcomputers at present are 32-bit with supercomputers being 64 or 128 bit.

Summary Question

2 What is the maximum amount of data that can pass down a 16-bit data bus in one stage of the 'fetch-decode-execute' cycle?

Summary Questions

3 What is the largest amount of addressable memory available with a 16-bit address bus?

4 Name and describe the function of the three different buses.

5 Identify three functions carried out by the control bus.

ADDRESS BUS

The address bus only goes in one direction – from the processor into memory. All the instructions and data that a processor needs to carry out a task are stored in memory. Every memory location has an address. The processor carries out the instructions one after the other. The address bus is used by the processor and carries the memory address of the next instruction or data item. The address bus therefore is used to access anything that is stored in memory, not just instructions.

The size of the address bus is also measured in bits and represents the amount of memory that is addressable. An 8-bit bus would only give 256 directly addressable memory cells. This means that a program could only consist of a maximum of 256 separate instructions and/or data items. If we assume that each memory address can store 8 bits (one byte) of data then we would have 256 bytes of memory available. This would be useless on modern computers.

You may have realised from Chapter 3 that each additional wire will double the capacity. Consequently 24 lines on the address bus would give 2^{24} combinations, which means it can access 16 Mb of memory. At the time of writing, 512 Mb of memory is common.

CONTROL BUS

The control bus is a bi-directional bus which sends control signals to the registers, the data and address buses. There is a lot of data flowing around the processor, between the processor and memory, and between the processor and the input and output controllers. Data buses are sending data to and from memory while address buses send only to memory.

The job of the control bus therefore is to ensure that the correct data is travelling to the right place at the right time. This involves the synchronisation of signals and the control of access to the data and address buses which are being shared by a number of devices.

For example, a signal on the control bus would dictate the direction of data transmission through the data bus; it would also indicate whether it was reading to or writing from an I/O port. The control bus will also be transmitting the pulses being delivered by the system's clock.

Input/Output (I/O) ports

In addition to the direct link between the processor and main memory, the processor will also receive and send instructions and data to the various input and output devices connected to the computer. Basic I/O devices would be the keyboard, monitor, mouse and printer though modern computer systems would typically include several other devices.

Physically, these I/O devices are connected via the 'ports' in the back of your computer. The ports are simply connections that allow I/O devices to be plugged in. For example, the printer will be plugged into one of the parallel ports. Signals will be passed in both directions through the printer cable, via the port and through the processor to send and receive the instructions. Parallel communications are explained in Chapter 20.

Inside the computer, the data buses carry the signals to and from the processor. In order to do this the processor is working in the same way as if it were sending data to or from memory. The difference, however, is that the processor does not communicate directly with the I/O devices. Instead, there is an interface called an I/O controller.

Controllers consist of their own circuitry that handle the data flowing between the processor and the device. Every device will have its own controller which allows new devices to be connected

to the processor at any time. As a minimum, therefore, a computer will have a monitor controller, a mouse controller, a keyboard controller and a hard disk controller.

Summary
Questions

6 Identify four different devices that could be connected to a PC via a port.

7 Give two reasons why I/O devices are handled by controllers rather than being connected directly to the processor.

Examination Questions

1. Newspapers and magazines are advertising many different specifications of personal computer systems. Such advertisements feature monitor, disk drives, processor, main memory and operating system.

   (a) What is the purpose of an operating system? [1]

   (b) What is the function of:

   (i) the processor; [1]

   (ii) main memory (immediate access store)? [1]

   (c) The system bus in a computer system is made up of three buses. Name each bus and give one example of its use. [6]

   AQA June 2001 Module 1

2.   Some of the components of a computer system are processor, main memory, address bus, data bus, control bus, I/O port and secondary storage. The diagram shows how these components are connected.

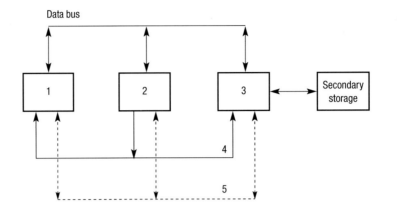

(a)   Name each of the five numbered components.   [5]

(b)   What is the function of the following components: processor; main memory; secondary storage?   [3]

(c)   Give two examples of a signal carried by the control bus.   [2]

(d)   Apart from data, what else is carried on the data bus?   [1]

AQA January 2003 Module 1

CHAPTER: **5**
Introduction to programming

What is a computer program?

In its simplest form a computer program (note the spelling) can be seen as a list of instructions that a computer has to work through in a logical sequence in order to carry out a specific task. In the case of most modern applications, such as word processing or spreadsheet programs, this list of instructions is going to be very long. We shall be looking at ways of making a program more manageable in Chapter 7.

A computer program is written in a programming language. In the same way that there are lots of different languages you can learn to speak, there are also lots of programming languages, and in the same way that some languages have many different dialects, there are also different versions of some of the more popular programming languages.

Another similarity with foreign languages is that each programming language has its own vocabulary and rules that define how the words must be put together. These rules are known as the 'syntax' of the language. The difference between learning a foreign language and a computer language is that there are far fewer words to learn in a computer language but the rules are much more rigid.

Generations of programming languages

Although computers have only been around since the mid-1940s they have changed beyond all recognition in that short time span. Programming the early computers was a very tedious business as programs were entered as a sequence of switch settings. Each switch was either on or off so by combining enough switches the programmer could represent different things. If you're not sure how, read Chapter 3 again. Thankfully programming computers has become a much simpler process, though the ever-increasing complexity of the computers themselves brings its own problems.

As computers have developed then so have the programming languages that can be used on them. These 'developments' are known as 'generations' of programming languages. There are said to be three 'generations' of languages as shown below.

Machine code
Assembly language } These are known as 'low level languages'
High-level languages

FIRST GENERATION – MACHINE CODE

The processor of a computer can only work with binary digits (bits). This means that all the instructions given to a computer must, ultimately, be a pattern of zeros and ones. Programs written in this format are said to be written in 'machine code'. Having to write everything down as a sequence of zeros and ones means that the programs are going to be very long-winded, and because everything is entered as bits there is a high risk of making a mistake. One way to make these bits easier to understand is to show a sequence of bits as either a denary or hexadecimal number.

Summary Question

1 Why is it difficult to write a program in machine code?

To compound the problem further it is also going to be very difficult to track down any errors or bugs that there are in the code. One final problem is that because machine code is written for a specific processor it is unlikely to be very portable. This means that it will only work on a computer with the same type of processor as it was written on.

Nevertheless because you are writing instructions that can be used directly by the processor they will be executed very quickly and the processor will do exactly what you tell it to do.

SECOND GENERATION – ASSEMBLY LANGUAGE

Summary Questions

2 Explain why some programmers still write programs in an assembly language.

3 Explain why assembly language and machine code are said to have a 'one to one' relationship.

4 Why must assembly language programs be assembled before they can be executed?

The need to make programs more 'programmer-friendly' lead to the development of assembly languages. Rather than using sequences of zeros and ones, an assembly language allows programmers to write code using words. There is a very strong connection between machine code and assembly language. This is because assembly language is basically machine code with words. The number of 'words' that can be used in an assembly language is generally small. Each of these commands translates directly into one command in machine code. This is called a 'one-to-one' relationship.

Most, but not all, assembly codes use a system of abbreviated words called mnemonics. In the small section of assembly code below the mnemonic 'LDA' stands for 'Load Accumulator' and STA means 'Store Accumulator'. ADD and SUB should be rather more obvious. In this simplified example all the numbers following each mnemonic refer to memory addresses – the place in memory where numbers are written to or read from.

```
LDA    20
ADD    43
STA    20
SUB    41
STA    45
```

This code does the following:

- **loads the accumulator with the contents of address 20**

- **adds the value held in memory location 43 to the value held in the accumulator**

- **stores the contents of the accumulator to address 20**

- **subtracts the value held in memory location 41 from the value held in the accumulator**

- **stores the contents of the accumulator to address 45**

Although assembly language uses words, some of which you might recognise, the code is not particularly easy to understand.

Before any code written in assembly language can be executed it has to be converted into machine code. This is because the processor can only understand binary digits (0s and 1s) – the words are meaningless to the computer, so the words must be converted into these binary digits. This conversion process is carried out by an assembler. The assembler will be able to identify some, but not all, of the errors that are likely to be hidden somewhere in the code. The code that the programmer creates is known as the source code. The assembler takes this source code and translates it into a machine code version that is known as the object code.

As with machine code, assembly languages are based on one processor so they are generally not very portable.

Machine code and assembly languages are known collectively as 'low level languages'.

THIRD GENERATION – HIGH-LEVEL LANGUAGES

The increasingly complex demands made on computers meant that writing programs in assembly code was too slow and cumbersome. High-level languages were developed to overcome this problem.

Whereas low level languages are machine-oriented, high-level languages are problem-oriented. This means that the commands and the way the program is structured are based on what the program will have to do rather than the components of the computer it will be used with. This means that a program written in a high-level language will be portable. It can be written on one type of computer and then executed on other types of computer.

There are many different high-level languages available – you can find details of the wide variety of languages in Chapter 9. Each high-level language has been written to cope with the demands of a specific type of problem. For example, some high-level languages are specifically designed for scientific applications, others for manipulating databases, whilst others are used to create web pages. The language the programmer chooses will depend to a large extent on the nature of the problem they are trying to solve.

The main characteristics of a high-level language are:

- **it is easier for a programmer to identify what a command does;**
- **like assembly languages, high-level languages need to be translated;**
- **unlike assembly code one command in a high-level language might be represented by a whole sequence of machine code instructions. This is called a 'one-to-many' relationship;**
- **they are portable;**
- **they make use of a wide variety of program structures to make the process of program writing more straightforward. As a result they are also easier to maintain.**

Translating high-level languages

One of the main features of high-level languages is that they are programmer-friendly. Unfortunately this means the computer will not understand any of the high-level language, so it will have to be converted into machine code.

This process is called translation and in order to carry it out a special piece of systems software called a translator is needed. There are two types of translator: an interpreter and a compiler. Translators carry out exactly the same function on a high-level language as an assembler does on assembly language – they create a machine code program that can be executed by a computer.

INTERPRETER

An interpreter works by converting just one statement of the source code into machine code at a time. The machine code is then executed. Typically an interpreter only converts what needs to be translated. For example when the line of code

```
If Age<17 Then Output = "Cannot drive a car"
```

needs to be translated, only the first section of the code 'If Age<17 Then' is translated and executed. The second part of the code is only translated if the condition is true. This saves time as only the code that is needed is converted. Some interpreters translate an entire line of code before they execute it. These are known as 'line interpreters'.

Benefits of using a interpreter:

- **If an error occurs during the execution of a program the interpreter can identify whereabouts in the source code the problem has occurred. Because of this, an interpreter is most likely to be used whilst a program is being developed.**
- **Because only one small section of code is being translated from the source code at any one time, the interpreter only needs a small block of memory in which to store the object code.**

Summary Question

5 Why are machine code and assembly languages said to be machine-oriented?

6 Explain why there are so many different high-level languages.

Drawbacks of using an interpreter:

- **No matter how many times a section of code is revisited in a program it will need translating from source to object code every time. This means that the overall time needed to execute a program can be very long.**

COMPILER

A compiler converts the whole source code into object code before the program can be executed. The good thing about this is that once you have carried out this process you will have some object code that can be executed immediately every time, so the execution time will be quick. This is ideal once you have sorted out all the bugs in your program.

Benefits of using a compiler:

- **Once the source code has been compiled you no longer need the compiler or the source code.**

- **If you want to pass your code on to someone else to use they will find it difficult to work out what the original source code was. This process of working out what the source code was is known as reverse engineering.**

Drawbacks of using a compiler:

- **Because the whole program has to be converted from source code to object code every time you make even the slightest alteration to your code, it can take a long time to debug.**

- **If an error does crop up in the compiled code it could be very difficult to find the source of the error.**

The obvious solution is to use an interpreter during the development of your program and, once you have sorted out all the problems, you run the program through a compiler and create a machine code version.

Summary Questions

7 If you want to use commercial software you often have to agree not to try to 'reverse-engineer' the code. What does this term mean?

8 Under what circumstances would you compile a high-level computer program?

9 Explain the benefits of using a high-level language compared to an assembly language.

10 Explain the differences between a compiler and an interpreter.

Study Questions

1. Explain why an assembly language uses mnemonics rather than full command words.

2. Many companies now offer 'open source' software. What does this term mean and what are the advantages to the user?

Examination Questions

1. Machine code is the first generation of programming languages. All other generations of programming languages need a program translator before the program can be executed. Name a type of translator suitable for:

   (a) second generation language programs; [1]

   (b) third generation language programs. [1]

   (c) Give two characteristics of high-level languages that distinguish them from second generation languages. [2]

   AQA June 2002 Module 1

2. (i) Machine code is the first generation programming language. What is the second generation? [1]

   (ii) A programmer writes a program in a second generation programming language. What has to be done to this program before it can be executed? [2]

   (iii) Some high-level languages are classified as imperative. What is meant by imperative? [1]

   (iv) Give an example of an imperative high-level language. [1]

   (v) What is the relationship between an imperative high level language statement and its machine code equivalent? [1]

   (vi) Give two disadvantages of programming in first and second generation programming languages compared with imperative high-level languages. [2]

   AQA January 2002 Module 1

CHAPTER:6
Programming constructs

Naming and storing data

In Chapter 5 we looked at how a computer program was made up of a list of instructions, but this is only part of the story. The instructions must have data to work with. For example, to add two numbers together requires an 'add' instruction and the two numbers. The programmer needs to give these two data items names so that the computer will know which data to use.

The data also has to be stored somewhere and the computer can use the names to find the data as and when it is needed. You could view the storage system rather like a series of pigeon-holes, each with a label stating what the contents are called. It is a really good idea to use names that indicate the purpose of the data – in the case of the example above the two numbers might be called Number1 and Number2. Using sensible names will help the programmer when they are trying to trace bugs and it also allows other programmers to follow the code more easily. Variable names are normally written with the first character in upper case and the rest in lower case.

This process of giving data values is called assigning, and it looks something like these two:

```
Number1 ← 23
Name ← "Derek"
```

The ← means 'becomes'. You may need to use the equals sign to make the assignment in the code you are writing.

Constants and variables

Data is stored either as constants or as variables. Constants (as you'd expect from the name) have values that are fixed for the duration of a program. For example, if you were writing a program that converted miles into kilometres you could set the conversion rate as a constant because it will never change. In this case we could call the constant **Convert_Miles_to_Km** and assign it a value of 1.6 as there are approximately 1.6 km to the mile. Then whenever we want to convert a distance in miles to its metric equivalent we would multiply it by the constant **Convert_Miles_to_Km**.

As you would expect, variables can change. For example the same conversion program will require the user to type in the number of miles they want to convert. This number will probably be different each time the user enters data. Therefore, you need to have a variable that you could call **Number_Of_Miles**.

There are lots of other examples – the number of answers a pupil has got right in a test would (hopefully) increase as they work their way through a test so the data

Summary Questions

1 Give two reasons why it is a good idea to use meaningful variable names.

2 Use examples to explain the difference between a constant and a variable.

would have to be stored as a variable. The password a user uses to access a network can be changed at any time, so it would also be classed as a variable.

Data types

So far we have only considered storing numeric data but in fact there are lots of other data types you might need to use. For example you might want to store a person's name, their date of birth and whether or not they wear glasses.

Here are some examples:

- An integer is the mathematical name for a whole number and that includes negative whole numbers. This might be used to store the number of cars sold in a particular month or the number of pupils in a class. As soon as you start storing anything on a computer you are automatically limited by the amount of memory that there is available and the number of bytes that are used to store that particular data type. For example Visual Basic limits the data type 'Integer' to numbers between −32 768 and +32 767. This is fine if you are using the variable to store the number of pupils in a school but probably not if you want to store the number of words in this book. Some programming languages allow you to tell the computer that you want to store a larger number. Visual Basic uses a variable called a long integer to achieve this.

- If you want to store a number that includes a decimal part, for example, a person's height in metres or their weight in kilograms, then you will need to specify it as 'real'.

- If you want to store a person's name or address, you will need to use a data type called an 'alphanumeric', 'string' or 'text'. You can actually store any character you want in a string whilst text implies it can only store letters. Text or string variables

are normally shown in quote marks. For example you might assign the name Frank to a variable like this:

```
Name ← «Frank»
```

- The simplest data type is a simple yes/no or true/false. This is called a Boolean data type. It is named after George Boole who discovered the principles behind logic statements.

- There are many other data types that you might want to use such as date, time and currency. Some programming languages allow users to define their own data types.

Declaring constants and variables

Declaring a constant or variable means that when you are writing code you describe the variables you are going to use before you actually use them in your program.

Whether the programming language forces you to or not, it is good practice to declare the variables and constants you intend to use in your program before you start writing any code. The benefits of doing this are that it forces you to plan first and the computer will quickly identify variables it does not recognise.

There are two parts to a declaration. You need to supply a suitable name for the constant/variable and you need to specify the data type that will be used. The declarations might look something like this:

```
Dimension Age As Integer
Dimension Name As String
Dimension Wears_Glasses As
Boolean
```

'Dimension' or 'Dim' is one of the command words used in Visual Basic to indicate that a variable is being declared. Once you have declared a variable it starts with a default value. In the above examples **Age** will start as zero, **Name** as nothing (also known as the empty string) and **Wear_Glasses** will start with the value False.

**Summary
Question**

3 Suggest suitable data types and variable names for:
(a) The current rate of VAT;
(b) Today's date;
(c) The total takings from a shop;
(d) A person's date of birth;
(e) Which wrist a person wears a watch on.

Local and global variables

As you will read in Chapter 7 it is highly likely that your program will be split up in some way. If you do this then you might want a variable to exist only in one specific section. This would then be described as a local variable. Limiting the existence of a variable to one section of your code means that you cannot inadvertently change the value being stored somewhere else in the program. It also means you could use the same variable name in different sections, and each could be treated as a separate variable.

A global variable is one that is available throughout the whole program. For example you might store the password to a program as a global variable if you wanted to make a password accessible to different sections of your code.

Programming constructs

Each high-level programming language has its own way of dealing with problems, but there are some similarities between them. There are a number of ways in which programming statements are constructed which are common to all high-level languages.

ASSIGNMENT

We met the concept of an assignment earlier in this chapter. An assignment gives a value to a variable. For example you might be using a variable called **Age** so the line

$$\text{Age} \leftarrow 34$$

will set the variable **Age** to have the value 34.

Assignments are the fundamental building blocks of any computer program because they define the data the program is going to be using.

SELECTION

The process of selection is what sets a true computer apart from a device such as a pocket calculator.

The selection process allows a computer to compare values and then decide what course of action to take. For example you might want your program to decide if someone is old enough to drive a car. The selection process for this might look something like this:

```
If Age < 17 Then
   Output = "Under age"
Else
   Output = "Old enough to drive"
End If
```

In this case, the computer is making a decision based on the value of the variable **Age**. If the value of "Age" is less than 17 it will output the text string "Under age". For any other age it will output the text string "Old enough to drive". This is a very simple selection statement with only two outcomes.

You can carry out more complex selections using constructs such as this Case statement.

```
Select Case Exam_Mark
   Case < 26: Grade = "D"
   Case < 51: Grade = "C"
   Case < 76: Grade = "B"
   Case < 101: Grade = "A"
End Select
```

This routine takes the value of the variable **Exam_Mark** and compares it against the different criteria. So if **Exam_Mark** is currently 76 then the variable **Grade** will be assigned the letter 'B'.

ITERATION

It is useful to be able to repeat a process in a program. This is called iteration. For example you might want to count the number of words in a block of text or you may want to keep a device moving forward until it reaches a wall. Both these routines involve repeating something until a condition is met – either you run out of words to count or the device comes to a wall. An iterative process has two parts – a pair of commands that show the start and finish of the process to be repeated and some sort of condition.

There are two basic forms of iteration – conditional and unconditional. A conditional loop is repeated until a specified condition is met – so it uses a selection process to decide whether or not to carry on (or even whether to start) a process.

Summary Questions

4 Explain the difference between a local and a global variable.

5 Give two benefits of using a local variable in a program.

6 Explain the difference between the declaration and the assignment of a variable.

This routine moves a device forward until the sensor detects an obstacle.

```
Repeat
   Move forward 1 unit
Until Sensors locate an obstacle
```

There is no way of knowing how many times this loop will be repeated so potentially it could go on for ever – a so called infinite loop,

If you want a process to carry out a set number of times you will need to use an unconditional loop. The following code will move the device forward 40 units irrespective of whether it meets an obstacle or not.

```
For Counter = 1 To 40
   Move forward 1 unit
Next
```

Structures such as those mentioned in this chapter are one of the characteristics of a high-level language. They are easy to understand when they are viewed in isolation, but the problems start when you try to put a series of constructs together to do something more useful than deciding if someone is old enough to drive a car or to move a device forwards. In order to create larger, more useful programs, you need to plan ahead.

Study Questions

1. A variable called `Licence_Type` is used to indicate the type of driving licence a person has. It can contain the code N, P or F. These codes indicate the type of licence a person has. They indicate a person has none, a provisional or a full licence, respectively. Write code to output the type of licence a person has. The output will need to be 'none', 'provisional' or 'full'.

2. Some computer languages support 'user defined variables'. Explain this term and give an example of a user defined variable.

3. Give two examples where an iterative process might be used.

Examination Questions

1. A program has been written to analyse the results of a survey. For each of the following, name a suitable data type and give a reason for your choice:

    (a)   number of cars owned by a household;   [2]

    (b)   a telephone number such as 0122456789;   [2]

    (c)   whether a household's accommodation has central heating or not;   [2]

    (d)   the average number of cars owned by the households.   [2]

    AQA June 2002 Module 1

2. The following code is part of a high-level language program to manage a telephone contact list:

```
Const Max = 200

Type TMember = Record
Name: String
TelNo: String
Age: Integer
EndRecord

Var Member : Array [1..Max] Of TMember

    Procedure FindTelNo (WantedName: String)
    Var EndOfList : Boolean
    Begin
    EndOfList :=False
    Ptr :=1
    While WantedName <> Member [Ptr].Name And Not
    EndOfList Do
    Ptr :=Ptr + 1
    If Ptr > Max Then EndOfList :=True
    EndWhile
    If EndOfList
    Then Print ('Name not in list')
    Else Print (Member[Ptr-1].Name, 'tel:',
    Member[Ptr-1].TelNo)
    EndIf
End
```

(a) Identify the following by copying one relevant statement from the above code.

   (i) constant definition; [1]

   (ii) assignment statement; [1]

   (iii) selection statement; [1]

   (iv) iteration. [1]

(b) Identify the following by copying one relevant statement from the above code.

   (i) user-defined type; [1]

   (ii) parameter; [1]

   (iii) local variable. [1]

(c) Why is it considered to be good programming practice to use named constants such as Max? [1]

(d) (i) Why is it not good design to use a field Age when storing personal details? [1]

   (ii) What could the programmer have done instead? [1]

(e) What values can a Boolean expression take? [1]

AQA January 2003 Module 1

CHAPTER: **7**
Procedures and functions

Introduction

This book has a structure. Each chapter deals with a different aspect of computing and each chapter is in turn broken down under various headings. The format of the book and each chapter should make it easy to find what you are looking for.

As computer programs have become ever more complex there has been an increasing need to give them more 'structure'. Procedures and functions are one way of doing this – you might say they are the chapters of the program.

Procedures

Modern computer programs are often very large and the only sensible way to cope with them is to break them up in some way. This is done by using blocks or procedures. Procedures are also known as subroutines or modules.

A procedure is self-contained and it carries out one or more related processes. These processes are sometimes called algorithms. An algorithm is a small section of code that carries out just one process.

For example you may want to write a program to maintain the contents of a file. You would need to write code to handle tasks such as adding a new record, amending existing details and deleting an old record. In this case you might have a procedure to handle events that are generated from a main menu and then each of the three tasks has its own procedure. For example if the variable 'Selected' is set to 'Add' then the procedure `Add_Record` would be called.

```
Procedure Main_Menu
Input Selected
If Selected = 'Add' Then Procedure_Add_Record
If Selected = 'Amend' Then Procedure Amend_Record
If Selected = 'Delete' Then Procedure Delete_Record
End Procedure
:
Procedure Add_Record
' Code to add a new record to a file
End Procedure
:
Procedure Amend_Record
' Code to locate and amend an existing record
End Procedure
:
Procedure Delete_Record
' Code to delete an existing record
End Procedure
```

Breaking up a program into manageable blocks like this has many benefits.

- They allow you to gain an overview about how the program is put together.

- You can use a top-down approach to develop the whole project.

- The program is easier to test and debug because each procedure is self-contained.

- Very large projects can be developed by more than one programmer.

Summary Questions

1 Describe three benefits of using procedures in writing computer programs.

2 What is meant by the term 'algorithm'?

3 Explain the difference between a procedure and a function.

Visual Basic forces you to work with procedures, though in Visual Basic they are actually called subroutines. As soon as you try to write code that is connected to a control, Visual Basic creates a procedure for you.

Object-oriented programming takes this concept one stage further by putting all the code and the relevant data in the same module. See Chapter 10 for more details.

Functions

Most modern pocket calculators have a large range of functions. The most basic are probably the square and square root keys. The idea is that you enter a number, press the function key you want and the calculator gives you a result based on that number.

A function in a computer program performs much the same task as the buttons on a calculator. The user supplies the function with data and the function returns a value. For example you could create a function that calculates the volume of a cylinder – you supply the height and radius and the function returns the volume.

This process is not limited to numeric data, for example, you could create a function to count the number of times the letter 'h' occurs in a given block of text, or to check to see if a file has read/write or read-only access restrictions in place.

There are two benefits of using functions in a program:

- Some processes are very complex and involve many lines of code, but in the end they produce a single answer. Including all those lines of complex code in the middle of your program will probably make it harder to understand, so instead you could put the code in a function and put the function itself somewhere else in the program, away from the main body of the program. This also means that if you want to alter the function it is easier to find. It also makes the main body of the code easier to work through.

- If you have to carry out the same process in lots of different places in the program, then instead of having to rewrite the same code over and over again, you would create the code once and call it from the various places through the program. This has the benefit of keeping programs smaller, and if you need to alter the way the function works, you only have to alter one version of it.

Parameters and arguments

In order for a function to operate efficiently you need a way to control the data that it takes in. This is usually done by using parameters or arguments. A parameter is a value that you want a function to take in and use.

Strictly speaking, parameters are used to transfer data to/from procedures, whilst arguments transfer data to functions, but these terms tend to be interchangeable.

For example, you may want your program to calculate the volume of a box (cuboid). In this case your program may contain the following code. The first line calls the function **Calculate_Volume** and sends it the parameters 3, 4 and 5.

```
Box_Volume = Calculate_Volume (3, 4, 5)
```

When the function receives the data, it is stored as the local variables **Length**, **Breadth** and **Height**.

```
Define Fn Calculate_Volume(Length, Breadth,
Height)
= Length * Breadth * Height
End Fn
```

Once the function has been executed the variable **Box_Volume** would contain the value 60. This call to the function is not very useful – it will return the same value every time it is used. It would be much more useful if the programmer used variables in the parameters.

```
Box_Volume = Calculate_Volume(Length, Breadth,
Height)
```

Using variables rather than constants as parameters gives the programmer much more flexibility.

Summary Question

4 A program contains a function that calculates the number of occurrences of a given character in a given piece of text. So a typical call to this function might look like this: **CharacterCount ("e","elephants have big ears")**, and this would return a value of 4. The 'e' and the text are both examples of parameters. Use this example to explain what parameters are.

Examination Questions

1.   The structured approach when writing programs uses functions and procedures.
      (a)   Give two reasons why procedures are used.   [2]
      (b)   Why are parameters used in conjunction with procedures and functions?   [1]

2.   When programming in some higher level languages, the use of parameters and local variables is helpful.
      (a)   Explain the following terms:
             (i)   parameters;   [1]
             (ii) local variables.   [1]

      (b)   For each of these features, give two reasons why this is useful to the programmer.   [4]

AEB Summer 1998 Paper 2

CHAPTER:8
Fundamentals of structured programming

Time and effort spent on designing a computer program are always well spent, and good program design should result in a more efficient and error-free result. It will also make creating the code easier if you plan ahead. There are a number of planning techniques that can be employed.

Structure charts

Structure charts are also known as Jackson Structure Diagrams. A structure chart uses a 'top down approach' to explain how a program is put together. Starting from the program name, the programmer breaks the problem down into a series of steps.

Each step is then broken down into finer steps so that each successive layer of steps shows the modules and procedures that make up the program in more detail.

The text at each level consists of only a few words – if you want more detail about what the process involves you need to move further down the diagram. The component parts for each section are organised from left to right to show how the system will work.

This diagram shows just part of a structure diagram of a program.

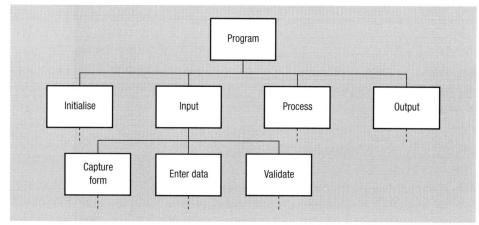

Figure 8.1 **Part of a structure chart**

Flowcharts

A flowchart uses a set of recognised symbols to show how the components of a system or a process work together. Some of the more common symbols are shown in the next diagram.

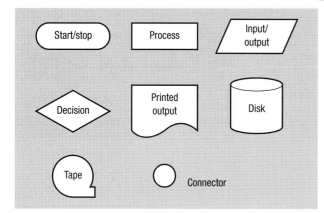

Figure 8.2 **Some flowchart symbols**

Systems flowchart

A systems flowchart shows the tasks to be completed, the files that will be used and the hardware that will be needed but only as an overview. It is normally possible to create just one flowchart that shows the whole system, but this is not always a good idea as modern programs can be very large and cramming every process on to one flowchart might make it too complex to be of any real use. It might be more advantageous to create a separate systems flowchart for each section of the project.

The systems flowchart in Figure 8.3 shows the first few processes that are used when a person starts to use an ATM (Automated Teller Machine) at a bank.

Pseudo-code

So far we have looked at diagrammatic ways of organising a program, but the code that a programmer creates does not use diagrams, it uses lines of code.

Pseudo-code is a way of writing code without having to worry too much about using the correct syntax or constructs. It consists of a series of commands that show the purpose of the program without getting bogged down with the intricacies of the chosen high-level language. The programmer will need to convert the pseudo-code into high-level code at a later date.

Pseudo-code is not a true programming language though it may well use some of the constructs and language of a high-level language. There is only one rule that needs to be adhered to if pseudo-code is to be of

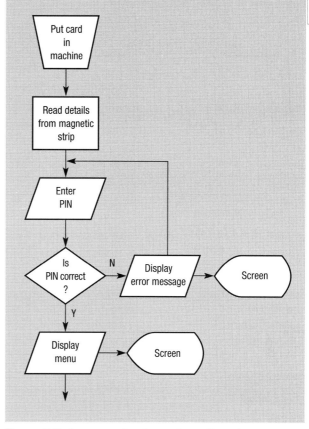

Figure 8.3 **An example of a systems flowchart**

any use and that is that the language used needs to be consistent. Using the command 'Save to File' in one place then 'Write to File' in another will only make the job of converting to a true high-level language harder.

Pseudo-code can be used at many levels. The line

```
Sort NameFile by surname
```

does exactly the same as these lines

```
Repeat
  Loop
    Compare adjacent values,
    swap if necessary
  End Loop
Until No more swaps are needed
```

It will be up to the programmer to decide how far down they need to break their pseudo-code before they can start to actually write the code.

1 Draw a systems flowchart that shows how the computer system at the supermarket handles the sale of goods at the POS (point of sale terminal).

2 The customers at a supermarket have the option of paying for their goods by credit or debit card. Draw a systems flowchart to show how this process works.

Pseudo-code is very useful in that it allows a programmer to sort out the overall structure of the program as it will eventually appear. The fact that it can be used at many levels means the programmer does not have to work out all the fine detail from the start.

Defining and naming variables and functions

Adding variables to a program as you go along is a recipe for disaster and it shows a serious lack of planning. Before you start your actual code you should draw up a list of all the variables you intend to use including details of the data types and whether they are going to be local or global variables.

These are some variables that are being declared so they can be used in a Visual Basic program. A 'Single' is a 'real' data type. If necessary it will be able to store decimal numbers.

```
Dim Load_File_Name As String
Dim Counter As Integer
Dim Average_Score as Single
Dim Reject_Flag As Boolean
```

Giving the variables, constants, modules, functions and procedures in a program meaningful names is good practice. It makes a lot more sense to call a variable that stores the number of pupils in a group 'GroupSize' than to call it Size or C3.

In the same way that programmers should sort out the variables, they should also draw up a list of the functions and procedures they intend to use along with details of what that procedure will do, what it will be called, and what parameters it will need to have assigned to it.

The final step to good program construction is to use the features of the program to make the code itself as programmer-friendly as possible. This might include adding suitable comments, especially to more complex or unusual sections of code, and using gaps and indents to show the overall structure of a program. Indenting loops can help to identify where a

loop begins and ends. It also helps when you are trying to debug a program.

The following two sets of code do the same thing – they place the first 12 values from the two times table in an array.

This first example provides no support for the programmer at all.

```
For X = 1 To 12
    W(X)= 2 * X
Next
```

This second example has made use of a number of features:

```
    'routine to place multiples of 2 in array
    TwoTimes()
For Count = 1 To 12
'counter counts from 1-12
    TwoTimes(Count) = 2 * Count
    'result in array TwoTimes
Next Count
'end loop
```

- **Comments to show the purpose of the algorithm itself.**
- **Comments on the purpose of each line.**
- **Sensible variable names such as 'Count' and 'TwoTimes'.**
- **Contents of the loop have been indented.**
- **The initial comment has been separated from the code.**

Dry runs and trace tables

No matter how careful a programmer is, even the simplest programs are likely to contain bugs. These come in a number of guises and some are trapped when the program is compiled, and others are trapped by the operating system. However some bugs can remain elusive and the programmer might have to resort to dry running the appropriate section of code.

Dry running is the process of following code through on paper. The variables that are used are written down in a trace table.

Summary Questions

3 A programmer might choose to use both a flowchart and pseudo-code when developing a program. Describe the benefits and drawbacks of using each of these systems.

4 High-level languages support 'user-defined variable names'. Explain what is meant by this term.

5 What steps can a programmer take to make the code they write easier for another programmer to follow?

6 Dry running a section of code is often seen as the last resort. Explain what the term 'dry run' means and explain why dry running is itself prone to errors.

This is a simple example of a dry run:

```
For Counter = 1 To 3
  If StoreName(Counter) > StoreName(Counter
+ 1) Then
    TempName ← Store Name(Counter)
    StoreName(Counter) ← StoreName(Counter
+ 1)
    StoreName(Counter + 1)
      ← TempName
  End If
Next Counter
```

The array called **StoreName** has four elements. The initial values for **StoreName** and the other variables are shown in the trace table below.

Counter	TempName	StoreName			
		1	2	3	4
0	<empty>	Kevin	Jane	Beth	Linda

The program is now dry run.

Counter is set to 1 and the contents of **StoreName(1)** is compared with the contents of **StoreName(2)**. Because 'Kevin' is greater than 'Jane' (alphabetically speaking) **TempName** takes the value 'Kevin', **StoreName(1)** takes the value 'Jane' and finally **StoreName(2)** takes the value held in **TempName** – 'Kevin'.

Counter	TempName	StoreName			
		1	2	3	4
		~~Kevin~~	~~Jane~~	Beth	Linda
1	Kevin	Jane	Kevin		

Counter now increments to 2 and **StoreName(2)** is compared to **StoreName(3)**. 'Kevin' is greater than 'Beth' so **TempName** becomes 'Kevin'. Even though **TempName** already contains 'Kevin' it is

important to realise that this is overwritten by the same name.

Counter	TempName	StoreName			
		1	2	3	4
		~~Kevin~~	~~Jane~~	~~Beth~~	Linda
~~1~~	~~Kevin~~	Jane	~~Kevin~~		
2	Kevin		Beth	Kevin	

Counter now increases to 3, and 'Kevin' is compared to 'Linda'. 'Kevin' is less than 'Linda' so the program jumps to the **End If** statement.

Counter	TempName	StoreName			
		1	2	3	4
		~~Kevin~~	~~Jane~~	~~Beth~~	Linda
~~1~~	~~Kevin~~	Jane	~~Kevin~~		
~~2~~	Kevin		Beth	Kevin	
3					

Counter has now reached the end value of the loop so the program moves on to whatever comes next.

You have probably realised by now that this algorithm is part of a simple sort routine.

Whilst a program is being developed a programmer might also use techniques such as single stepping, where the program is executed one line a time and the programmer can see the values of the variables being used, inserting breakpoints. A breakpoint stops the execution of a program either so the programmer can check the variables at that point or possibly just to show that a program, has executed a particular section of code.

Examination Questions

1. Data is entered via a keyboard from documents, validated and then saved to disc if no errors are found. A report is generated if errors occur during the validation process. Draw a system flow chart to show this. [5]

2. The operators **DIV** and **MOD** perform integer arithmetic. **x DIV y** calculates how many times y divides into x, for example 7 DIV 3 = 2. **x MOD y** calculates the remainder that results after the division, for example, 7 MOD 3 = 1.
    The following algorithm uses an array **Result**. Dry run this algorithm by copying and completing the trace table below. [6]

```
x ← 5
Index ← 0
Repeat
      y ← x MOD 2
      x ← x DIV 2
      Index ← Index + 1
      Result(Index) ← y
Until x = 0
```

y	x	index	Result (3)	Result (2)	Result (1)
-	5	0	-	-	-
1	2	1	-	-	1

What is the purpose of this algorithm? [1]

AQA June 2002 Module 1

3. The algorithm below rearranges numbers stored in a one-dimensional array called **List**. **Ptr** is an integer variable used as an index (subscript) which identifies elements within **List**. **Temp** is a variable, which is used as a temporary store for numbers from **List**.

```
Ptr ← 1
While Ptr < 10 Do
   If List [Ptr] > List [Ptr+1] Then
      Temp ← List [Ptr]
      List [Ptr] ← List [Ptr+1]
      List [Ptr+1] ← Temp
   Endif
   Ptr ← Ptr+1
Endwhile
```

(a) Dry run the algorithm by completing the table. It is only necessary to show those numbers which change at a particular step. [7]

Ptr	Temp	List									
		[1]	**[2]**	**[3]**	**[4]**	**[5]**	**[6]**	**[7]**	**[8]**	**[9]**	**[10]**
		43	25	37	81	18	70	64	96	52	4

(b) What will happen when **Ptr** = 10? [1]

(c) If the whole algorithm is now applied to this rearranged list, what will be the values of:

(i)   List[1]; [1]

(ii) List[9]; [1]

(iii) List[10]? [1]

AQA January 2003 Module 1

CHAPTER:9
Advanced classification of high-level languages

Selecting a high-level language

High-level languages are usually problem-oriented. This means that most (but not all) high-level languages are written to solve problems in specific areas. As a result there are lots of different high-level languages available to the programmer – some sources on the Internet list over 2000 of them. This can make the process of selecting the most suitable language a daunting task.

The criteria that a programmer uses to select a suitable language include:

- **matching the facilities offered by the language to the problem;**
- **the ability of the program to interact with other existing programs;**
- **suitability of the input/output to match the user needs;**
- **the level of expertise of the programmer;**
- **the cost of the program;**
- **how long it will take to acquire the skills to learn a new language.**

No one programmer can hope to have a working knowledge of all the computer languages that there are on the market. Existing languages are always being upgraded and added to and new languages are being developed to cope with new situations. At this stage of your computer career you cannot be expected to know more than a little about a small number of these languages.

High-level programming languages can be classified by the way in which they are organised. This method of organisation is better known as a paradigm (pronounced 'paradime'). There are a number of recognised paradigms.

IMPERATIVE/PROCEDURAL PROGRAMMING LANGUAGES

An imperative is a command that must be obeyed, and that is exactly how an imperative language works. An imperative language consists of a list of instructions that the computer has to follow. Every time you rerun the program the computer follows exactly the same instructions in exactly the same way. The user can exercise control over what the program does, but if selecting option A makes the computer carry out process B now, then it will make it carry out process B every time option A is selected.

> **Summary Questions**
>
> 1 Describe three criteria that a programmer might use when selecting a high-level programming language to solve a problem.
> 2 High-level languages are said to be problem-oriented. Explain this term.

You could define an imperative language as one that tells a computer what, when and how to do something. Imperative languages have been around for a long time, and some of the most well known are also the oldest:

- **Fortran (Formula Translation) was developed in the 1950s to help with mathematical and scientific problems. As you would expect, Fortran has a large built-in set of mathematical functions, and it has been designed to store numbers to a high level of accuracy.**

- **COBOL (Common Business Oriented Language) was originally created around 1960 and it was designed specifically to handle files of data and is supported by powerful search and report creation routines.**

- **BASIC (Beginners All-Purpose Symbolic Instruction Code) was developed to allow students to learn how to create computer programs. Early versions of BASIC were said to lack 'structure', but BASIC has come a long way since those early days and the Microsoft product Visual Basic has moved towards an object-oriented approach.**

- **Pascal (named after the seventeenth century French mathematician) was created in the 1970s. Pascal was originally designed for teaching programming. It makes use of structured programming constructs and data structures. Pascal has lead to the development of Turbo Pascal which in turn has lead to the creation of Delphi.**

- **Java (named after the favoured coffee beans of the team that developed it) was developed in the 1980s. Although it is now associated with the Internet, it was originally designed to program the chips used in electronic devices such as mobile phones and pagers. A key feature is the ability to create 'applets' which are self-contained programs that will run independently.**

- **C is called C because its predecessor was called B. It is widely used for operating systems and applications. Many versions of Unix-based operating systems are based on C. Although it has the characteristics of a high-level language it also shares many features with low-level languages. It is both simple and flexible to use. The latest derivative of C is rather unimaginatively called C++. It is possible for languages to be based in more than one paradigm. C++ is an imperative object-oriented language.**

LOGIC AND DECLARATIVE LANGUAGES

A declaration is telling somebody about something. In the case of a declarative programming language you give the computer facts and rules and the language can then be interrogated to extract data. There is no need to 'tell' the computer how to carry out the request – it decides and deduces for itself. If the program cannot find a solution by one route it can backtrack and try to find a solution by an alternative route.

Declarative languages are also referred to as very high-level languages. More advanced programming languages (the so-called fifth generation languages) take this a stage further. They make use of the results of previous searches and requests to alter how they come to their conclusions. You might look on this as a computer thinking for itself and ultimately this will lead to true artificial intelligence.

Logic programming is a specific type of declarative language, and Prolog (Programming Logic) is probably the best-known logic programming language. Prolog has been used to develop both knowledge-based and expert systems. See Chapter 11 for further details.

Summary Question

3 Explain the difference between an imperative and a declarative language.

Study Questions

1. What is meant by the term 'artificial intelligence'?

2. What features would you expect to find in a programming language that was designed to work in a control environment?

3. What is an applet, and where might one be used?

4. Only a few of the many hundreds of high-level languages are included in this chapter. Find out about other imperative and declarative languages. Explain why the language was originally developed.

Examination Questions

1. It has been decided to rewrite an existing system. What factors should be considered when deciding on the programming language to use? Give three factors, and explain why each is important. [6]

    AQA June 2002 Module 4

2. When designing a solution to a particular problem, a systems analyst may have to choose an appropriate high-level language. Give two criteria which the analyst might consider in making this choice, justifying the choice of each of these criteria. [4]

    AEB Summer 1999 Paper 2

CHAPTER: **10**
Object-oriented programming

An object-oriented program puts all the data and the processes that can be carried out on that data in one place. This 'place' is called an object.

One of the big problems programmers have when working with most high-level languages is that although they can write separate modules or procedures, the data these routines refer to is often held elsewhere in the program. This means that the routines can be hard to use in other programs. It also means that changes carried out to data might inadvertently affect the results of another routine. This is a common cause of bugs in software programs.

Encapsulation

The answer to these problems is to use an object-oriented language. The main concept behind object-oriented languages is that the routines, or, as they are more correctly called, the objects, are self-contained. This means that they contain all the data and all the functions – the things you might want to do with that data. This concept of keeping all the relevant parts together is called encapsulation.

Classes and objects

A class is a 'blueprint' or master copy, that defines a related group of 'things'. It sets down the facts and rules that the group has in common, but it does not store any data about the 'things'. An object is a member of a class. It takes the definition from the class and adds data. So a class might be called 'birds' and this would contain characteristics or rules such as 'body covered in feathers', or 'has wings', but an object from that class might be 'ducks'. This object would add extra rules such as 'has webbed feet' and it would also contain data about the different species of ducks.

Objects belong to classes and it is the classes that set down the basic format or blueprint for all the objects that are part of that class. If you think of this in practical terms you could say that all cars have similar features – so they could be said to belong to the same class. For example, they all have a power source, brakes, somewhere for the driver to sit, and so on. These features are the data – the physical features of a car. But a car can also do things – it can accelerate, use fuel, create exhaust emissions, and so on. These are the rules.

So each individual car forms an object: they have all the characteristics and attributes of the class 'car' (they all have brakes and they all use fuel), but they have their own specification – their own particular version of those details.

A class definition details all the data and attributes that that class can contain.

Visual Basic uses this concept. When you are writing a program, you have to place various objects on the form. All command buttons start out with the same

Summary Question

1 Explain the term encapsulation.

characteristics – they all come from the same class. It is up to the programmer to change the characteristics to create a unique object.

Inheritance

Inheritance is the principle of taking an existing class and adding to the features and abilities that that class has.

Inheritance in object-oriented languages acts in a similar way to the biological definition of inheritance. You start out with a set of characteristics and add to what already exists. You cannot delete or change existing features or abilities, you can only add to them.

If you started with a base class called 'vehicles' then you might state that a vehicle has a power source and it can move. You could then create a new class called 'road vehicles' that would inherit the two characteristics 'has a power source' and 'can move', and add some new ones such as 'movement is achieved by using wheels' and 'direction is controlled by a steering wheel'. You could then create another class based on the road vehicle class that was called 'buses'. This would inherit all the characteristics of road vehicles and add additional characteristics such as 'designed to carry paying passengers'. This relationship between the objects can be shown as an inheritance diagram like this one.

In Visual Basic a new command button will automatically start out with a built-in set of instructions about what it will look like and what it can do, but if you want to you can create a brand new object by copying and pasting. The new object will then inherit all the characteristics of the old one.

Polymorphism

Two (or more) classes are said to be polymorphic if they share a common base class. They will share some characteristics, but have others that are unique. You could create a number of classes based on base class 'vehicles'. The class 'road vehicles' is described above, but you could also create a class called 'water vehicles' that had its own extra characteristics. The classes 'road vehicles' and 'water vehicles' share some characteristics such as 'has a power source' and 'can move' but each has its own unique features as well. These two classes are said to be polymorphic.

Object-oriented languages

When high-level languages were first being developed they were targeted at particular problems. Most modern computer languages are much more general purpose, and object-oriented languages set out to be general purpose. As you would expect from such an important concept, there are a number of important object-oriented languages.

Visual Basic has already been mentioned but other well-known examples include Java, C++, Perl and Python.

Containment

Containment is the concept of an object that can contain other objects – you might have an object called 'vehicles' that can contain other objects such as 'engine' and 'equipment'.

Summary
Questions

2 Explain the difference between a class and an object.

3 (a) Draw a suitable inheritance diagram to show the relationship between the classes: meals, breakfast and supper.
  (b) Use this inheritance diagram to explain the term 'inheritance'.

4 Starting with a copy of the vehicle inheritance diagram, add classes for air vehicles, jet skis, taxis and ferries.
  (a) Are the classes 'jet skis' and 'ferries' polymorphic? Explain your answer.
  (b) Are the classes 'taxis' and 'ferries' polymorphic? Explain your answer.

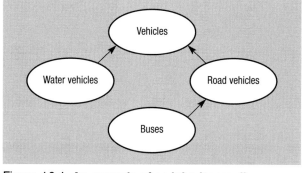

Figure 10.1 **An example of an inheritance diagram**

Examination Questions

1. A supermarket has a section labelled 'Bottled Water'. Bottled water comes as 'still bottled water' or 'carbonated bottled water' In an object-oriented program, 'bottled water', 'still bottled water' and 'carbonated bottled water' are three defined classes. The classes 'still bottled water' and 'carbonated bottled water' are related by single inheritance, to 'bottled water'.
    What is meant here by:
    (a) Class? [1]
    (b) Inheritance? [1]
    (c) Draw an inheritance diagram for the given classes. [3]
    (d) Give three advantages of the object-oriented approach to programming over a structured approach. [3]

    AQA June 2002 Module 4

2. One of the concepts of object-oriented programming is containment.
    Class 'Tform1' inherits from class 'Tform'.
    A form, 'Form1', of class 'Tform1', contains two buttons, 'Button-1' and 'Button-2', of class 'Tbuttons'.
    Write the class definition for 'Tform1'. [3]

    AQA June 2003 Module 4

CHAPTER:11
Logic programming

Logic programming is a specific type of declarative language, and Prolog (Programming Logic) is probably the best-known logic programming language. One way to explain the basic structure of logic programming is to look at an example that is based on the relationships between a group of people.

A logic programming language has two basic features, 'Facts' and 'Rules'.

```
Facts       Father (Wayne, Andrew)
            Father (Charles, Felicity)
            Father (Charles, Jennifer)
            Father (Andrew, Lionel)
            Mother (Belinda, Edwin)
            Mother (Debbie, Felicity)
            Mother (Debbie, Jennifer)
            Mother (Felicity, Lionel)
            Mother (Jennifer, Sam)
```

A fact is used to define a connection. In this case, the definition is that the first named person is the parent of the second, so Wayne is the father of Andrew, and Debbie is the mother of Felicity and Jennifer.

```
Rules       Grandfather (W,X) if Father (W,Z) AND Mother (Z,X)
            Grandfather (W,X) if Father (W,Z) AND Father (Z,X)
            Grandmother (W,X) if Mother (W,Z) AND Mother (Z,X)
            Grandmother (W,X) if Mother (W,Z) AND Father (Z,X)
```

The letters in the 'Rules' will contain variables – the program can substitute different names from the 'Rules'.

A 'Rule' is used to explain how the facts can be connected. The first of these 'rules' states that a person (W) is a grandfather of person (X) if he is the father of another person (Z) AND that person (Z) is the mother of another person (X). So, because we have the facts **Father (Charles, Felicity)** and **Mother (Felicity, Lionel)** the rule **Grandfather (W,X) if Father (W,Z) AND Mother (Z,X)** can be used to show that Charles is Lionel's grandfather.

You can then use this program to pose questions. For example you might want to identify Lionel's grandfather. To do this you would enter:

```
                    Grandfather (Who,Lionel)
```

and the program will respond

Who = Wayne

You can develop other rules to cover other circumstances. For example if you wanted to find out if two people had the same mother you would need to set up a set of rules including:

```
ShareMother (W, X) if Mother (Y, W) AND
Mother (Y, X)
```

Summary Questions

1 Explain the difference between a rule and a fact.

2 Use the facts and rules in the example above to answer:
 (a) Grandmother (Who,Lionel)
 (b) Grandmother (Debbie,Who)
 (c) Grandfather (Who,Sam)

Study Questions

1. Write down a rule that could be applied to the facts in the example given above that would find:

(a) the parents of a given person;
(b) if two people are siblings.

2. What details would you need to add to the 'Facts' if you wanted to check if two people were sisters?

Examination Questions

1. A simple logic processing language is used to represent, as a set of facts and rules, the valid constructions of numbers for a particular task. The set of facts and rules are shown below in clauses labelled i to vi.

   i.   digit (1 | 2 | 3 | 4 | 5 | 6 | 7 | 8 | 9 | 0)
   ii. sign (+ | -)
   iii. integer IF digit
   iv. integer IF digit AND integer
   v.   number IF integer
   vi. number IF sign AND integer

Clause i has the meaning '1, 2, 3, ...0 are all digits'.

Clause iv has the meaning 'something is an integer if it is a digit followed by an integer'.

(a) State whether or not the following numbers are valid and list the clauses used to justify your answer.

    (i)   79   [3]

    (ii)   148.5   [2]

    (iii) −2003598   [3]

(b) One of these numbers is invalid according to the above facts and rules.
Write the clause(s) that would make this number valid.   [2]

AQA January 2002 Module 4

2. A simple logic processing language is used to represent, as a set of facts and rules, the valid constructions of sentences in a subset of the English language. The set of facts and rules are shown below in clauses labelled 1 to 16.

    1) Determiner (a)

    2) Determiner (the)

    3) Adjective (small)

    4) Noun (elephant)

    5) Noun (lettuce)

    6) Noun (dog)

    7) Verb (ate)

    8) Verb (followed)

    9) Adverb (slowly)

  10) Noun_phrase (X) IF noun (X)

  11) Noun_phrase (X,Y) IF determiner (X) AND noun (Y)

  12) Noun_phrase (X,Y, Z) IF determiner (X) AND adjective (Y) AND noun (Z)

  13) Verb_phrase (X) IF verb (X)

  14) Verb_phrase (X,Y) IF adverb (X) AND verb (Y)

  15) Sentence (A, B, C) IF noun_phrase (A) AND verb_phrase (B) AND noun_phrase (C)

  16) Sentence (A, B, C, D, E) IF noun_phrase (A, B) AND verb_phrase (C) AND noun-phrase (D, E)

(a) Using the given set of facts and rules (1–16 above), give one example of:

    (i) a fact;   [1]

    (ii) a rule.   [1]

(b) Using the given set of facts and rules (1–16 above), state whether or not the following sentences are valid indicating which rules have been applied in the process.

    (i) The dog ate the lettuce;   [2]

    (ii) A cat ate the elephant.   [2]

CHAPTER:12
Dynamic and static data structures

In Chapter 6 we looked at the different ways individual items of data might be stored. For example, we looked at storing a person's age as an integer and their name as a string. These are known as data types. In this chapter we will look at the ways in which data types might be stored. These are called data structures.

The ways that the data can be stored can be split into two broad categories – dynamic and static.

A static data structure stores a set amount of data which is usually set up by the programmer.

The word dynamic means changeable, and this is just what happens to a dynamic data structure – although the amount of memory that is allocated by the operating system to a structure is finite, the actual amount of data in a dynamic system is always changing.

There are a number of dynamic structures we need to look at including stacks, queues and binary trees.

Stacks

A stack is a dynamic data structure. A stack is an example of a LIFO (last in first out) structure that means that the last item of data added is the first to be removed. A stack in a computer works in exactly the same way as a stack of books waiting to be marked or a stack of dishes waiting to be washed up – whichever item was added to the top of the stack last will be the first one to be dealt with.

However, unlike the washing up where items are literally taken off the stack as they are needed, the data in a computer stack is not actually removed. What happens is that a variable called the stack pointer keeps track of where the top of the stack is.

The process of adding a new item of data to the stack is called 'pushing' and taking an item off the stack is called 'popping'. When an item is pushed onto the stack the stack pointer moves up and when an item is popped off the stack the pointer moves down, but a copy of the data is still left on the stack.

Here is a simplified example of a stack in use. Note that this stack can only store six data items.

Summary Question

1 Explain the difference between a static and a dynamic data structure.

Bert
Cynthia
Cedric
Albert

Stack pointer ➜ (points to Bert)

The stack pointer is used to show where the top of the stack is.

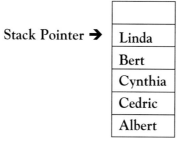

Stack Pointer ➜

| Linda |
| Bert |
| Cynthia |
| Cedric |
| Albert |

'Linda' is pushed on to the stack so the pointer moves up.

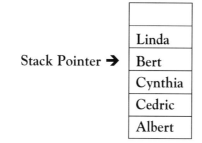

Stack Pointer ➜

| Linda |
| Bert |
| Cynthia |
| Cedric |
| Albert |

The stack is 'popped' so the data at the pointer (Linda) is read and the pointer moves down. Linda stays in the stack, but it will be overwritten the next time data is pushed on to the stack.

A more detailed explanation of this process can be found in Chapter 13.

It is possible for the stack to need more memory than has been allocated to it. In the example given above if the CPU tried to push on three more data items, the last one would have nowhere to go. In this case a 'stack overflow' error would occur.

USES OF STACKS

- If something happens to stop the normal operation of a program, for example another program asks for some data from a hard disk, then the first program is 'interrupted'. Whilst the new demand is being dealt with the details of the first program are stored on the stack. As soon as the 'interrupt' has been dealt with the details are taken back off the stack and the first program can carry on wherever it left off.

- Stacks also play a vital role in a process called recursion. You can read more about this in Chapter 14.

- It is common practice to 'nest' program constructs. For example, you might want to put one selection process inside another, or you might have a selection process being carried out inside an iterative loop. In this case the details of the successive nested loops are stored on the stack.

```
For HourCounter = 0 To 23
   For MinuteCounter = 0 To 59
      For SecondCounter = 0 to 59
         Output Hour , Minute , Second
      Next SecondCounter
   Next MinuteCounter
Next HourCounter
```

This pseudo clock won't keep very good time, but it does show how For/Next loops can be nested inside each other.

Queues

A queue is a called a FIFO (first in first out) structure. A queue in a computer acts just like people queuing for a bus – the first person in the queue is going to be the first person to get on the bus and the first item of data to be put into the queue in a computer will be the first to be taken out.

The commonest use of queues is when a peripheral such as a hard disk or a keyboard is sending data to the CPU. It might be that the CPU is not in a position to deal with the data straight away, so it is temporarily stored in a queue. Data being sent from the CPU might also need to be stored, and this is certainly the case when a document is sent to a printer. In this case your document is placed in the queue until the printer (which is a very slow device compared to the CPU) has the time to deal with the job. Queues that are used in this way are also known as 'buffers'.

Here is a simplified example of how a queue is used. This queue can only store six data items.

Pointer ↓

		Bert	Cynthia	Cedric	Albert

The queue has already been sent four data items, but none has yet been removed. The first name in was Albert.

Pointer ↓

	Linda	Bert	Cynthia	Cedric	Albert

Linda has now been added to the queue. When a new name is added, it gets added to the end of the queue

Pointer ↓   Pointer ↓

	Linda	Bert	Cynthia	Cedric	Albert

When a name is taken from the queue it is taken from the start. In this case Albert is read from the queue and the pointer moves to the next item in the queue.

A more detailed explanation of this process can be found in Chapter 13.

If documents are being sent to print on a network printer then it might be possible for the user or systems manager to control the queue in some way. For example they may be able to force print jobs to the top of the queue or to put print jobs on hold whilst others are pushed through.

Binary trees

A binary tree is another type of dynamic data structure. Whilst stacks and queues are primarily used to control the actual processing being carried out by the computer, a binary tree is used to store data.

The first item of data to be used is stored in the 'root node'. The next (and any subsequent) data item is dealt with by the following routine:

- If the value of the new data item is less than the value in the current node then branch left, otherwise branch right.

- Keep repeating this process until you come to an 'empty' branch, then put the new value in the node at the end of the branch.

This sounds awkward but look at the diagram below and try to follow through how the name 'Fred' has been added to the binary tree.

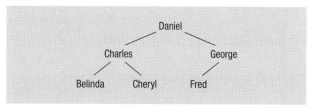

Figure 12.1 **An example of a binary tree**

Daniel is the root node. Belinda, Cheryl and Fred can be classed as 'leaf' nodes because they have no nodes below them. Charles can be described as the 'parent' and Cheryl the 'child'.

Binary trees are also useful if you want to be able to sort data as it is entered rather than waiting until it has all been typed in. There are more details of how this sort routine works in Chapter 13.

Lists and arrays

An array is a list or table of data that has just one variable name – the variable name identifies the list or table. Each item in the table is called an element.

As you will read below, an array can have many 'dimensions' but most arrays are either one-dimensional in which case they form a 'list' or can be visualised as a two-dimensional table.

Lists and arrays are static data structures that are created by the programmer to store tables of data. Programmers need to define just how big an array is

Summary Questions

5 A stack can be described as a LIFO and a queue as a FIFO. Use examples to explain the terms LIFO and FIFO.

6 Explain why stacks and queues are considered to be dynamic data structures.

7 Create a binary tree to store the following names – Sarah, Martin, Kevin, Tim, Susan and Tom. What would happen if the names were added to the tree in a different order?

going to be at the start of their program. This means that the size of the array and the amount of memory put aside for it does not change – it is static.

You might find that you want to store a sequence of data in some way. For example you might want to store the names of pupils in a class. You might decide to store the names like this:

```
Name1 = 'Derrick'
Name2 = 'Peter'
Name3 = 'Jill'
Name4 = 'Lynn'
```

Carrying out any sort of work even on just these four names is going to be very cumbersome. Imagine how difficult this would be if you wanted to store 30 names.

The best solution to this problem is to use an array. In the example above, we could call the array **Student_Name**. The third element in the array is Jill. This would be shown as

```
Student_Name(3) = 'Jill'
```

Another example could be to set up an array called **Days_In_Month**. The third element would be set to 31 as that is the number of days in March.

Because this table contains just one row of data it is actually called a list though to the computer it is a one-dimensional array.

A true array has one or more dimensions – for example you might want to store the mock exam results of a group of pupils. The array then might be called '**Results**' and it would have two dimensions – one

for the pupils and the other for the subjects and might look something like this:

	1	2	3	4	5	6	7
1	54	67	76	65	75	32	
2	32	45	98	32	54		
3	12	32	54	56			
4	32	21	12	43			
5	15						

You will note that the rows/columns are not labelled – it is up to the programmer to remember which 'axis' refers to the pupil and which to the subject.

In this diagram the 65 might represent the mark obtained by Hilary in the French exam. If the table were called **Results** then Hilary's French mark would be stored in **Results(4, 1)** where the 4 identifies the pupil and the 1 the subject.

It is possible to work with multi-dimensional arrays. If you take the exam paper array further, you might decide to store the exam results by paper. In this case the value in **Results(4, 1, 2)** could store the mark Hilary got in the second paper of the French exam.

In fact you can have many more dimensions than this – a four-dimensional array might store the marks gained for each question in each paper, so **Results(4, 1, 2, 12)** might store the mark Hilary was given for question 12 in paper 2 of the French mocks. As you add more and more dimensions to the array it becomes increasingly difficult to conceptualise.

Element in **Days_In_Month**	1	2	3	4	5	6	7	8	9	10	11	12
Contents of that element	31	28	31	30	31	30	31	31	30	31	30	31

Study Question

1. Peripherals such as printers make use of a method called double buffering. Research how this process works. Explain the benefits of this method.

Examination Questions

1. A binary tree can be used to represent the alphabet in a code. Part of the tree is shown below. Starting at the root of the tree, branch left is a dot and branch right is a dash. So N has the code: dash dot, and SOS has the code

    dot dot dot   dash dash dash   dot dot dot.

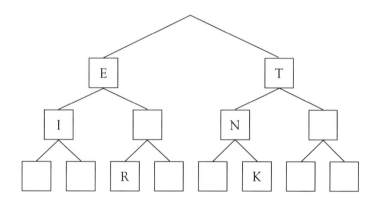

    (a) Place the missing letters S and O into the correct positions in the diagram.   [2]
    (b) What does the following two letter code spell: dot dot dash ?   [2]

    AQA January 2001 Module 1

2. The following numbers are to be entered in order to be stored in a binary tree for subsequent processing.

    13, 28, 30, 22, 6, 16, 4, 5, 21

    Show, with the aid of a diagram, how this data structure will store these values.   [3]

3. Multi dimensional arrays, records and binary trees are three different data structures. Listed are three examples of collections of data

    Details of directories and sub-directories of files in a computer system.
    Personal details such as name and address, held by a university.
    Analysis of the marks gained by a group of students in an examination

    For each of these examples choose which of the above data structures would be suitable.   [3]

4. The following data is input to a program, in alphabetical order, and is stored.

    Anne, Bob, Claire, Dean

    Draw a diagram to show how this data is stored for:
    (a)   a stack;
    (b)   a queue.   [4]
    One item is retrieved from these data structures for processing, and Eden is input.
    Draw the diagrams of this new situation for:
    (c)   a stack;
    (d)   a queue.   [3]

    AQA June 2002 Module 4

CHAPTER:13
Advanced standard algorithms (1)

Commonly used programming constructs

A variable normally stores a value such as a client's name or the number of students in a class. This data has an immediate use for the user. Other variables play an important role an controlling this data. In this chapter we will be looking at how variables can be used to create flags, counters and pointers.

FLAGS

A flag in a computer program is used to indicate whether or not something has happened.

Flags once played an important part in communication, and some flags are still used to day to signify something has happened, for example, white flags and flags at half-mast. A computer flag serves a similar purpose. For example, you might want to know if a password has been entered correctly; if a person has access rights to a file, or if the details in a file need saving because they have been changed. This example shows how you might use a flag to see if a specific file is in a particular folder.

```
Found_Flag ← False
Repeat
  Load the next file name from the folder
  If this is the file name you want then
  Found_Flag ← True
Until end of folder
```

On exiting the algorithm the value of **Found_Flag** will be **true** if the file name has been found, and **false** if it has not.

COUNTERS

As the name implies a counter counts how many times an event has occurred. For example, you might want to count how many times a pupil gives the right answer to a quiz.

```
Counter ← 0
Repeat
  Ask a question and input the answer
  If the answer is correct Then Counter ← Counter + 1
Until you have asked all the questions
```

On exiting this algorithm the variable **Counter** will contain the number of answers the pupil got right. The formal term for adding one to a variable is to increment it.

POINTERS

If you are working your way down a long list of names and you don't want to lose your place you need to mark where you are in some way. You might put a ruler under the current name, or if you are interested in a particular holiday in a table of holiday dates and prices you might put a circle around the one you are interested in. These are both examples of pointers.

You can use pointers in exactly the same way with arrays – you can use a pointer to show which element of the array you are working with. There are examples of pointers at work in Chapter 14. As you will see later in this chapter, pointers have an important part to play in controlling the contents of queues and stacks.

Pushing and popping a stack

The theoretical aspects of stacks were covered in Chapter 12. This section will show you how to push and pop a stack. In the following two routines a single dimension array called **StackArray** has been used to represent the stack. The variable **StackPointer** is being used to keep track of how far up or down the stack the pointer should be and **StackMaximum** stores the maximum number of values that can be stored in the stack.

```
' routine to push on to a stack

' check there is room on the stack
If StackPointer <= StackMaximum then
  ' push on to the stack
  StackArray(StackPointer) ← DataItem
  StackPointer ← StackPointer + 1
Else
  Error message "Data not saved - stack
  full"
End if
```

The error trap carries out an important task. The stack will only be allocated a limited number of memory locations, which in this case is kept in the variable **StackMaximum**. If the error routine was not there the stack would 'overflow' – there would be too much data to store in it.

This second routine shows how an item can be popped off a stack.

```
'Routine to pop off a stack

'check the stack is not empty
If StackPointer > 0 then
  'pop off the stack
  DataItem ←
  StackArray(StackPointer)
  'decrease stack pointer
  StackPointer ← StackPointer - 1
Else
  Error message «There is no data
  to pop from the stack»
End if
```

Circular queues

The popular concept of a queue is a line of people (or vehicles) gradually moving towards a 'goal' such as the till at a supermarket or a set of traffic lights. One of the main features of this system is that all the elements in the queue move forward in turn to take up the space just vacated by the person or vehicle in front of them.

In practical computing terms this would mean moving all the data in the queue forward as well. Moving data in any computer-based situation is a slow process so instead a system of pointers keeps track of which item is next in the queue.

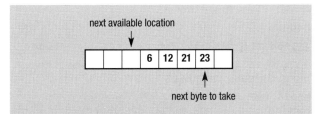

Figure 13.1 **An example of a queue**

It is important to realise that once an item has been put in the queue it does not move again until it is

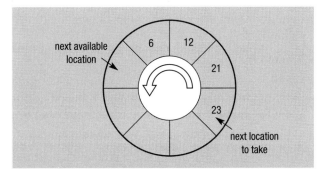

Figure 13.2 **An example of a circular queue**

taken out of the queue and even then it is overwritten rather than removed from the queue. In fact you need two pointers – one to point to the next item that is due to go out, and a second to keep track of where the next incoming item goes. Both these pointers move back along the queue, but when they get to the end of the queue, they go back to the start of the queue and start all over again.

It would be easier to imagine the queue as a circle. In that case the pointers can just keep on moving round the circle. This is why the implementation of a queue in a program is often referred to as a circular queue.

In the following pseudocode the variable **Next_In_Pointer** is used to point to the end of the queue, where the next item joining the queue will be put. The variable **Next_Out_Pointer** is used to show where the item at the head of the queue is.

The code for adding a new item to an eight element queue looks something like this:

```
'routine to add to a queue
Put Data_Item at Next_In_Pointer
  'increment Next_In_Pointer
Next_In_Pointer ← Next_In_Pointer + 1
  ' Check to see if the end of the queue has been reached.
  ' If so go back to the start of the queue
If Next_In_Pointer  = 9 Then Next_In_Pointer ← 1
```

The code for taking an item from the 'front' of the queue might look like this:

```
 routine to extract from a queue
  'remove data
Take data from byte at Next_Out_Pointer
  'move Next_Out_Pointer on
Next_Out_Pointer ← Next_Out_Pointer + 1
  ' Check to see if the end of the queue has been reached.
  ' If so go back to the start of the queue
If Next_Out_Pointer = 9 Then Next_Out_Pointer ← 1
```

Creating a binary tree

The process of creating a binary tree was explained in Chapter 12. The code for creating a binary tree needs three arrays. The first (called 'Node' in the example below) stores the data itself. The second ('Left' in the example) stores which node the left branch from a node moves to and the third ('Right') copes with branches to the right.

The data to add to the tree is stored in the variable **Add_Item** and the root node has already been set up with the name 'Jim'.

```
  ' Find next gap in the Node array
NodeCount ← 1 While Node(NodeCount) is not empty
  NodeCount ← NodeCount + 1
End While
  ' NodeCount stores the next blank
Node(NodeCount) ← AddItem

  ' start at the root node
PresentNode ← 1 While Node(PresentNode) is not empty do

  ' Branch Left or Right?
  If AddItem < Node(PresentNode) Then
```

```
      ' If Left branch is empty then assign NodeCount
      If Left(PresentNode) = 0 Then
        Left(PresentNode) ← NodeCount
      End If
      PresentNode ← Left(PresentNode)
    Else
      ' If Right branch is empty then assign NodeCount
      If Right(PresentNode) = 0 Then
        Right(PresentNode) ← NodeCount
      End If
      PresentNode ← Right(PresentNo)
    End If

  End While
```

If the root starts with the name 'Jim' the arrays should look like this after you have added the names Kevin, Alice and Belinda to the tree.

	Node ()	Left()	Right()
1	Jim	3	2
2	Kevin	0	0
3	Alice	0	4
4	Belinda	0	0

The binary tree this represents will look like this.

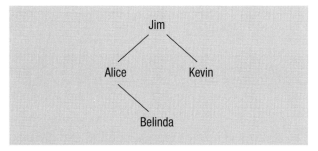

Figure 13.3 **The resultant binary tree**

Linked lists

Moving data about is expensive in terms of time, and many techniques have been developed to overcome this problem. One such solution is called a linked list. A linked list is a set of data with pointers added after each set or item of data to show the computer which record to go to next.

The problems with working with a list is that it is a static structure. If your list consisted of a sequence of data, for example, the names Alice, Belinda, Carly, Daphne and Erica and you wanted to add Beth to the list there are three choices.

- Append the data – append means 'add to the end of' and in this case you would literally add Beth to the end of the list. The problem with this is that, tempting though this may seem, you will destroy the alphabetical order the list had, and as you will discover later, keeping data in some sort of order can make maintaining the list much easier.

- The second option is to squeeze it into place, but the only way to do this would be if you copied the old data and inserted Beth in the appropriate slot as you copied the data across. Again this sounds like a quick fix, but imagine that there were 500 000 names in the list rather than the five shown here. This would then be a much more drawn-out system.

- The third system is to give each name a number (Position in the diagram below) that shows where it physically is in the list. After each name we need to add a number that will tell the computer which item is the next in the list. In the diagram, this number is in the next column. Finally we will also need a pointer that shows where the first item is stored. In this case it would be 1. This process is called a 'linked list'.

At first the list of names would look like this:

Position		Next
1	Alice	2
2	Belinda	3
3	Carly	4
4	Daphne	5

5	Erica	0
6	empty	
7	empty	

To read through the list the computer starts at the name in Position 1. The pointer after 1 links to 2, and so on. To fit Beth in the list, you add her name in the first available 'empty' space – in this case Position 6. Then you sort out the pointers. Beth comes between Belinda (number 2) and Carly (number 3) in the list so the pointer after Belinda is changed to point to Beth, and the pointer after Beth is set to point to Position 3 – which is Carly. The next diagram shows the state of the table after Beth has been added.

Position		Next
1	Alice	2
2	Belinda	6
3	Carly	4
4	Daphne	5
5	Erica	0
6	Beth	3
7	empty	

The big benefit of using this system is that none of the data has had to be moved – the only change is the order in which you visit the data. As you add more and more data this process becomes more and more convoluted. After a while the list is likely to become very untidy and at that stage you might want to create a brand new file with all the names in order.

This simple example is only storing the name of a person. It is possible to set up a set of pointers on any of the fields that are used in the records held in a file. Using linked lists in this way ensures that data can be quickly extracted.

This example shows some names, dates of birth and telephone numbers. Each field has its own pointer so a program could extract the data in any order the user needed to.

	Name	1	Date of Birth	3	Phone Number	3
1	Alice	2	05/03/1978	0	788453	2
2	Belinda	6	24/04/1967	6	788532	0
3	Carly	4	12/10/1956	2	612321	6
4	Daphne	5	05/03/1977	1	654641	5
5	Erica	0	09/11/1976	4	788009	1
6	Beth	3	16/06/1976	5	612342	4
7	<Empty>		<Empty>		<Empty>	

```
' Routine to add an item to a linked list
' Find next gap in the Item array
  ItemCount ← 1
  While Item(ItemCount) is not empty
     ItemCount ← ItemCount + 1
  End While
' ItemCount stores the next blank
  Item(ItemCount) ←AddItem
' set pointer to first name
  Pointer ← Startup

  While Next(ItemCount) <> 0
'check to see if AddItem fits here
     If Item(Pointer) < AddItem Then
' If it does, store what pointer was in LastPoint then move pointer to next Index value
        LastPoint ← Pointer
        Pointer ← Next(Pointer)
     Else
' the item fits in here so move round the pointers
        Index(LastPoint) ← ItemCount
        Index(ItemCount) ← Pointer
     End If

  End While
```

Like the binary tree, a linked list uses arrays to store both data and pointers. In the example below the data will be stored in an array called 'Item' and the pointers in an array called 'Index'. The variable 'Startup' stores the start up value.

If you apply this algorithm to this linked list:

and add in the name 'Daphne', then the resulting list will look like this.

	Item()	Index()
1	Helen	3
2	Colin	1
3	Jim	0

You will notice that the index of the last item (Jim) is set to 0. This is used to indicate the end of the list.

	Item()	Index()
1	Helen	3
2	Colin	4
3	Jim	0
4	Daphne	1

READING DATA FROM A LINKED LIST

And finally to access all the data stored in a linked list.

```
' set pointer to first name in the list
  Pointer ← Present

  Repeat
' output data from Item array
    Output Item(Pointer)
' move to next item in the list
    Pointer = Index(Pointer)

' check to see if all items have been output
  Until Index(Pointer) = 0
```

Summary
Questions

1 Explain the benefits of using a linked list to store a long list of names.

2 The secretary of a hang-gliding club stores the details of over 2000 members on a database. Explain how linked lists could be used to maintain lists that allow the data to be accessed either by membership number, surname, first name or address.

3 Draw a table to illustrate how a linked list could be used to store the names Sarah, Martin, Kevin, Tim, Susan and Tom. The names should appear in this order in your table, but your pointers should show how the names can be 'visited' in alphabetical order.
 (a) Show how the table would change after Jack has been added to the table.
 (b) Show how this second table would change after the name Tim has been removed from the list.

Study Questions

1. Explain how a circular queue can be used to cope with a user entering data via a keyboard.

2. Create pseudo-code that demonstrates the use of a flag to indicate if a user has pressed an invalid key.

3. Create pseudo-code that shows how a counter can be used to show how many files on a floppy disk are over 200 Kb.

4. Create pseudo-code to show how a pointer can be used to indicate the highest value held in a 20 element array.

Examination Questions

1.   (a)   (i)   The animals Rabbit, Dog, Wallaby, Elephant and Cat are entered, in the order given, into a linked list so that they may be processed alphabetically. Draw this linked list.   [2]

        (ii)   Redraw the list after two additional items, Gerbil and Pig, have been added.   [2]

  (b)   This linked list is said to be a dynamic structure. What is meant by the term dynamic structure?   [2]

2.   Describe how the elements in a non-empty queue are reversed with the aid of a stack.   [4]

CHAPTER:14
Advanced standard algorithms (2)

Searching

One of the main benefits of using a computer is the ability to search. Consider how many everyday activities involve searching, for example:

- **a cash machine searches for your bank account details to find how much (or little) money you have left in the account;**

- **the computerised till at your local supermarket searches for the cost of the goods you are buying;**

- **a search engine on the Internet looks for the cheapest holiday to the Algarve.**

Most searches are carried out on data storage systems, but they are used in other applications as well, for example, in the search and replace process on a word processor.

A simple search might just look for one keyword, but most search routines allow you to construct more complex queries using logic statements such as OR, AND and NOT.

LINEAR SEARCH

A linear search works by looking at every item or set of data until the details that you are searching for are found or you fail to find it altogether.

The efficiency of a search can be strongly influenced by the way that the data is organised. If there is no logical or rational method in the way the data has been stored then the only option is to use a linear search. This is the simplest and slowest system.

Summary Question

1 Explain why a linear search for data is inefficient.

You might use a linear search when you try to find a CD in a rack – you know it is there somewhere but unless the CDs are organised in some way, say by title or artist, then you will have to check every title until you find the one you want. A search might be coded something like this:

```
Repeat
  Look at the 'Title'
Until 'Title' is the one you want OR there are no more CDs
```

A standard search on the Internet uses a similar technique. In this case most search engines look in the 'metatags' for the keywords you have entered.

BINARY SEARCH (BINARY CHOP)

If the data you want to look through is in some sort of logical order then you might be able to make use of a technique called a binary chop or binary search. This method works in the same way as the children's game where someone thinks of a number between say 1 and 100 and you have to guess what it is by being told if your guesses are higher or lower than the number.

A logical person would start with 50, because they could then discount half of the numbers straight away. Guessing half way into the middle of the remaining numbers (either 25 or 75) will allow half of the remaining numbers to be discarded and so on. Each time you make a guess you halve the number of options that are left to you, and you alter the range within which the answer must be.

These 15 'cells' contain 15 numbers arranged in ascending order:

```
  1   2   3   4   5   6   7   8   9  10  11  12  13  14  15
  ■   ■   ■   ■   ■   ■   ■   ■   ■   ■   ■   ■   ■   ■   ■
```

Use this method to find the number 51 which is contained in one of these cells. Start in the middle – block 8.

```
  1   2   3   4   5   6   7   8   9  10  11  12  13  14  15
  X   X   X   X   X   X   X  37   ■   ■   ■   ■   ■   ■   ■
```

Block 8 contains the number 37, so blocks 1 to 8 can now be discarded. Half way between 9 and 15 is 12 so look there next.

```
  1   2   3   4   5   6   7   8   9  10  11  12  13  14  15
  X   X   X   X   X   X   X  37   ■   ■   ■  57   X   X   X
```

Block 12 contains the number 57 so blocks 12 to 15 can be discarded. Half way between blocks 9 and 11 is block 10 so look there.

```
  1   2   3   4   5   6   7   8   9  10  11  12  13  14  15
  X   X   X   X   X   X   X  37   ■  51   ■   X   X   X   X
```

Block 10 contains the number we are looking for. This has taken three 'looks' to find the missing number.

This pseudo-code shows how you might set out the process in a program. In this case the record number that needs to be found is stored in a variable called FindMe.

```
FindMe stores the record title that we are searching for
Lowest_Pointer  ← 1
Highest_Pointer ← Number_of_Records
Do
  Middle_Pointer ← (Lowest_Pointer + Highest_Pointer) / 2
    If Record at Middle_Pointer < FindMe Then
      Lowest_Pointer ← Middle_Pointer
    End If
  If Record at Middle_Pointer > FindMe Then
    Highest_Pointer ← Middle_Pointer
  End If
Until Record at Middle_Pointer = FindMe
```

The pointers **Lowest_Pointer** and **Highest_Pointer** point to the first and last locations in the file where the record you are looking for might be located. The pointer **Middle_Pointer** stores the number roughly half way between the two extremes.

This process will only work if you are accessing a direct or random access file – see Chapter 35 for more details about random access files. The process is called a binary chop because every time you look at a possible match you halve the number of records that are still 'in'.

At first this seems like a very slow system, but in fact it is very efficient. If you want to search through just three records it will take a maximum of two 'looks' before you find a match and with seven records you will need three 'looks' and so on. This is an exponential growth – doubling the number of records you want to look for takes just one more 'look'. So that if you have one million records you would need to take a maximum of just

Summary Questions

2 What condition must be true before a binary chop search can be used?

3 A set of 255 records is to be searched. Write down the minimum and maximum number of looks a program will have to take if the data is to be searched:
   (a) by a linear search;
   (b) by a binary chop search.

20 'looks', and it would take a maximum of 33 looks to find one person in the world which currently has a population of over six billion.

Sorting

After searching, sorting is the most common process you would normally want to carry out on a set of data. There are lots of different ways of sorting data, and one of the skills that programmers need is to decide which method suits their needs best. Some are particularly good when there is a lot of data to sort, others are particularly good when the data is almost, but not quite in the right order, and so on. The sort routine described below is the simplest. It is in known as a ripple or bubble sort.

BUBBLE OR RIPPLE SORT

The only realistic way to sort data is if it is stored in an array. If the data is held in an array you can sort the data by comparing each element in the array with the data in the following element. If the first is bigger than the second then you swap them. If you repeat this process enough times the data will eventually be sorted in ascending order.

In this example the data is stored in an array called **Storage** and the array holds **Number_Of_Records** records.

The numbers at the start of each line are there to help with the explanation – they are not part of the program.

```
1 For Loop1 = 1 To Number_Of_Records - 1
2   For Loop2 = 1 To Number_Of_Records - 1
3     If Storage(Loop2)> Storage(Loop2 + 1)
      Then
4       Temporary ← Storage(Loop2)
5       Storage(Loop2) ← Storage(Loop2 + 1)
6       Storage(Loop2 + 1 ) ← Temporary
7     End if
8   Next Loop2
9 Next Loop1
```

Suppose the array **Storage** had eight elements.

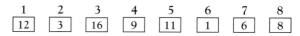

The routine would work like this:

- **For now we will ignore lines 1 and 9 and start with lines 2 and 8.**

- **Lines 2 and 8 are a For/Next loop – a form of iteration. In this case the process is going to be repeated seven times. The process that is going to be repeated is the lines 3 to 7.**

- **Line 3 compares each element in the array in turn with its neighbour. So the first time the loop is processed Loop2 is 1 so Storage(1) is compared with Storage(2). In this case these would be 12 and 3, respectively,**

- **12 is greater than 3 so lines 4, 5 and 6 are carried out and the values are swapped round to leave the array looking like this.**

- **The value of Loop2 is now incremented to 2 so Storage(2) is compared and swapped if necessary with Storage(3) and so on.**

- **This whole process of comparing and swapping carries on until all the elements in the array have been swapped. At the end the array now looks like this.**

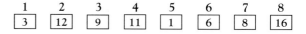

- **As you will have noticed this isn't very sorted yet. That is why lines 1 and 9 are there. They now repeat the process all over again until the array is finally sorted like this.**

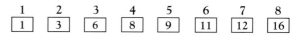

This process is called a ripple or bubble sort because each time the program carries out one pass of the array the larger numbers are rippling or bubbling to one end of the array and the smaller ones to the opposite end.

This first example is actually very inefficient – it gets carried out regardless of whether it needs to be or not, and there is a lot of unnecessary work for the computer to do.

This second algorithm carries out exactly the same process, but in a more sophisticated way. This time the program uses a flag called **Completed_Flag** to record whether or not a swap has been made. If no swaps have been made then the data must be sorted so there is no point in carrying on.

```
Repeat
 Completed_Flag ← True
 For Counter = 1 To Number_of_Records - 1
   If Storage(Counter)> Storage(Counter + 1)
   Then
     Temporary ← Storage(Counter)
     Storage(Counter)← Storage(Counter( + 1)
     Storage(Counter + 1) ← Temporary
     Completed_Flag ← False
   End if
 Next
Until Completed_Flag = True
```

Searching a binary tree

The concept of binary trees was introduced in Chapter 12. Now it is time to make use of this dynamic data structure. There are two main operations that you might want to carry out on a binary tree – searching and 'traversing'.

The process of searching a binary tree uses a technique similar to the binary chop method described above. In this routine the variable **FindMe** contains the name we are looking for, and you will remember that the 'Root node' is the node the tree is built from.

```
Current_Node ← Root_Node
Repeat until Current_Node equals FindMe
  If Current_Node > Find_Me then
    Move left to child node
  Else
    Move right to child node
  End If
Loop
```

TRAVERSING A BINARY TREE

The word traversing means to move across and that is what you do when you traverse a binary tree – you move across it visiting nodes as you go.

The process of traversing a binary tree extracts all the data from the tree in some sort of order. There are three ways of traversing a binary tree – pre-order, in-order and post-order.

To traverse a binary tree you start at the root node and move left, right or visit depending on the type of traversal you are using. Moving left or right entails 'looking' to see if there is a node in that direction and moving if there is. Visit entails extracting the data at that node.

Traversing the binary tree shown below gives the following results:

Pre-order	Visit, Left, Right	John, Helen, Kim
In-order	Left, Visit, Right	Helen, John, Kim
Post-order	Left, Right, Visit	Helen, Kim, John

Note that pre/in/post tells you when you do the visit stage.

**Summary
Question**

4 Explain how a ripple sort works on the set of numbers 4, 7, 2, 8, 1.

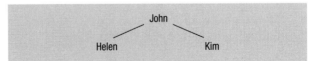

Figure 14.1 A simple binary tree (1)

This algorithm carries out an 'in-order' traversal.

```
Set current node as root
Traverse
End

Define Procedure Traverse
  If there is a node to the left then
    Move left to child node
    Traverse
  End If
  Visit
  If there is node to the right then
    Move right to child node
    Traverse
  End If
  Move back up the branch
End Procedure
```

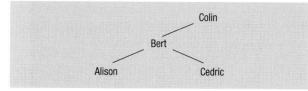

Figure 14.2 **A simple binary tree (2)**

Here is how this algorithm traverses this binary tree.

1. The root node is set as the current node ('Colin').

2. The procedure **Traverse** is called for the first time.

3. There is a node to the left of the current node so move to the node to the left so that we are now on the node containing 'Bert'.

4. The procedure **Traverse** is called for the second time. The details of the first call of **Traverse** are pushed on to the stack.

5. There is a node (Alison) to the left on 'Bert' so move left. Current node now becomes 'Alison'.

6. **Traverse** is called again. This time there is nothing to the left of the current node.

7. Visit the node – the term visit is deliberately vague. It might mean 'print it out' or it might mean enter the person's date of birth or any other process you want to carry out on each node.

8. Now we need to check if there is a node to the right of 'Alison' but there is not, so move back up the branch to 'Bert'.

9. This call of **Traverse** has now been completed so the details of the previous call can be popped off the stack.

10. We jumped out of the second call of **Traverse** after the first question so we now 'visit' the node 'Bert'.

11. Now we look to the right of 'Bert'. There is a node there ('Cedric') so we go to that node.

12. **Traverse** is called again so the details of the previous call of **Traverse** are placed on the stack.

13. Now we are at 'Cedric' we look left, then visit then look right.

14. This call is now finished so back up the branch to 'Bert'.

15. We have now finished the call to 'Bert' so that call of **Traverse** is also complete, so its back up to 'Colin'.

16. Visit 'Colin'.

17. Try to go right, but there is nothing to go to.

18. Finish the first call to **Traverse**.

If you have followed this process through you should find that you have visited the nodes in alphabetical order – Alison, Bert, Cedric and finally Colin.

This looks and sounds like a very complex process, but in fact it is a very elegant solution to the problem. You must remember that although we have only traversed a tree with four nodes, the process would be exactly the same for a tree with four hundred nodes. The only limitation is the number of calls of **Traverse** that the stack can handle.

Traversing a binary tree in pre-order follows the same routine but in this case you visit the root node as soon as you get to it. Traversing the tree given above in pre-order would result in Colin, Bert, Alison and Cedric.

The only detail you would need to make the code carry out a pre-order traversal would be to move the visit to before the first **If** statement like this.

```
'Pre order traversal
Visit
If there is a node to the left then
  Move left to child node
  Traverse
End If
If there is a node to the right then
  Move right to child node
  Traverse
End If
```

A post-order traversal would result in the list Alison, Colin, Bert and Cedric. In this case you visit the node after you have tried to go both left and right from the node.

An interesting feature of all this is that no matter how you set out the four nodes an in-order traversal will always produce a sorted list, but pre-order and post-order produce a different set of data if the data are rearranged.

Recursion

Recursion is the process of calling a function from within itself. The concept is very elegant, but trying to understand how it works is rather more difficult.

The algorithm described above that traverses a binary tree uses recursion. Each time a call is made

the current contents of the procedure must be stored on the stack.

The process to traverse a binary tree in order goes like this:

```
Define Procedure Traverse
  If there is a node to the left Then
    Go Left
    Traverse
  End If
  Visit
  If there is a node to the Right Then
    Go Right
    Traverse
  End If
End Procedure
```

After the procedure **Traverse** has been called for the first time the program will check to see if there is a node to the left. If there is it goes left then calls the procedure **Traverse**. This means that **Traverse** has been called from inside the procedure **Traverse**, and if the next node also has a node to its left then **Traverse** will be called from inside itself again.

Summary Question

5 Each member of a club has a unique four-digit membership number. Details of the members are stored in a database that is sorted by membership number. A member contacts the secretary to notify them about a change of address but they do not supply their membership number. Explain how the database program will locate the record.

Study Questions

1. The only sort routine that has been discussed in this chapter is the ripple or bubble sort. Research other sort routines and identify what circumstances suit each type of sort routine best.

2. Rewrite the algorithm that carries out a ripple sort to make it as efficient as possible.

3. Explain the term recursion and give an example where it might be used.

4. Create a binary tree using the following data: Rose, Jasmine, George, Naomi, Trevor and Stanley.

(a) List the nodes that will be visited in order to find the node that stores George.

(b) Traverse the tree in pre-order and write down the value at each node when you visit it.

(c) Repeat this process for a post-order traversal.

(d) Repeat this process for an in-order traversal.

Examination Questions

1. The diagram shows a binary tree. The letter at each node is printed as the tree is traversed. What will be printed when the traversal is:

   (a) in order; [1]

   (b) pre-order; [1]

   (c) post-order. [1]

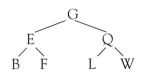

2. Show the steps needed to look up Manchester using a binary search on the following list. [3]

   Antrim, Bristol, Cardiff, Edinburgh, Manchester, Newry, Swansea

   AEB Summer 1997 Paper 2 Question 7

3. (a) The series of characters J, F, H, U, S, X, T are to be entered into a binary search tree in the order given. Draw a diagram to show how these values will be stored. [4]

   (b) The following data are held in arrays **Data**, **L** and **R**:

Data	[1]	[2]	[3]	[4]	[5]	[6]	[7]
	J	F	H	U	S	X	T

L	[1]	[2]	[3]	[4]	[5]	[6]	[7]
	2	0	0	5	0	0	0

R	[1]	[2]	[3]	[4]	[5]	[6]	[7]
	4	3	0	6	7	0	0

Using the arrays on page 72, dry-run the following pseudocode by completing the trace table opposite:

```
Item 'T'
Ptr 1
WHILE Data[Ptr] < > Item DO
   PRINT Data[Ptr]
   IF Data[Ptr] > Item
     THEN Ptr L[Ptr]
     ELSE Ptr R[Ptr]
   ENDIF
ENDWHILE
PRINT Data[Ptr]
```

Item	Ptr	Printed Output
T	1	J

[6]

AQA January 2002 Module 1

4. A binary search tree is a data structure where items of data are held such that they can be searched for quickly and easily. The following data items are to be entered into a binary search tree in the order given:

London, Paris, Rome, Berlin, Amsterdam, Lisbon, Madrid

(a) Draw a diagram to show how these values will be stored. [4]

(b) Circle the root node in your diagram. [1]

(c) If Madrid is being searched for in this binary tree, list the data items which have to be accessed. [1]

AQA June 2001 Module 1

5. The following section of pseudo-code processes a one-dimensional integer array called **List**. The numbers in **List** are in ascending order, and **x**, **Low**, **Medium** and **High** are all integer variables. (The function **Int** returns the whole number part of its parameter.)

```
Proc Process(Low, High, x)
Found  ←  False
Repeat
   Middle  ←  Int((Low + High)/2)
   If List (Middle) = x
     Then Found  ←  True
     Else If List(Middle) > x
       Then High  ←  Middle - 1
       Else Low  ←  Middle + 1
Until Found = Tree
End Proc
```

(a)   Copy and complete the following dry-run table for Process (1, 10, 19), given that the integers in **List** are 2, 4, 6, 7, 11, 13, 19, 21, 27, 29.

Low	High	Middle	Found
1	10		

[7]

(b)   What type of routine does this pseudo-code define?   [1]

AEB Summer 1999 Paper 2

6.   A binary search and a linear search are two different methods of searching a list.
A given list contains 137 items.

(a)   (i)   What is the maximum number of items accessed when searching for a
particular item from the given list using a binary search?   [1]

(ii)   Explain your answer.   [1]

(b)   (i)   What is the maximum number of items accessed when searching for a
particular item from the given list using a linear search?   [1]

(ii)   Explain your answer.   [1]

AQA January 2003 Module 4

CHAPTER:15
Data and information

Data

In Chapter 3 we looked at how sequences of zeros and ones could be used to represent different items of data. In its 'raw' form, this data has no meaning – it is simply a series of numbers or characters. For example, if you look at the following data, it is impossible to tell what it represents:

2267, 2356, 2427, 3567, 4352, 4552

4353, 4234, 3542, 2333, 1343, 4352

Without data, there would be no need for computers. The purpose of any computer is:

- **to have data input into it;**
- **to process that data in some way;**
- **to output that data in some way.**

If you consider the typical applications that computers are used for, you can see that data is critical to its use. For example, databases are collections of data on a related theme, spreadsheets handle numeric data and carry out calculations on that data, word processors process text data, and so on.

Data has become a valuable commodity in its own right. Companies are able to collect data and use it in a way that benefits their organisations. For example, most of the major grocery retailers now have loyalty cards which are designed to collect data on the purchasing habits of their customers (see case study); market research companies carry out extensive surveys to collect data about consumers' opinions; governments collect data about the population to help them plan public services.

Information

Data becomes information when it is given some structure that is meaningful to the user. To return to the raw data used in the previous section, by adding structure to the data, it becomes meaningful:

Sales of cars by sales person 2003					
	Jan	Feb	Mar	Apr	May	June
John Smith	2267	2356	2427	3567	4352	4552
Mary Jones	4353	4234	3542	2333	1343	4352

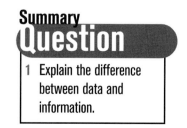

Summary Question

1 Explain the difference between data and information.

It is usually the job of application software to turn raw data into meaningful information. More specifically, it is the job of the IT specialist to use the appropriate software tools to process the data in a way that is most useful for their organisation. In this example, spreadsheet software could be used to add the necessary structure to the data. You will notice that the data has not changed, but it now has meaning. Databases are widely used to store large volumes of data and to provide features that enable the data to be processed and output in a variety of ways, for example, in table or graph form.

Direct data sources

Direct data collection is when the data is collected with a specific purpose in mind. For example:

- **A bank collects data on cash withdrawals from an automatic teller machine (ATM) in order to ensure there are sufficient funds.**

- **A school will collect exam results to analyse overall performance.**

- **A retailer will collect a customer's name and address in order to make a delivery.**

- **The government may collect data on the number of pensioners in an area to plan health care provision.**

Indirect data sources

Indirect data collection is when data is collected and then used for a different purpose. For example:

- **A manufacturer of an electrical product may collect your name and address to validate your warranty on a product and then use the data to send direct mail.**

- **A grocery retailer may collect data from a loyalty card in order to calculate the discount due and then use the data to decide on which products to stock in its stores.**

- **The government may sell data collected from the Census to commercial organisations to help them with their marketing activities.**

- **A bank may share data collected on an application form for a loan with other departments within the bank.**

Case study

Supermarket loyalty cards

For many years the major supermarkets had no idea who their customers were. Other big businesses such as the banks knew a great deal about their customers because every time they bought a 'product' from the bank, the customer had to fill in a detailed application form about where they live, how much they earn and what other financial services they use.

Supermarkets on the other hand had millions of customers passing through the stores without knowing who they were, where they lived, how often they shopped there, or how much money they spent. This presented the supermarkets with a problem. How could they decide where to build new stores, what prices to charge, what products to stock or even what hours to open without a detailed understanding of the customers and their habits?

The loyalty card solved many of these problems and provided a rich source of data to be used for marketing purposes. A loyalty card looks like a credit card and uses a magnetic stripe to record details about customers and their purchases. Every time the customer presents the card at the checkout, it is swiped through a card reader. Customers liked the loyalty card because it gave them discounts – the more they spent, the greater the discount. However, the supermarket benefited more because indirectly, they were able to collect the following data:

- **the name and address of their customers allowing them to send direct mail to their homes;**
- **how far people are prepared to travel to the store helping them to decide where to locate any new stores;**

- **how loyal customers are and how often they shop at the store;**
- **how much customers spend on the average shopping trip;**
- **which special offers are the most successful;**
- **which product ranges sell best in which parts of the country.**

Study Questions

1. Identify two different organisations that collect data and for each explain two ways in which the data is used.

2. Identify one source of data available to:

(a) a car manufacturer;

(b) a hospital;

(c) a charity.

3. Why might some people object when organisations store personal information about them?

4. Some people in the UK would like to have a national identity card which would be issued by the government.

(a) What information might the government record on this card and for what purpose?

(b) How might the information be misused?

5. Identify all the organisations who store your personal details. Are there any of these organisations who you think should not have your details? Why?

6. Why do you think that data and information has become so important to modern businesses?

7. It is common for checkout operators in shops to ask customers for their postcode even though they do not collect any other information from them. Why do you think they collect just this piece of information?

Examination Questions

1. Janlori Goldman wrote "There is barely a piece of information about people that isn't used for purposes different from what it was initially gathered for, and always without their approval".

Give two different pieces of information in addition to name and address that a supermarket chain might gather about a customer who makes regular purchases from its many branches and who can be identified by the supermarket. For each piece of information, state one purpose that the supermarket might use the information for. The purpose must be different in each case. [4]

AQA January 2002 Module 2

2. Customers at supermarkets are offered loyalty cards which give them discounts on the products they buy. It also provides the supermarket with a rich source of information about the customers.

   (a) With reference to this example describe the difference between direct and indirect data sources. [2]

   (b) Explain the difference between information and data. [2]

3. "The consumer pays for every purchase twice over: first with money, and second with information that's worth money." Alvin Toffler.

   (a) State two uses for information, gathered about customers, that support the view that information is worth money. [2]

   (b) Imagine that you are asked to advise lawyers who are drafting a law entitled 'Fair practices in the gathering of information'. State two key principles of such a law. [2]

   AQA June 2001 Module 2

CHAPTER: 16
Number and data representation

Binary number system

The binary system is a fundamental principle of computing and was introduced in Chapter 3. It is important because most of what computers do is carried out digitally, that is, as a series of 'ons' and 'offs'. In binary terms this means ones and zeros. By combining ones and zeros, any type of data, be it characters, numbers, sound, pictures or video, can be represented by the computer. The instructions that make up software are also handled by the computer purely as a sequence of ones and zeros.

There are a number of ways in which binary codes are used to represent different types of data. This chapter covers how binary is used to represent integers and keyboard characters. Chapter 17 covers number bases and character coding systems, Chapter 18 covers real numbers including negatives and decimals, and Chapter 19 looks at binary representation of graphics and sound.

Pure binary representation of denary integers

This has been covered in Chapter 3 and is revised here. Denary is number base ten. It is referred to as denary so that it is not confused with the word 'decimal' which in this context refers to numbers with a decimal point. This is important as a different method is used to represent 'real' numbers, as opposed to 'integers', which are whole numbers.

To recap, binary numbers are converted to denary integers as follows:

- **Write down a binary number (e.g. 10000111).**

- **Above the number, starting from the 'least significant bit' (LSB) write the number 1.**

- **As you move left from the LSB to the 'most significant bit' (MSB) increase the number by the power of 2 as shown:**

MSB   LSB

128	64	32	16	8	4	2	1
1	0	0	0	0	1	1	1

- **Wherever there is a 1, add the denary value: the above example represents one 128, one 4, one 2 and a 1 giving a total value of 135 (128 + 4 + 2 + 1 = 135). Therefore 10000111 in binary equals 135 as a denary integer.**

To convert a denary integer to a binary number, use the same method as above, but working the other way. For example, to convert the number 98:

- **Write down the power of 2 sequence. (Eight bits are used here but you will notice that you only need seven for this example.)**

MSB   LSB

128	64	32	16	8	4	2	1

- **Starting from the MSB put a 1 or 0 in each column as necessary to ensure that it adds up to 98 as follows:**

0 under 128
1 under 64
1 under 32
0 under 16
0 under 8
0 under 4
1 under 2
0 under 1

Therefore 01100010 = 98.

Another way of carrying out this calculation is to carry out repeated divisions on the denary number as follows:

98 divide by 2 = 49 with a remainder of 0
49 divide by 2 = 24 with a remainder of 1
24 divide by 2 = 12 with a remainder of 0
12 divide by 2 = 6 with a remainder of 0
6 divide by 2 = 3 with a remainder of 0
3 divide by 2 = 1 with a remainder of 1
1 divide by 2 = 0 with a remainder of 1

Reading from the bottom this gives us 1100010 which equals 98. (Note that the leading zero is omitted.)

Check your answer by working it back the other way:

128	64	32	16	8	4	2	1
0	1	1	0	0	0	1	0

64 + 32 + 2 = 98

Binary Coded Decimal (BCD)

Binary Coded Decimal represents denary integers using blocks of four binary digits. A BCD code typically looks like this:

1001 0011 1000

Each block of four binary digits is converted to denary using the same method as above, as follows:

8	4	2	1	8	4	2	1	8	4	2	1
1	0	0	1	0	0	1	1	1	0	0	0

The result of each block then comprises the final number. In this case this is:

8 + 0 + 0 + 1 = 9
0 + 0 + 1 + 1 = 3
8 + 0 + 0 + 0 = 8

Therefore the answer is 938.

To convert from denary integer to BCD is the reverse of this process. For example, 236 in BCD would be 0010 0011 0110. The space between each block of four is shown here for clarity. There would be no physical space between the blocks within the computer.

8	4	2	1	8	4	2	1	8	4	2	1
0	0	1	0	0	0	1	1	0	1	1	0

Check your answer by converting it back again.

Summary Questions

1 Convert the following binary codes into denary:
   (a) 110;
   (b) 11001001;
   (c) 10010;
   (d) 10101010;
   (e) 1011010.
2 Convert the following denary values into binary:
   (a) 25;
   (b) 121;
   (c) 87;
   (d) 142;
   (e) 255.

The main use of BCD is to enable fast conversions of denary to binary for applications such as pocket calculators. Each digit on a calculator can only be from 0 to 9. Therefore, each block of four bits can be used to represent each number on the calculator's display.

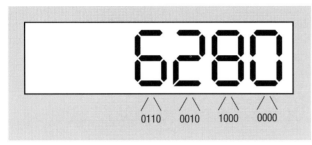

Figure 16.1 **Calculator display and BCD conversion.**

Storing characters

In addition to the various number systems discussed in this chapter, binary codes can also be used to represent text and characters.

EBCDIC

EBCDIC (pronounced eb-sid-ic) stands for Extended Binary Coded Decimal Interchange Code. In addition to fast conversions of denary integers, EBCDIC applies a similar process for the quick conversion of other keyboard characters including all the letters and special characters. This method was devised by IBM and uses an 8-bit code. It is most commonly used when encoding data onto magnetic tape.

ASCII AND UNICODE

ASCII or the American Standard Code for Information Interchange (covered in Chapter 3) was until recently the standard method of converting keyboard and other characters into binary codes. Initially a 7-bit code was used which allows for 128 different characters. More recently, extended ASCII was introduced which is an 8-bit code allowing for 256 characters.

A new standard has emerged called Unicode which follows the same principles as ASCII in that it has a unique 8-bit code for every keyboard character on a standard English keyboard. Unicode also includes international characters for over 20 countries and even includes conversions of classical and ancient characters.

Unicode is being constantly developed and updated to include more of the "diverse languages of the modern world", for example, the Arabic and Chinese alphabets are significantly different to English and even alphabets that are similar to English, such as French and German, still contain specific characters not found on standard English keyboards.

The importance of any 'standard' is that it is universally adopted, which in this case involves everyone in the computing industry throughout the world. The increased use of the Internet has meant that much more data is being passed around global networks. If different encoding systems are used it means that data can be corrupted when used on any system other than that on which it was created. Unicode aims to cover every platform in terms of hardware and operating systems, every foreign language and every program.

**Summary
Questions**

3 Convert the following BCD codes into denary:
(a) 0110 0101 0011;
(b) 1000 0011 0101;
(c) 0001 0111 0000;

4 Convert the following denary values into BCD:
(a) 49;
(b) 132;
(c) 687;
(d 756.

5 What is the purpose of ASCII and Unicode?

6 What is the main difference between ASCII and Unicode?

7 ASCII uses an 8-bit code. Why are eight bits needed?

Study Questions

1. ASCII and Unicode both claim to provide the 'standard' method for representing characters. However, both systems are different.

(a) What are the implications of having more than one 'standard' in this context?

(b) At what point does something become 'industry standard'?

(c) Identify which organisations are involved in the development of the Unicode standard.

2. Identify two common uses of BCD.

Examination Questions

1. (a) (i) Convert the decimal integer 13 into pure binary. [1]

(ii) Convert the decimal integer 13 into BCD (Binary Coded Decimal). [1]

(iii) Give one advantage of BCD. [1]

(b) What is the relationship between data and information? [1]

AQA June 2001 Module 1

2. Bit patterns can be interpreted in a number of different ways.

(a) A computer word contains the bit pattern 0001 0111. What is its decimal value if it represents:

(i) a pure binary integer; [1]

(ii) a BCD (Binary Coded Decimal)? [1]

AQA January 2003 Module 1

CHAPTER:17
Advanced number representation – number bases

Number bases

A number base indicates how many different characters are available. Denary is number base 10 which means that it uses ten digits: 0, 1, 2, 3, 4, 5, 6, 7, 8 and 9 and binary is number base 2 which means that it uses two digits: 0 and 1. Different number bases are needed for different purposes. Humans use number base 10 whereas computers use binary as this represents digital data.

The size of the number base determines how many characters are needed to represent a number. Looking at the example in the previous chapter, the number 98 in denary (base 10) requires two digits. The binary (base 2) equivalent is 1100010 which requires seven digits. As a consequence of this there are many occasions in computing when very long binary codes are needed. To solve this problem, computers also use other number bases which require fewer characters to represent numbers. For example, some aspects of computing involve number base 8 which is referred to as 'octal'. This means that the characters 0 to 7 are used. When you reach 7, the next number is 10 as there is no 8 and 9. The next number after 17 in octal is 20 and so on.

The accepted method for representing different number bases (in text books and exam questions) is to show the number with the base in subscript. For example:

43_{10} is denary

1011_2 is binary

167_8 is octal

$2A7_{16}$ is hexadecimal

Hexadecimal

A more common number base in computing is base 16 referred to as 'hexadecimal' or 'hex'. Hex is particularly useful for representing large numbers as fewer characters are required. Hex is used in a number of ways. Memory addresses are stored in hex format as are colour codes. The main advantage of hex is that two hex characters represent one byte.

Consider the number 11010011_2. This is an 8-bit code which when converted to denary equals 211_{10}. The same number is hex is $D3_{16}$. This basic example shows that an 8-bit code in binary can be represented as a two character code in hex. Consequently hex is often referred to as 'shorthand' for binary as it requires fewer characters.

Summary Question

1 Explain why computers can only process in binary form.

As it is number base 16, hex uses 16 different characters: 0 to 9 and A to F. The table below shows denary numbers up to 31 with the hex equivalents:

Denary	Hex	Denary	Hex
0	0	16	10
1	1	17	11
2	2	18	12
3	3	19	13
4	4	20	14
5	5	21	15
6	6	22	16
7	7	23	17
8	8	24	18
9	9	25	19
10	A	26	1A
11	B	27	1B
12	C	28	1C
13	D	29	1D
14	E	30	1E
15	F	31	1F

There is scope for confusion here as humans rarely use letters as numbers. Also, the numbers in hex convert to different numbers in denary. For example, the number 16 in denary is the equivalent of the number 10 (one zero) in hex.

DENARY TO HEX CONVERSIONS

A common approach to convert denary to hex is to first convert the denary to binary as described in Chapters 3 and 16, and then convert the binary to hex. Taking the denary number 211 as an example:

128	64	32	16	8	4	2	1
1	1	0	1	0	0	1	1

Therefore $11010001_2 = 211_{10}$

Split the binary number into two groups of four bits and convert each into the hex equivalent.

8	4	2	1		8	4	2	1
1	1	0	1		0	0	1	1

$8 + 4 + 1 = D$ (the hex equivalent of 13) and $2 + 1 = 3$

Therefore $211_{10} = 11010011_2 = D3_{16}$.

HEX TO DENARY CONVERSIONS

The process here is to convert the hex to binary, and then the binary into denary. Hex to binary conversions are the reverse of the above process. Take the hex number, and then convert each character in turn into its binary equivalent using groups of four bits. Take $2A3_{16}$ as an example:

8	4	2	1		8	4	2	1		8	4	2	1
0	0	1	0		1	0	1	0		0	0	1	1

$2 = 0010$

$A = 1010$ (10 in denary)

$3 = 0011$

Therefore 1010100011_2 is the binary equivalent of $2A3_{16}$.

Summary
Questions

2 Some programming languages use hexadecimal numbers. Explain what a hexadecimal number is and explain what the benefits are of using this system.

3 Convert the following denary (base 10) numbers into binary:
(a) 10;
(b) 12;
(c) 15;
(d) 65;
(e) 165.
Use your answers to convert the same numbers into hexadecimal.

This binary code can then be converted into denary in the usual way:

512	256	128	64	32	16	8	4	2	1
1	0	1	0	1	0	0	0	1	1

$512 + 128 + 32 + 2 + 1 = 675_{10}$

When carrying out a conversion, it is useful to remember the binary equivalent of the 16 characters used in hex as shown in the table above.

Summary Questions

4 Convert the following hexadecimal numbers into binary:
(a) 10;
(b) 12;
(c) 1F;
(d) F1.

5 Convert the following hexadecimal numbers into denary:
(a) E;
(b) 21;
(c) 17;
(d) AB.

Examination Questions

Examination questions for this chapter are combined with the topics covered in Chapter 18.
See questions at the end of Chapter 18.

CHAPTER:18
Advanced number representation – real numbers

Integers and real numbers

In computing terms it is important to distinguish between different types of numbers. Chapters 3 and 16 concentrated on converting integers into binary. An integer is a whole number. More specifically we have only looked at 'unsigned' integers which means that all the numbers have been positive. Computers also need to handle 'real' numbers – positive and negative numbers which may be shown to several decimal places. Many computer applications will require very large or very small numbers to be handled to a high degree of accuracy.

Summary
Question

1 Use examples to explain the difference between an integer and a real number.

Twos complement

Twos complement is a method used to represent 'signed' integers in binary form. This means that it can be used to represent positive and negative integers. This method is very similar to the methods described in Chapter 3 and 16 so it is assumed that you already have a good understanding of this before attempting this section. The purpose of this section is to show how twos complement can represent negative integers.

Assume we want to convert the binary code 10011100 into denary using twos complement:

- **Write out the denary equivalents as shown:**

MSB							LSB
−128	64	32	16	8	4	2	1

You will notice that with twos complement, the most significant bit becomes negative. Using an 8-bit code, this means that the MSB represents a value of −128

- **Now write in the binary code:**

MSB							LSB
−128	64	32	16	8	4	2	1
1	0	0	1	1	1	0	0

- **Now add up the values:**

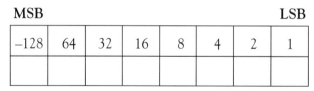

$$-128 + 16 + 8 + 4 = -100$$

Converting from denary to binary using twos complement can be slightly more difficult for negative numbers as you will be starting from a negative number and working forward. Remember that with twos complement, when the MSB is 1 it means that the number must be negative. You may find it easier to use the following method:

To convert −102 into binary, first write out the binary equivalent of +102 as shown:

MSB							LSB
128	64	32	16	8	4	2	1
0	1	1	0	0	1	1	0

- Starting at the LSB write out the number again until you come to the first 1.
- Then reverse all the remaining bits, that is, 0 becomes 1 and 1 becomes 0.
- The number becomes 10011010.
- The number is now in twos complement.

MSB							LSB
−128	64	32	16	8	4	2	1
1	0	0	1	1	0	1	0

To check, add these up: −128 + 16 + 8 + 2 = −102.

ADDING AND SUBTRACTING USING TWOS COMPLEMENT

Adding numbers together using twos complement is the same as adding numbers together in denary in that you add up the total and carry values across to the next column. For example, in denary to add 48 to 83:

$$
\begin{array}{r}
4\,8 \\
8\,3\ + \\
\hline
1\,3\,1 \\
\hline
1\,1
\end{array}
$$

Binary addition is the same. To add 01101100 to 10001000

$$
\begin{array}{r}
0\,1\,1\,0\,1\,1\,0\,0 \\
1\,0\,0\,0\,1\,0\,0\,0\ + \\
\hline
1\,1\,1\,1\,0\,1\,0\,0 \\
\hline
1
\end{array}
$$

Remember that in binary 1 + 1 = 10 and that 1 + 1 + 1 = 11.

The only true arithmetic that the computer can carry out is addition. In order to carry out subtractions, the only method is to convert the number to be subtracted to a negative number, and then to add the negative number. For example 20 − 13 in denary would actually be performed by adding 20 to −13 giving the answer of 7. To do this in binary:

- Calculate the binary equivalent of 20 which equals 00010100
- Calculate the binary equivalent of -13 which equals 11110011.
- Add 20 to -13 in binary form:

$$
\begin{array}{r}
0\,0\,0\,1\,0\,1\,0\,0 \\
1\,1\,1\,1\,0\,0\,1\,1\ + \\
\hline
0\,0\,0\,0\,0\,1\,1\,1 \\
\hline
1\,1\,1
\end{array}
$$

- Check your answer back by converting it to denary and the answer is 7 which is correct.
- You may notice that this calculation would have a final 1 to be carried. This is called an 'overflow bit' and is handled separately to the calculation.

Summary Questions

2 Explain the term 'unsigned integer'.

3 Explain why a computer needs to use twos complement to store negative numbers.

4 Show how an 8-bit twos complement integer would be used to store:
(a) +64;
(b) −64;
(c) +100;
(d) −100.

5 Add the binary numbers 1001 and 1100. Leave your answer as a binary number.

6 Use twos complement to carry out the following calculations:
(a) 12 + 8;
(b) 25 − 17.

Fixed point numbers

In order to represent real decimal numbers, that is, numbers with decimal places, fixed point representation can be used. In the same way that denary has a decimal point, binary has a binary point. The numbers after the binary point represent fractions. For example, if you had an 8-bit binary code, you may place the binary point after the fourth bit as shown:

1	0	0	0	1	1	0	0

The binary point is not actually stored in the 8-bit code, its position is fixed by the programmer. It is shown here purely to aid understanding.

To convert this to a denary number is a similar process to the other conversion we have done. This time, the numbers after the binary point become fractions as follows:

8	4	2	1	$\frac{1}{2}$	$\frac{1}{4}$	$\frac{1}{8}$	$\frac{1}{16}$
1	0	1	0	1	1	0	0

The conversion of the bits before the binary point are handled in the same way as before with each value doubling as you move from right to left. The numbers after the binary point halve each time as you move from left to right as shown.

Therefore the number above is

$$8 + 2 + \frac{1}{2} + \frac{1}{4}$$

giving a total therefore, of $10 \frac{3}{4}$ or 10.75.

The binary point can be placed anywhere within the byte but the position of the binary point restricts the size of the number that can be represented and also the accuracy of the number. With the binary point in the position shown in this example:

- the smallest number we could represent (apart from 0) is 0000.0001 which is $\frac{1}{16}$ or 0.0625;

- the next number we could represent is 0000.0010 which is 2/16 or 0.125. It is not possible to represent any number between 0.0625 and 0.125;

- the largest number we could represent is 1111.1111 which is 15 $\frac{15}{16}$ or 15.9375;

- moving the binary point to the left means that we can have more accurate decimals but reduces the range of whole numbers available;

- moving the binary point to the right increases the range of whole numbers but reduces the accuracy;

- it remains the case that with an 8-bit code, we can represent 256 different combinations regardless of where we put the binary point.

Floating point numbers

The big problem with all the 8-bit systems we have investigated so far is that they can only store a very limited range of numbers. The biggest positive number we have been able to store so far is only 255 and the smallest positive number is 0.0625. There will be many scenarios when a program needs to cope with numbers that are larger or smaller than this. There are two ways round this problem:

- The first is to allocate more bits to store the number. For example, a 16-bit unsigned code would allow you to store all the integers from 0 to 65 535; a 24-bit code would allow you to cope with 16 777 215 different combinations; and so on.

- If you wanted to store negative and positive numbers you would need to use the twos complement system outlined above. Using 16 bits would allow you to store between −32 768 and 32 767.

Summary Questions

7 Describe the benefits of using a fixed point number system.

8 Convert $3\frac{1}{4}$ into a binary number.

9 Convert the binary number 10.11 into its decimal equivalent.

The problem with allocating an ever-increasing number of bits to store large numbers is knowing when to stop. The solution to this is to use a floating point number representation.

In floating point, the binary point can be moved depending on the number that you are trying to represent. It 'floats' from left to right rather than being in a fixed position. In the previous example, the binary point was fixed after the fourth bit and this presented serious limitations on both the range and accuracy of numbers that can be represented. Floating point extends the fixed point technique described in the previous section and also involves twos complement so you should not attempt this section until you are happy with these two concepts.

A floating point number is made up of two parts – the mantissa and the exponent. In denary, we often have to calculate large numbers on our calculators. Most calculators have an eight or ten digit display and often the numbers we are calculating need more digits. When this happens, an exponent and mantissa are used. For example, the number 450 000 000 000, which is 45 and ten zeros, would be shown as 4.5×10^{11}. This means that the decimal place is moved 11 places to the right.

In binary, the exponent and mantissa are used to allow the binary point to float as in the following example. Remember that the mantissa and/or the exponent may be negative as twos complement method is also used. Consider the following 12-bit code: 000011000011.

The code can be broken down as follows:

- **the first eight bits are the mantissa which can be broken down further as:**
  - **the MSB is 0 which means that the number is positive;**
  - **the next seven bits are the rest of the mantissa: 0001100.**

- **The remaining four bits are the exponent: 0011**

It is common to show the mantissa and exponent more clearly as follows:

Mantissa	Exponent
00001100	0011

First, work out the exponent in the usual way remembering that twos complement is being used:

Therefore the exponent is +3.

–8	4	2	1
0	0	1	1

This means that the binary point will 'float' three places to the right.

Now calculate the mantissa. The binary point is always placed after the most significant bit as follows:

–1	$\frac{1}{2}$	$\frac{1}{4}$	$\frac{1}{8}$	$\frac{1}{16}$	$\frac{1}{32}$
0	0	0	0	1	1

The point now floats three places to the right. The values for the conversion have changed because the binary point has now moved.

8	4	2	1	$\frac{1}{2}$	$\frac{1}{4}$
0	0	0	0	1	1

Therefore, 00001100 0011 = 0.75.

This is a simplified example to show the concept. The real power of floating point is that the binary point can be moved several hundred places to the

Summary
Questions

10 A computer uses a 5-byte word to store a 'real'. Explain what a word is in this context.

11 A computer uses 12 bits to store numbers in floating point format. Seven bits are used to store the mantissa and the other five bits the exponent. Both parts use twos complement. The following numbers are stored using this system. Work out their decimal equivalents.
(a) 011100001111;
(b) 101000011111.

left or right as necessary to represent either very large or very small numbers.

Normalisation

Normalisation is a technique used to ensure that when numbers are represented they are as precise as possible in relation to how many bits are being used. Another benefit is that normalisation ensures that only one representation of a number is possible. The easiest way to think about this is to consider how many decimal places you would choose to use when representing a denary number.

Assume that you are creating a system to record the results of various athletic events: 100 m, 400 m and 1500 m, and that you allow six digits to store the time taken for each race.

- **The winner of the 100 m event ran it in 10.4357 s. Four numbers have been used after the decimal place to provide a precise number.**

- **The winner of the 400 m event took 47.3453 s. Again four numbers are used after the decimal place.**

- **The winner of the 1500 m race took 150.435 s. This time, the number is only precise to three decimal places as three digits are needed for the integer. The decimal point has floated here in order to represent the number. However, the result is not as precise as the results for the 100 m and 400 m races.**

- **The result of the 100 m race could be stored as 010.436. However this would not be sensible as the**

Summary

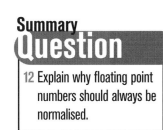

Question

12 Explain why floating point numbers should always be normalised.

number is not as precise as it could be with six digits available.

The same thing happens when using a mantissa and exponent. With a fixed number of bits that can be used to represent the mantissa, the precision of the number can be affected by where the binary point is positioned. The exponent is used to ensure that the floating point is placed to optimise the precision of the number. For example:

234 000 can be represented as $23\,400 \times 10^1$
$$2.34 \times 10^5$$
$$0.00000234 \times 10^{11}$$

The second option is the best way to represent the number as it uses the least number of digits yet provides a precise result. This number is referred to as being in 'normal form' or 'normalised'.

With binary codes, normalisation is equally important. In order to be 'normalised' the first bit of the mantissa, after the binary point, should always be a 1. For example, consider the binary equivalent of 108 in denary using an 8-bit code would be 01101100:

- **the normalised mantissa would be 0.1101100;**

- **the binary point will have to be moved seven places to the right in order to convert it back to the original number;**

- **therefore the exponent must be 7;**

- **twos complement for 7 is 0111.**

Therefore the normalised representation of 108 is 0.11011000111.

You might be wondering why it is worth showing 108 in this way when it could be shown more simply as 01101100. The reason for this is that with an 8-bit mantissa and a 4-bit exponent it is possible to represent a much wider range of positive and negative numbers than using eight bits alone.

Examination Questions

1. (a) (i)   Convert the hexadecimal number BD93 to binary.   [1]
        (ii) The contents of register A is 1010 0000 0011. These bits are a representation
              of a number in twos complement, with the leftmost ten bits as the mantissa
              and the rightmost six bits as the exponent. Convert this number into decimal.   [3]

    (b) Give two reasons why floating point numbers are normalised.   [2]

    AQA January 2003 Module 4

2. A 2-byte register holds numbers in floating point form with a 10-bit mantissa and
    a 6-bit exponent.
    (a) Explain the terms:
        (i)   mantissa;   [1]
        (ii) exponent.   [1]

    (b) Each of these holds data in twos complement form. At one moment, this register holds the
         following bits: 0110101100000011.
        (i)   Label the mantissa in this data.   [1]
        (ii) How can you tell if the number is positive or negative?   [2]

    (c) Explain, or show, how you would subtract 3 from 5 using twos complement.   [2]
    (d) Give one advantage of floating point notation over fixed point notation for storing
         real numbers.   [1]

    AQA January 2002 Module 4

3. A binary pattern might represent a decimal integer or a decimal real number.
    In a computing context, give an example of:
    (a) a decimal integer;   [1]
    (b) a decimal real number.   [1]
    (c) The binary data 00110111 represents an unsigned real number in fixed point
         form, with the binary point between bits 1 and 2. E.g. 1101.11.
         Convert this number into decimal, showing all your working.   [2]
    (d) Convert the binary data 10110111 00111110 into hexadecimal.   [1]
    (e) Give one example of where hexadecimal numbers are used, and explain why
         they are used here rather than binary numbers.   [2]

    AQA June 2002 Module 4

CHAPTER:19
Representing sound, images and other information

Bit-mapped graphics

Graphics are the display of pictures on your computer. Graphics can range in complexity from simple line drawings through to full animations. All computer graphics are represented using sequences of binary digits (bits). In order to understand this fully, you first need to understand how monitors display information. This is covered in detail in Chapter 47 so is only touched upon here.

The display on a monitor is made up of thousands of tiny dots or picture elements called pixels. A typical monitor will have a grid 1024 by 768 pixels. Each of these pixels can be controlled to display different colours. By combining the pixels, a picture is created on the screen. You can see this more clearly on a television screen as it has a lower resolution (less pixels) than a computer monitor. If you go very close to a television you can see the pixels and you can see them change as the overall picture changes.

At a very simple level, each pixel could be controlled by one bit. This means that each pixel is 'mapped' to one bit in memory. The bit could be set to either zero or one representing off or on which in this case would be black or white.

Summary Questions

1 What is a bit-mapped graphic?
2 If eight bits of memory are mapped to each pixel, how many megabytes of memory are needed to store a 1024 × 768 display?

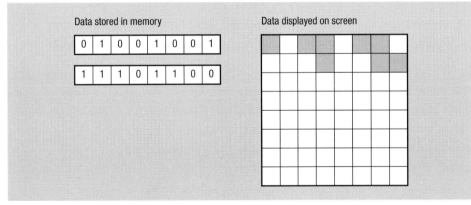

Figure 19.1 **Bit-mapped display**

To create colour graphics, each pixel is mapped to at least one byte (eight bits) in memory. This means that each pixel could be any one of 2^8 or 256 different colours. If you are not sure why this gives 256 combinations, you should reread Chapter 3. Your computer will contain a 'card' for controlling graphics. The amount of memory allocated for bit-mapping depends on the amount of memory on this graphics card.

Modern computers allocate 24 bits to each pixel which give 2^{24} combinations or 16 777 216 different colours. 24 bits are used as eight bits are allocated to the three primary colours: red, green and blue (RGB) from which all other colours are created. This means that with a 1024 × 768 display with 24 bits per pixel you get 18 874 368 bits or 2.25 Mb of memory to make one picture.

Vector graphics

Vector graphics are created using lines and coordinates. A vector is a measure of quantity and direction. It is easier to think of vector graphics as geometric shapes. For example, if we had a vector graphic of a square it would be made up of four coordinates with lines drawn between them. To rescale the object requires an adjustment of the coordinates. Therefore, the graphics are being controlled mathematically rather than being completely regenerated as with a bit map. An image created on the screen will be made up of lines and the scale and position of the lines will be adjusted as the screen display changes to create an image.

Consider the following two images:

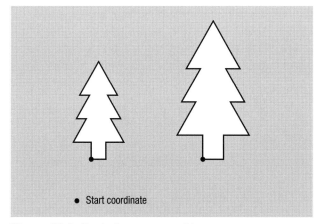

• Start coordinate

Figure 19.2 **Scaled vector graphic**

The first image is a series of lines, the second image is the same series of lines but the dimensions are different. If this second image was stored as a vector graphic, the file would contain the new dimensions as numbers and calculations. One of the advantages of this method is that the file would be much smaller than a bit-mapped file containing the same image. As vector graphics files contain the mathematical codes required to create an image rather than storing the actual image as with a bit-mapped graphic, they are not practical for every scenario where graphics are needed such as scanning and digital photography. Many software applications convert vector graphics to bit-mapped to allow alterations to be made.

CAD/CAM packages make use of vector graphics as these packages tend to use line-based drawings. Some two- and three-dimensional animation programs also use vector graphics. This is because an animated image is a series of still images combined together. Once the still image has been created, the vectors can be manipulated to create the various frames within the animation.

Analogue and digital signals

All the processing carried out by a computer is digital, yet there are occasions when either the input or output required is analogue. For example, much of the data sent around the Internet is sent in analogue form over the telephone network. This is because the telephone lines were originally designed to carry voice data which is analogue. A microphone takes speech input which is analogue, or a musical instrument digital interface (MIDI) takes in data from a musical instrument which may be analogue.

Analogue data is data that is infinitely variable and is often represented in the form of a wave. Figure 19.3 shows a typical sound wave:

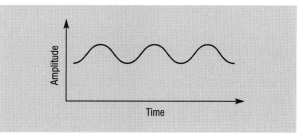

Figure 19.3 **An analogue wave**

Digital data is often represented as shown below with the ons and offs shown as set 'peaks' and 'troughs'. As we have seen in this section, digital data is a sequence of zeros and ones.

Summary Questions

3 What is a vector graphic?

4 Give two examples where analogue data needs to be converted to digital data.

5 Give two examples where digital data needs to be converted to analogue data.

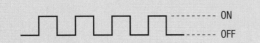

Figure 19.4 **A digital signal**

Analogue to digital conversions

The problem arises when we need to put analogue data on to the computer or when we want to output digital data from the computer in analogue form. In order to do this, an analogue to digital converter (ADC) is needed. Perhaps the most well-known converter is the modem which changes (modulates) a digital signal into analogue so that it can be sent down a telephone wire. When it is received at the other end, another modem demodulates the signal, converting it back into digital form.

Another example is a (MIDI) device for an acoustic guitar. This device fits beneath the strings on the guitar and when the strings are played they generate an analogue sound wave. The sound waves are picked up and converted to digital form.

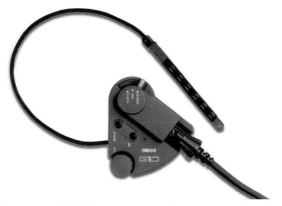

Photograph 19.1 **MIDI device for an acoustic guitar**

Sound sampling and synthesis

Sampling is the process of converting analogue sound waves into digital form to create what is commonly known as digitised or digital sound. An analogue sound wave is infinitely variable so in order to store this digitally, a series of readings at fixed intervals are taken from the wave. These readings are then stored as binary codes. It is called sampling because you do not record every single change in amplitude of the wave form. Instead, you choose set points at which a reading (or sample) will be taken.

The diagram below shows the points at which the sample readings are taken:

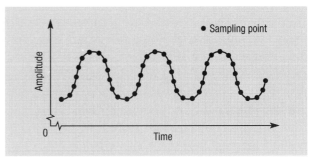

Figure 19.5 **Sampling an analogue wave (1)**

The amplitude of the wave is only recorded at the point where each sample is taken. Other variations in the amplitude are not recorded. Therefore, to create an exact replica of the analogue sound would require a sample to be taken every time the amplitude of the wave changed even by a small amount. However, the human ear doesn't notice very small changes, so sound can be faithfully created with fewer samples. Taking more samples allows more accurate production of the original analogue sound. Consider the following example:

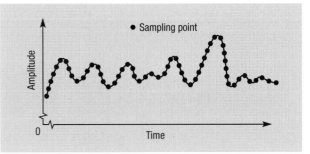

Figure 19.6 **Sampling an analogue wave (2)**

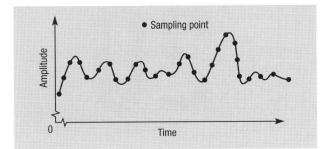

Figure 19.7 **Sampling an analogue wave (3)**

Imagine that the sound wave shown represents part of a song. The first would create a more accurate recording as it involves more   samples. However, it would require much more memory and storage space than the sample in the second diagram where fewer samples have been used. Samples can be edited to remove any background noise or interference from the original sound wave. Some people argue that CDs produce 'better quality' sound than vinyl disks for this reason.

Sound synthesis is another term that is used to refer to sound that is produced digitally rather than in analogue format. It means that the sound is synthesised or manufactured rather than being in its 'original' analogue format. By definition, all sounds created by a computer are digital.

Summary Questions

6 'Analogue produces a purer sound than digital'. Give one reason why this statement could be true.

7 Explain why video with sound requires a large amount of disk space.

Study Questions

1. Identify one application where it would be more appropriate to use vector graphics rather than bit-mapped graphics.

2. Identify one application where it would be more appropriate to use bit-mapped graphics rather than vector graphics.

3. What is the standard sampling rate for CD audio quality?

4. Video messages sent via mobile phone often appear slightly jagged and jerky. Explain why this is the case.

Examination Questions

1.   Traditionally, sound was recorded in analogue form, such as on vinyl records.
     For digital audio systems, the signals received from the microphone are sampled
     and the measurement of the amplitude can be stored as digital data. To reproduce
     the sound, the digital data is fed through a digital-to-analogue converter.
     (a)   Give two factors which affect the quality of sound.   [2]
     (b)   What is possible when using the digital method of representing sound that
           could not be done with the sound recorded in analogue form?   [1]
     (c)   What is sound synthesis?   [1]

AQA January 2003 Module 1

CHAPTER:20
Communication methods

One of the key aspects of computing is communication. For example, input and output devices need to communicate with the processor, the hard disk needs to communicate with memory and so on. Communication in this sense takes place through the transmission of data and instructions. We have already looked at many examples of data transmission inside the computer. In this section, we are more concerned with communication between computers and peripheral devices and also between one computer and another across local and global networks. This section will also include a detailed analysis of the infrastructure that makes up the Internet.

Computer data can be transmitted using a variety of media. For example, there are a number of different cable types that can be selected, or microwave links can be used where wireless applications are needed. As we saw in the previous chapter, data is transmitted either in digital form, or is modulated into analogue. In either case, you should view the transmission of data as a series of signals being sent that represent different binary codes which in turn can represent text, numbers, sound or graphics. It is important to understand the difference between analogue and digital as most communication methods involve converting one to the other. Therefore, it is recommended that you read Chapter 19 before reading this chapter.

Serial and parallel transmission

Serial transmission sends and receives data one bit at a time in sequence. Serial connections are usually used for long distance transmission which in computing terms means anything over about one metre. Therefore, it will usually be a serial cable that connects most of the peripherals to the computer such as the mouse and keyboard, and serial cables that connect computers together to form a network.

The speed of the transmission will depend on the type of cabling used so it is not necessarily the case that serial transmission is slow. A recent development has been the use of the Universal Serial Bus or USB. This is a high-speed serial connection that allows peripheral devices to be connected to your computer. The standard specification for serial network cables is a transmission rate of 100 Mbps (million bits per second).

Parallel data transmission will use a number of wires to send a number of bits simultaneously. The more wires there are, the more data can be sent at any one time. We have already come across parallel transmission in relation to the buses used inside the computer. A 32-bit parallel connection, for example, may connect the processor and memory together. Parallel cables are also used for printer cables as large volumes of data are being sent that need to be handled quickly.

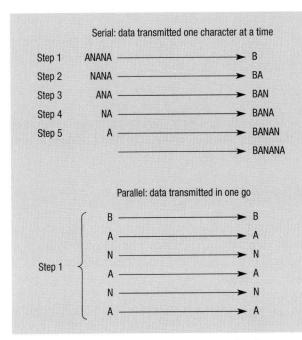

Figure 20.1 **Serial and parallel communication**

Parallel cables use more wires and are therefore more expensive to produce than serial cables. The signal will also degrade as distance increases due to interference between the lines. Another problem is timing the signals so that the data sent down each wire arrives at the other end at the correct time and in sequence with data being transmitted through the other wires. This is known as synchronisation and this becomes more difficult as the number of wires increases.

Bandwidth

Bandwidth is the term used to describe the amount of data that can be transmitted along a communication channel. It relates to the range of frequencies that are available on the cable that can be used to carry data. As the range of frequencies increases so does the amount of data that can be transmitted within the same time-frame. We have already touched on the relative speed at which data can be transmitted. Speed is a vital factor in communications.

Bandwidth is measured in bits per second or bps. This simply expresses how many binary digits (zeros and ones) can be transmitted in one second. A modem for example, may operate at 28.8 Kbps which translates to 28 800 bits per second. A 56 Kbps modem therefore has twice the bandwidth and will transmit twice the amount of data within the same time-frame.

In common with other aspects of computing, bandwidths get bigger and therefore can transmit more data more quickly as each year passes. You can now see transmission rates quoted in Mbps which is Megabits per second.

Bit rate

Bit rate is the term used to describe the speed at which a particular transmission is taking place. It is closely linked to the bandwidth because the bit rate will be limited by how much bandwidth is available.

Bit rate is measured in bits per second (bps) in exactly the same way as bandwidth. Bandwidth represents the frequencies and therefore the capacity that is available and bit rate represents the actual speed of transfer.

It is important to note that bandwidth and bit rate are not the same thing. A 56 K modem can in theory transmit 56 K bits of data per second. However, the bit rate is likely to be lower than this as not all of the bits are used for the data being transmitted. Some bits are used as parity bits or start/stop bits as explained later in the chapter.

Baud rate

Baud rate is another term used to describe the speed at which data is transmitted. One baud represents one electronic state change per second. An electronic state change is a change in frequency of the carrier wave. Therefore, one baud roughly equates to one bit per second. It is more common now to find speeds quoted in terms of bits per second as this is a more accurate measure of actual transmission rates.

Summary Question

1 Define bandwidth, bit rate and baud rate.

This is slightly confusing but reflects the fact that the baud was invented before the widespread use of computers and networks. It is accurate enough to describe one baud as one bit per second.

Synchronous and asynchronous data transmission

Synchronous means 'occurring at the same time' or 'having the same speed'. In the context of transmissions this means that the two devices which are communicating will synchronise their transmission signals. Using the system clock, the computer sending the data will control the transmission rate to be in time with the device or computer receiving the signal. If the two devices are not synchronised then data could be lost during transmission. Once they are synchronised the two devices can send and receive data without need for any further information.

Asynchronous transmission does not use the system clock to synchronise the signal. Instead, it sends data one character at a time, but each character is sent with additional bits of information that tell the receiving device what to do with the signal it is receiving.

For example, to send a Unicode character may require an 8-bit code to be transmitted. In addition to the eight bits, asynchronous data transmission requires at least two other bits. At the start of the eight bits there is a 'start bit' and at the end, a 'stop bit'. The character may also include a 'parity bit' as described in the next section. The start bit informs the receiving device that a piece of data is on its way. At this stage, the baud rates of the two devices are synchronised to allow correct interpretation of the data. The stop bit indicates that the data has arrived so the baud rates will revert to their original settings.

If the baud rates are different on the two devices, the signals will be interpreted incorrectly and the data will not make sense. You may have experienced corrupt data on web pages or even a 'time out' error when downloading from the Internet. This is often due to your computer being unable to synchronise with the computer you are downloading from.

To send a character requires an 11-bit code of which only eight bits are the actual data. This is necessary so that the receiving device knows where each byte of data starts and stops. However, it does reduce the amount of actual data that can be transmitted in a given time-frame. Transfer rates are measured in bits per second. In this case we are using three additional bits for every character we send. With synchronous data transmission, we could use all eleven bits for data.

Parity bits

A parity bit is a method of detecting errors in data during transmission. The way it works is quite simple, but it will not identify all errors in transmission.

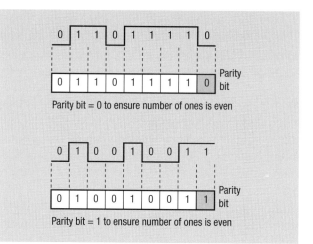

Figure 20.3 **Even parity**

When you send data, as shown, the data is being sent as a series of zeros and ones. In Figure 20.3, a Unicode character is transmitted as the binary code 01101111. It is quite possible that this code could get corrupted as it is passed down a wire. Remember that the code is being sent on a carrier wave. Any slight variation in the frequency could mean that a 0 is misinterpreted as a 1. This would make the data very unreliable. Depending on the nature of the data, this could be critical. In the top example the parity bit is set to a 0 to maintain an even number of ones. The bottom example shows another binary code where the parity bit is set to 1 in order to ensure an even number of ones.

One method for detecting errors is to count the number of ones in each byte before the data is sent to see whether there is an even or odd number. At the receiving end, the code can be checked to see whether the number is still odd or even.

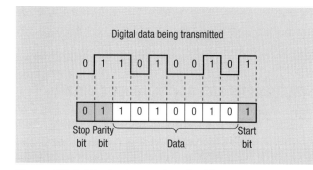

Figure 20.2 **Start, stop and parity bits**

EVEN PARITY

The number of ones in the code are counted. If there are an odd number of ones, the parity bit is set to one to make the total number of ones even. When the data is received, it is checked to ensure that there are still an even number of ones. If there are, then the data is assumed to be correct.

ODD PARITY

The number of ones in the code are counted. If there are an even number of ones, the parity bit is set to one to make the total number of ones odd. When the data is received, it is checked to ensure that there are still an odd number of ones. If there are, the data is assumed to be correct.

Handshaking and protocols

One of the biggest problems with computer communications is getting the various computers, networks, and peripheral devices to talk to each other. If we just take the example of logging on to the Internet, there are a number of different transmissions that take place in order for this to happen: the mouse has to transmit data to the serial port, which in turn passes a signal to the processor. The processor transmits to the modem which transmits over the telephone system, probably via a satellite to your ISP and so on.

There are so many different manufacturers of hardware and so many different ways of transmitting data that it is essential that there are accepted standards for data transmission. It might help to think of this in terms of the way that people from around the world communicate with each other. We all have our own languages and customs. When we deal with each other, we agree on what the rules of communication are going to be. For example, we may all agree to speak in the same language.

Handshaking and protocols are two methods for ensuring that different computers can communicate with each other.

HANDSHAKING

Handshaking is the process of two devices sending signals to each other to indicate that they are ready to send and/or receive data. A human handshake is often used to confirm an agreement. A communica-tions handshake is the same – in this case, the two devices agree on the protocols that they are going to use. They also agree on the speed of transmission. The two devices may not have the same capabilities in terms of the speed at which they can send and receive data. One part of the handshake therefore is to identify the fastest transmission speed that both devices are capable of.

PROTOCOLS

A protocol is a set of rules. In the context of communications, there are a number of rules that have been established in relation to the transmission of data. Protocols cover aspects such as the format in which data should be transmitted and how items of data are identified.

From using the Internet, you will already have come across three common protocols:

TCP/IP – Transmission Control Protocol/Internet Protocol relates to the set of rules that govern the transmission of data around the Internet. Data sent around the Internet is split into 'packets'. TCP/IP handles the routing and re-assembly of these data packets.

HTTP – Hypertext Transfer Protocol. You may have seen http preceding Internet addresses, for example, http://www. bbc.co.uk, though you do not need to type it in yourself these days. HTTP is the set of rules governing the exchange of the different types of file that make up displayable web pages. A key feature of this protocol is the ability to handle the various links that exist within the pages (hyperlinks).

FTP – File Transfer Protocol is similar to HTTP in that it provides the rules for the transfer of files on the Internet. FTP is commonly used when downloading program files or when you create a web page and upload to the ISP's server.

Summary Questions

4 Explain the difference between odd and even parity giving an example of each.

5 Odd and even parity checks do not detect all errors in data transmission. Explain why not.

6 Give two different situations where devices may need to handshake.

7 Why are protocols needed in computing?

8 Identify three different protocols and briefly describe the purpose of each.

Study Questions

1. Identify three devices that connect to a computer:

(a) using serial connections;

(b) using parallel connections.

2. Identify two uses of parallel communication.

3. What are the advantages of USB connections over traditional serial connections?

4. What is 'FireWire' and how does it differ from traditional serial cabling?

Examination Questions

1. Many computer systems and printers have both serial and parallel ports.
   - (a) Data can be sent to a printer from either port. What is meant by:
     - (i) serial transmission of data; [1]
     - (ii) parallel transmission of data? [1]

   - (b) (i) When could parallel data transmission be used? [2]
     - (ii) Justify the answer you have given in (b) (i). [2]

   - (c) Asynchronous data transmission is a method of data transmission in which a character is sent as soon as it becomes available, for example, when a key is pressed on the keyboard. In this situation, what is the reason in having the start and stop bits? [2]

   AQA January 2001 Module 1

2. The ASCII coding system uses seven bits to code a character. The eighth bit is used as a parity bit.
   - (a) Explain how a parity bit is used when transmitting ASCII codes using even parity. [3]
   - (b) What is the relationship between bit rate and bandwidth? [1]

   AQA June 2002 Module 1

3. One method of sending data to a printer is by using parallel transmission.
   - (a) What is meant by parallel data transmission? [1]
   - (b) Parallel transmission should not be used over long distances. Why not? [1]
   - (c) How should data be transmitted over long distances? [1]

   AQA June 2002 Module 1

Introduction

A network is any number of computers connected together sharing processing power, storage capacity and other resources. In its simplest form this could be two or three computers connected in someone's home or in a small office. At the other end of the scale, there are large global networks and, of course, the Internet, which is a global network of networks.

Connections between the computers are usually made using various types of cables though, more recently, wireless networks have been introduced using radio signals as a means of connection.

Network adapter

In order to connect to a network, a computer must have a 'network adapter', more commonly known as a Network Interface Card or NIC. The NIC is a printed circuit board which is contained inside the computer like any other card (graphics and sound cards, for example). The NIC will be specifically designed to allow the computer to connect to the particular network topology being used. The type of card also dictates the speed of data transmissions that will be available around the network.

Stand-alone computers

A stand-alone computer is a computer that has no connection to any other. Stand-alone computers are common in the home where a PC is used in isolation for much of the time. However, as soon as the computer connects to the Internet, the stand-alone computer, by definition, becomes a networked computer. The definition can get blurred when you consider that many Internet Service Providers claim to provide an 'always on' service which means that the computer is permanently part of a network.

Photograph 21.1 **A network interface card**

Stand-alone computers were common in businesses during the 1980s and early 1990s after which local area networks became the preferred option even for smaller organisations. The individual computers connected together to form a network are known as 'workstations'. Networking brings both advantages and disadvantages compared to the use of stand-alone computers as summarised in the table below.

Local area network

A Local Area Network or LAN is a number of computers and peripherals connected over a small geographical distance, covering one building or site. Some definitions limit a LAN to 1 km. LANs are common in businesses, educational establishments, hospitals and even the home.

Most LANs are made up of one or more servers and workstations. A server is a high specification computer with sufficient process-

Photograph 21.2 **A typical server room cabinet**

ing power and storage capacity to service a number of users. A workstation is any computer attached to the network. There are a number of different ways in which the network can physically be connected, and these are known as 'network topologies'. Topology in this context means layout.

Summary Questions

1 Identify three reasons why a user may prefer a stand-alone computer compared with a network computer.

2 Identify four advantages to the user of being on a local area network.

Advantages of networks	Disadvantages of networks
Users are able to communicate more easily with other users on the network through e-mail and messaging systems	Hardware costs are increased as cabling and hubs must be installed
Site licenses for software can be purchased at reduced unit cost	The operating system is more complex
Users can share peripherals such as printers	Networks are less secure as it is easier to hack into a networked computer than a stand-alone computer
All software used by computers in a network can be upgraded from the server	If the main server or cabling fails, then the whole system may be affected
Administrators have greater control over individual workstations, e.g. monitoring software and users	They usually require a Network Manager to keep them running which increases cost
Users can log on and access their work from any workstation on the network	Viruses are more easily spread
Information can be shared, e.g. multiple access to the same database, access to an intranet	Big brother – some network users might not like being watched

STAR NETWORK

A star network takes its name from the simplified way in which it can be represented on paper as shown below.

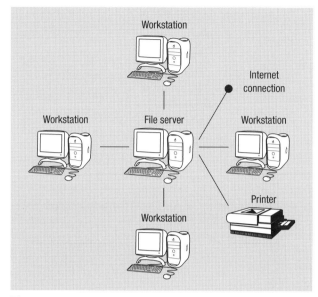

Figure 21.1 **Star network**

KEY FEATURES

The diagram shows each workstation connected to a central server via an individual connection. The main feature is the dedicated connection between server and workstation. The server will be a high specification machine with a large amount of processing power and storage capacity. The workstations have access to the server through the cabling.

Software may be stored centrally on the server and can be installed, upgraded and maintained via the server. The server will also contain a Network Operating System that controls the users' access to the system and also includes various administration functions such as managing the print queue.

The software can also be held locally at the workstation. If it is held locally the start up time is low, but it is harder to maintain and upgrade. Holding the programs centrally means the administrator has much better control over the software and who has access to it.

A real star network may not look anything like the diagram as it is unlikely that the workstations will just happen to make a star shape. Also, there are some additional hardware devices between the server and the workstations which are described in Chapter 23. For example, a star network uses a 'hub' to connect the workstations to the server. However, this is what topology is – it shows the *conceptual* rather than the *actual* layout.

Advantages of star networks	Disadvantages of star networks
Fast connection speed as each workstation has a dedicated cable	Expensive to set up due to increased cabling costs
Will not slow down as much as other network types when many users are on-line	If the cable fails then that workstation cannot receive data via any other route as it could with other network topologies
Fault-finding is simpler as individual faults are easier to trace	Difficult to install as multiple cables are needed. The problem is exaggerated where the LAN is split across a number of buildings
Relatively secure as the connection from workstation to server is unique	The operating system is more complex and more expensive than other topologies
New workstations can be added without affecting the other workstations	The server can get congested as all communications must pass though it
If one cable or workstation fails, then only that workstation is affected	

BUS NETWORK

KEY FEATURES

A bus network also has a file server though instead of having a dedicated cable between each workstation and the server, the server is accessed down one main cable. This cable carries data between the server and the workstations with each workstation branching off the main bus cable.

The bus network is the most common network topology in use at present and the industry standard implementation is the Ethernet network which is covered in more detail in Chapter 23.

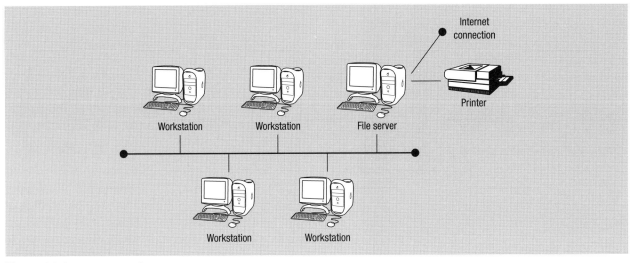

Figure 21.2 **Bus network**

Advantages of bus networks	Disadvantages of bus networks
Cheaper to install than a star network as only one main cable is required	Less secure than a star network as all data is transmitted down one main cable
Easier to install than a star network	Transmission times get slower when more users are on the network
High transmission speeds can be achieved using high specification coaxial cable such as Ethernet	If the main cable fails, then all workstations are affected
Easy to add new workstations	Less reliable than a star network due to reliance on the main cable
Multiple servers can be used	More difficult to find faults

RING NETWORK

KEY FEATURES

A ring network does not necessarily have a main server as the processing power is provided by each individual workstation. A server may still be used in this topology. If this were the case, one of the workstations would be replaced with a server. Workstations communicate with other workstations by passing data around the ring. This means that all data may need to pass through other workstations before reaching its destination. Ring networks are the common way of creating small home networks.

Wide area network

A Wide Area Network or WAN is a number of computers and peripherals connected together over a large geographical distance. This could mean any network that extends beyond a single site right up

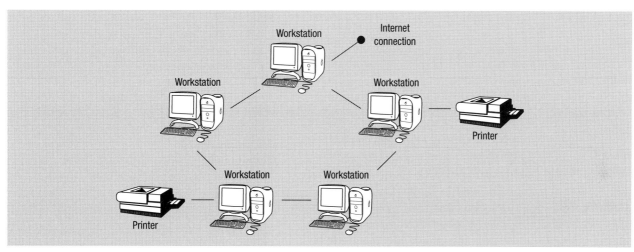

Figure 21.3 **Ring network**

Advantages of a ring network	Disadvantages of a ring network
Cheaper to install than a star network as there is only one cable between each workstation	Cable failure can cause the whole network to fail
File server not necessarily needed which also reduces cost	Less secure than a star network as data may pass through a number of workstations before reaching its target
High speed can be achieved as each workstation can boost the signal	Adding new workstations affects the whole network

Summary

Questions

3 Draw a diagram to show the following LAN topologies:
   (a) star;
   (b) bus;
   (c) ring.
4 Give three reasons why an organisation may choose to install a star network rather than a bus network.
5 Give two reasons why home networks may be installed using a ring topology.

to global networks such as the Internet. Definitions get a little blurred here as there is an intermediary level between the LAN and WAN called a Metropolitan Area Network (MAN). This network covers distances between 1 km and 10 km. Therefore, by this definition, a WAN is any network over 10 km.

The main difference between a LAN and a WAN is the media used to create the connections between the computers. WANs make use of a wider variety of communication media including telephone wires, microwave links, satellite connections and fibre optic cables. Modems may be needed when using the telephone wires and more recent technologies such as ADSL and ISDN can also be used to increase data transmission rates over long distances. These are covered in Chapter 24.

Another feature of the WAN is that there is less likely to be a central server controlling the workstations and acting as a central resource. Instead, WANs have 'distributed control' with each workstation retaining control of itself. For example, a supermarket may have a WAN to connect all of its stores. Each store will have control of their local computers and resources, yet they can connect to other computers in the WAN.

Typically a retailer will connect their Electronic Point of Sale (EPOS) system directly to Head Office. The EPOS system scans the products' bar codes which records the value and quantity of stock sold. Most supermarket systems also incorporate Electronic Funds Transfer at the Point of Sale (EFTPOS) which means that the customer can pay by card and the money is transferred directly from their bank account to the retailer's bank account using a WAN.

The Internet is often referred to as a WAN and this will be covered in detail in Chapters 25 to 29. However, many large organisations have been using WANs for many years, prior to the popularity of the Internet. Government organisations such as the Health Service and Police Force, and commercial organisations such as banks and grocery retailers use WANs to connect computers across regions, and even continents.

Modem

Modem stands for Modulator/ Demodulator. It is device that is either plugged into the serial port at back of your computer, or more commonly found inside the computer. Using standard telephone cable, the modem is connected to your telephone socket. A modem therefore acts as a telephone that allows computers to 'talk' to each other.

Computers process data in digital form – they work on zeros and ones. Telephone cables on the other hand usually handle data in analogue form, that is, as a wave. The modem converts (modulates) the digital signals from the computer into analogue form so that they can be transmitted along the phone lines. A modem is needed by the computer receiving the data, in order to demodulate the signal, that is convert it back into digital form.

Most modems are rated as 56 Kbps which indicates that the maximum rate at which they can convert data is 56 Kbits per second. Recent developments in communication technology may render the modem obsolete. ISDN and ADSL are both methods used to

Photograph 21.3 **EFTPOS**

Photograph 21.4 **An internal modem**

allow computers to connect to the Internet. Both of these methods send data in digital form over the telephone line so no modulation is needed. At the time of writing, the modem remains the most common method for accessing the Internet for home users but broadband is becoming increasingly popular.

Summary Question

9 Explain why a modem may be required to connect computers using telephone cables.

Study Questions

1. 'No more wires'. How likely is it that wireless networks will completely replace networks with cables?

2. Identify three advantages and three disadvantages of wireless networking.

3. Networking is the connection of computers and other devices. Explain how a network may incorporate:

(a) Mobile phones;
(b) PDAs.

4. What are the advantages of integrating these devices into a network?

5. It is suggested that the Internet cannot be referred to as a WAN. Give reasons to support this claim.

Examination Questions

1. (a) A college uses a LAN (Local Area Network) to share software and printers between its students. Describe a LAN. [2]

   (b) The diagram below shows the current topology.

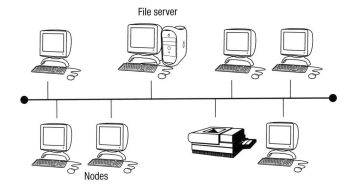

File server

Nodes

   (i) Name this topology. [1]
   (ii) Give one advantage of this topology. [1]
   (iii) Give one disadvantage of this topology. [1]

   AQA January 2001 Module 1

2. A small company has several stand-alone computers which staff use for word processing letters and accessing the products catalogue, stored in a database, to answer telephone enquiries from customers. A copy of the database is stored on each machine.

   (a) The company has been advised that networking the computers would be beneficial.
   (i) State two advantages for the business of a local area network (LAN). [2]
   (ii) What extra hardware is needed on each stand-alone computer to connect it to a LAN via cables? [1]

   (b) Computers could be connected in a topology such as a star network or a bus network.
   (i) State one advantage of a star network over a bus network. [1]
   (ii) State one advantage of a bus network over a star network. [1]

   AQA January 2002 Module 1

CHAPTER:22
Advanced networks

Baseband and broadband

Baseband and broadband are both used to describe the amount of bandwidth available when communicating between devices. Bandwidth is a measure of the amount of data that can be transmitted between two points in a given time-frame. Remember that data is usually carried on a wave – the greater the frequency range, the greater the amount of data can be transmitted in a given time-frame.

Baseband describes communications systems that use a single frequency band to transmit data. Many LANs use baseband technology and high-speed transmission can be achieved over small distances.

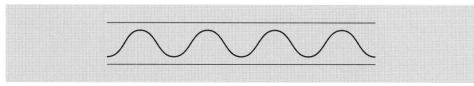

Figure 22.1 **Baseband carrier wave**

Broadband refers to communications systems that use a wide band of frequencies. The wider range of frequencies can be used in order to send more data within the same time-frame.

Broadband communication is widely used on the Internet to allow faster uploading and downloading. This is becoming more critical as the Internet is increasingly used for large volume data transmissions such as video and sound. Broadband communication can be achieved using a variety of media such as fibre optic cables and satellite links. It can also be achieved down standard telephone wires using ISDN and ADSL technologies which are explained in more detail in Chapter 24.

A technique called 'frequency division multiplexing' is used to take advantage of the wider bandwidth available.

Frequency Division Multiplexing (FDM) splits the cables into different frequencies or channels and transmits different signals down each channel simultaneously. Figure 22.2 shows the concept.

This technique is used on broadband Internet connections by having three channels. One to upload to the Internet, one to download from the Internet, and one for two-way voice com-

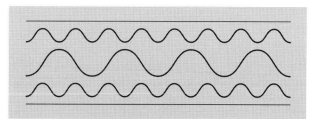

Figure 22.2 **Broadband carrier waves**

munications. This enables an Internet user to be on-line and make a standard telephone call at the same time.

Time Division Multiplexing (TDM) splits the transmission into a series of time-slices. Every item of data being transmitted gets as many slices of transmission time as needed to send the item. When a number of data items are being transmitted at the same time, they take it in turns to wait for their time-slice to come round again until all of it is sent. This way, many items of data can be sent down the same line at the same time.

The problem is that each item of data has been sliced up in order to send it. Therefore, where multiplexing is used, a demultiplexer is needed at the other end to re-assemble the slices into meaningful data.

This technique is commonly used to connect users on a local area network to the Internet. Local area networks will have many workstations but probably only one connection from the server to the Internet. A multiplexer is connected to the server which gives each user a time-slice for

transmissions to and from the Internet. This is why the Internet slows down when lots of users access it using a LAN.

Circuit switching

In any communication there must be a sender and a receiver and a connection must be established between the two. There are a number of ways in which this connection can be made. When you connect to the Internet, a connection is established between your computer and the web site that you are visiting. You probably realise that this is not a direct link. In the first instance, you connect to your Internet Service Provider (ISP) which in turn connects to the ISP hosting the web site.

In fact, there may be many more connections in the circuit. Data being transmitted around a WAN will be sent via a number of 'nodes'. A node is one of the connections within the network. In old-fashioned telephone terms we would call them 'exchanges'. In Internet terms, there are thousands of nodes and, therefore, thousands of routes that a communication may take to reach its destination. The diagram below shows the basic idea.

The transmission will be routed through a number of nodes before a connection is established between sender and receiver. With circuit switching, a route is established and is left open for the duration of the communication. This is how telephone conversations take place. You have a dedicated connection to the person you are speaking to until the receiver is put down and the connection broken.

Summary Questions

1 Explain the difference between baseband and broadband communication methods.

2 When using the school/college network, give two reasons why the speed of access to the Internet may slow down as the number of users increases.

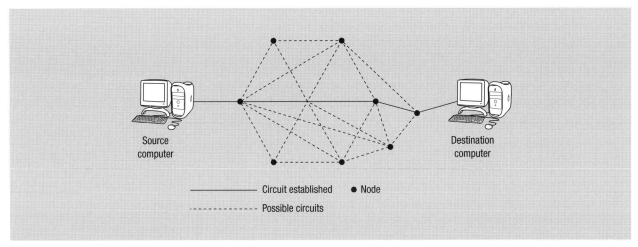

Figure 22.3 **Circuit switching**

Packet switching

Packet switching is a method of establishing a connection which is more suitable for non-voice data, for example, Internet transmissions. The concept was developed in the 1960s as an efficient and secure means of data transmission.

Data sent over the Internet is broken down into smaller chunks called 'packets' or 'datagrams'. Each packet of data will also contain additional information including a packet sequence number, a source and destination address and a checksum.

The packets are sent to their destination using the destination address. They are re-assembled at the other end using the packet sequence number. The checksum will identify any errors in the data (as described in Chapter 36) and if it finds any, that packet can be requested again using the source address.

Each packet can take a different route to its destination as it can be re-assembled at the other end regardless of the sequence in which they are received. Therefore, the packets are routed via the least congested and therefore the quickest route. Data is transferred quicker using this method and is more secure as the packets are taking different routes.

DATAGRAM VIRTUAL CIRCUIT

It is possible to establish a dedicated route through which the packets or datagrams can be sent. It is described as a virtual circuit because there are no switches involved. Instead, the sender and receiver agree on a route by which all datagrams will be sent and this series of connections remains open until all data has been received.

Asynchronous Transfer Mode (ATM)

ATM is a method of networking that has been designed to allow a range of different data types to be transmitted in the most efficient way. It supports transmission of text, numeric data, graphics, sound and video.

When sending data, the requirements for how the data is transmitted may vary. A key factor is the accuracy required in the transmission of the data. For example, as described in Chapter 19, sound is sampled when it is converted into digital form. If a few of the zeros and ones are corrupted in transmission then the user may not even notice as the overall effect on the sound will be minimal.

On the other hand, financial data must be transmitted very accurately as any minor corruption in the patterns of zeros and ones could have a serious effect on the actual number received at the other end.

ATM combines a number of techniques such as packet-switching and multiplexing (both explained in this chapter) to handle different types of data in different ways which overall provide a more efficient system than a standard network. All data is

Summary Questions

3 Identify the component parts of a datagram.

4 Identify the differences between circuit switching and packet switching.

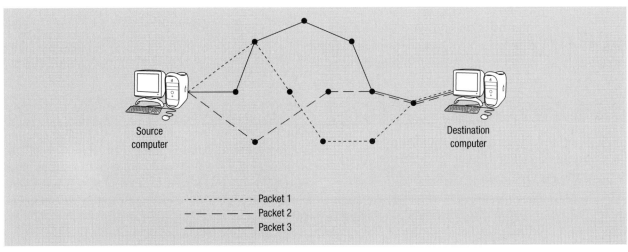

Figure 22.4 **Packet switching (showing three packets)**

split into 53 byte cells (packets) which are queued up to be sent using multiplexing techniques. Each cell will be routed via the most efficient route depending on the data within the cell.

Protocols

The concept of a protocol was covered in Chapter 20. Essentially it is a set of rules. In communications terms, it refers to the various rules that govern how data is sent around networks. In this section, we will be looking specifically at Transmission Control Protocol and Internet Protocol (TCP/IP) which set the rules relating to the transmission of data around the Internet.

Layers of TCP/IP

TCP/IP are the rules relating to transmission of datagrams or data packets. IP controls the delivery of the packets and TCP keeps track of the packets and reassembles them on receipt. TCP/IP is made up of a number of layers which are referred to as a protocol stack. The TCP/IP stack is in line with the International Standard communication protocol called the Open System Interconnection (OSI) model.

There are seven layers:

Layer 7: Application layer. The sender and receiver are identified and authenticated. Network resources are identified to ensure that they are sufficient for the communication to take place.

Layer 6: Presentation layer. Converts incoming and outgoing data from one presentation format to another. Standardises presentation formats so that different types of data (sound, graphics, video, etc.) can be understood by the receiving device. Also handles data that has been compressed or encrypted.

Layer 5: Session layer. Sets up, coordinates and terminates the communication session.

Layer 4: Transport layer. Ensures that all the packets have arrived and that there are no errors in the packets. Also handles multiplexed communications and creates virtual circuits.

Layer 3: Network layer. Defines the network addresses of devices that send and receive data and handles the routing of packets being sent and received.

Layer 2: Data-link layer. This layer provides synchronisation of devices so that the receiving device can manage the flow of data being received. It also identifies what network topology is being used and can identify transmission errors.

Layer 1: Physical layer. Controls the physical signals that transmits the strings of bits around the network, that is, the actual transmission of the zeros and ones. It also controls physical characteristics such as data transmission rates and the physical connections in a network.

The mnemonic *All People Seem To Need Data Processing* can be used to remember the seven layers.

The higher levels are closer to the user in that the top three layers are usually handled using either the operating system or application software. The bottom four layers are handled using a combination of hardware and software. Layer 1 is handled entirely by the cabling.

Sockets

A socket is a program that sends and receives data being communicated around a network. Each computer in the network will be assigned a socket address. For example, if data was being transmitted from Workstation A to Workstation B, the data would be sent through the socket of A to the socket of B.

The socket acts like a port in that it is an identifiable entry and exit point for other devices, in this case the other workstations in a network. However, unlike a port, it is not a physical device, but a software module that handles the data being sent to and from it.

Sockets can be managed using the TCP/IP stack which will allocate a unique address to every workstation using a combination of the IP address of the host computer and a port number assigned to that particular computer. Sockets can be created at any time to enable a network connection to be established to or from a computer.

Summary
Questions

5 Identify two of the seven layers of TCP/IP and explain the purpose of each.

6 Give two reasons why TCP/IP is needed.

For example, two workstations are being used on a LAN with a local IP address 122.111.233.100. Workstation A is assigned port 01 and Workstation B is assigned port 02. Therefore:

Workstation A has the socket address
122.111.233.100 01

Workstation B has the socket address
122.111.233.100 02

This means that any data being transmitted will be sent from one unique address to another unique address. Therefore, the source and destination of every single packet of data is unique. If the LAN was connected to the Internet, all data being received would be identifiable by the socket address of the computer sending the data in the same way. Consequently, if a server receives many requests for different web pages from different workstations, it can handle each one uniquely using the socket addresses.

Summary Questions

7 What is a network adapter?

8 What is a socket?

Study Questions

1. Identify three applications that would benefit from broadband communications.

2. Broadband is a term used commonly on the Internet. What are the advantages of broadband to an Internet user. What are the disadvantages?

3. Why might a user choose to use one type of NIC over another?

Examination Questions

1. Explain the difference between baseband and broadband communication. [2]

    (a) Give one example of where baseband might be used explaining why it is appropriate for that use. [2]

    (b) Give one example of where broadband may be used explaining why it is appropriate for that use. [2]

    (c) Explain how multiplexing may be used to enable several users to gain access to the Internet using the same cable connection. [2]

2. (a) What is meant by a wide area network? [1]

    (b) Explain the term protocol in the context of data transmission over a wide area network. [2]

    (c) Why is a protocol needed for a wide area network? [1]

    Summer 1999 Module 3

3. A computer connects to a LAN using port 60. The port is a socket address.

    (a) What is a socket? [2]

    A socket address is added to the IP address to identify this computer on the network.

    (b) What is an IP address? [2]

    (c) How can the network uniquely identify every computer connected to it? [1]

CHAPTER:23
Advanced local area networks

Chapter 21 introduced the concept of local area networks. This chapter looks in more detail at the hardware required to set up a LAN.

Cable types

By definition, a network is made up of a series of computers connected together. Although it is possible to use radio waves as the method of connection, at present most local area networks use physical connections such as cable, and it is this that we will concentrate on in this chapter. There are a number of cable types which differ in terms of their physical constructions, the speed at which they transmit data, and cost.

It is worth noting that at the time of writing there has been major growth in the development of wireless local area networks (WLAN) although it is not yet included in the A level specification. Students should use Appendix 2 for links to useful web sites on developing technologies.

TWISTED PAIR

Twisted pair cable comprises two insulated copper wires twisted around each other. The wires are encased by an outer layer of insulation. This is the standard cabling used in the telephone network. There are different grades of twisted pair, which allow different transmission rates. Better quality twisted pair cables are used to connect computers within LANs, particularly in Ethernet networks.

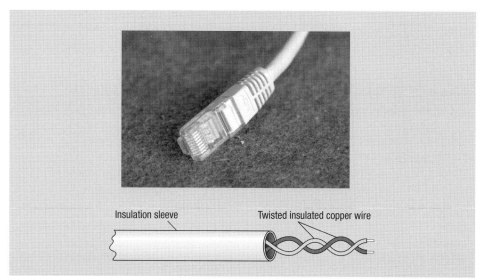

Insulation sleeve   Twisted insulated copper wire

Figure 23.1 **Twisted pair cable**

The different grades of twisted pair are defined by a CAT standard. A CAT is a category defined by the American National Standards Institute (ANSI). Currently there are seven categories running from CAT1 to CAT6. The most common cable at the time of writing is CAT 5E which allows transmission rates of 100 Mbps.

Some cables have more than one pair of twisted wires within the outer insulation. This allows more data to be transferred within a given time-frame. For home use, it would allow two lines, one for voice data and the other for Internet use.

COAXIAL

Baseband coaxial cable consists of a single copper wire encased within a layer of insulation. In turn, this is encased within copper braid which in turn is covered by a further layer of insulation. You will be familiar with this cable as it is used for television aerial connections. However, it is also used in LANs.

High rates of data transmission can be achieved mainly due to the fact that the cable is very well insulated and, therefore, there is less degradation in the signal. The copper braiding in the cable acts as a ground thus reducing the amount of interference. Coaxial cable is more expensive to produce than twisted pair.

Broadband coaxial transmission is achieved by having a series of carrier wires all contained within the layers of insulation. By increasing the number of wires, the amount of data that can be transmitted is increased.

OPTICAL FIBRE

Optical fibre or fibre optic cable, as it is more commonly known, is made up of a number of glass or plastic strands encased within an outer layer of insulation. Each strand or fibre is capable of transmitting data using pulses of light. Consequently, by using many fibres, a lot of data can be transmitted simultaneously down each of the strands.

The pulses of light are less prone to interference than the electrical signals sent down copper cables, so fibre optic transmissions are more reliable. Transmissions can also travel much further before the signal needs to be boosted.

However, there are physical constraints in that the cable is physically bigger and cannot be bent like other cables. It also requires greater levels of physical insulation than copper as it is more fragile.

Hubs

A hub is a device at the centre of a network. It connects all the computers and other devices in a network

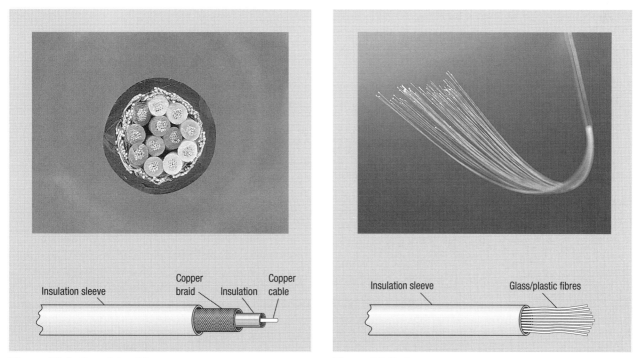

Figure 23.2 **Coaxial cable**

Figure 23.3 **Fibre optic cable**

to the central file server. Whenever data is transmitted to the server from a workstation, it passes through the hub. When data is transmitted to workstations from the server, or to a printer from the server, it is sent via the hub. Consequently, all data being passed around the network must pass through the hub, which presents a problem in that data packets may collide if a workstation is receiving data from two other workstations at exactly the same time. Therefore, a 'router' is used. A router is a communications device that receives every packet of data being transmitted, reads the header of the packet and then sends it along the appropriate cable to its destination.

In Chapter 21 we looked at various topologies for constructing a network. We also identified that these layouts were only an illustration and were over-simplified. One critical element of hardware missing from these diagrams is the hub. It is also likely that a network will contain a number of hubs and a number of workstations.

The hub serves two main purposes. It acts as a 'router' to ensure that the correct server is communicating with the correct workstation or peripheral, and it boosts the signal. Depending on the type of cable used, signals needs to be boosted as they degrade over distance. For example, in the case of CAT 5E, the signal needs boosting every 90 m which means that you need a hub every 90 m. A LAN spread over a large site, therefore, will need a number of hubs. Bridges can also be used to boost signals and this is covered below.

Segments

When constructing a LAN it is quite likely that the workstations will need to be spread around various rooms or even various buildings. In your school or college, you probably have a number of computer rooms. There will also be an office or room that houses the server or servers. All the computers in your network must link up to that server somehow. This usually involves a convoluted collection of wires running through ceiling, under floors, down walls and around the edges of rooms.

Consequently, a computer room next to an office with the server in it will not need as much cabling as another computer room which may be several hundred metres away. Also, the computer room that is several hundred metres away will need an additional hub or bridge to boost the signal.

To make this more manageable, networks are often broken up into smaller segments. Each segment can be configured to optimise the performance of the workstations in it. Additional servers may also be added to some or all of the segments.

Bridges

A bridge is needed when a network has been split into segments as described in the previous section. A bridge is a device that connects the segments so that there is a route by which data can be transmitted to every part of the network. It can also boost the signal.

A bridge can also be used to connect different LANs together. For example, a large organisation may have a number of LANs spread over a single site, particularly if there are a large number of users. Even if these LANs are made up of different topologies, a bridge can be used to connect them together. The diagram below shows two segments, one of which is a bus network and the other a star network. Both have their own servers and hubs and a bridge connects the two segments. In this context the bridge is acting as a 'gateway' between the two different parts of the network.

Ethernet

Ethernet is the most common model for LANs. It combines many of the techniques and cable types discussed in this chapter to create high data transmission rates. The most common system at the time of writing is 10BASE-T which provides transmission rates of 10 Mbps using either coaxial or twisted pair connections. Ethernet 100BASE-T is also available and provides transmission rates of 100 Mbps. 100BASE-T is used as a 'backbone' to connect LANs over larger distances, for example, two buildings.

Ethernet is modelled on the bus network in that there is one central cable which carries all the data around the network. Ethernet cards are installed in each workstation to allow them to connect using the relevant protocols. There are various ways in which Ethernet can be implemented. One possibility is the use of 'switched Ethernet' where the traditional hub is replaced with a switching hub. A traditional hub sends every packet of data to every workstation. A switched hub directs packets to the

Summary Questions

1 Describe the two main functions of a hub in a local area network

2 Give two reasons why a large LAN may be broken down into segments.

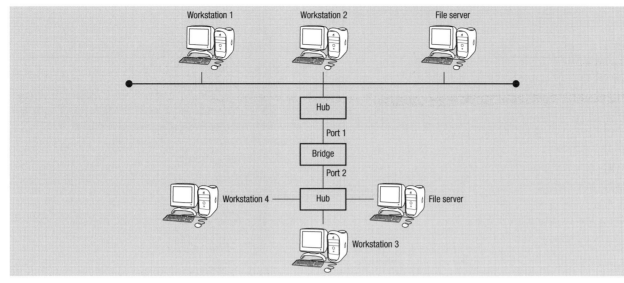

Figure 23.4 **LANs connected by a bridge**

appropriate workstation using the address of the port or socket for the designated workstation. This makes better use of the bandwidth as redundant packets are not being transmitted.

Ethernet also uses a protocol called Carrier Sense Multiple Access with Collision Detection (CSMA/CD) which was developed to enable the various workstations and devices to use the cable at high speeds without interfering with each other, that is, the packets of data would not collide.

Ethernet sends data in frames. This is a similar concept to the packets in packet switching networks. Any device on an Ethernet may attempt to send frames. Before each frame is sent, the device uses the CSMA/CD protocol to see whether the cable to the workstation or device is idle or whether another device is using it. If the line is busy, the device will wait and try again later. If two devices try to send at exactly the same time, a collision occurs and both frames will be discarded. Each device will then wait a random amount of time before sending the frame again.

Client–server networks

In the star and bus topology in Chapter 21, the diagram shows a main server. Although the workstations have local resources in terms of processing power, and storage capacity, they are controlled by the server. This means that when new software is installed, for example, it can be installed on the server and then distributed to the workstations. When one workstation wants to print, it sends its request to the server.

In this context, each workstation is a 'client' which is served by the server. This is the most common way of constructing a LAN with a large number of users. The server will be a 'high-end' computer with a large amount of processing power and storage capacity. It needs to be big enough and fast enough to cope with the demands placed upon it by the workstations.

The workstations on the other hand do not need to be of such a high specification. The current trend is to have a 'thin client' which refers to the fact that the workstation will not have a CD drive or expansion slots, thus reducing the cost of the workstation.

Peer-to-peer networks

In a peer-to-peer network, no one computer is in overall control of the network. Instead the resources of each workstation are available to all the computers in the network. Each workstation therefore can act either as a client or as the server, depending on the current task.

This is more common among smaller networks of up to ten workstations. Peer-to-peer networks can be created without the need for a special network operating system. With the growth in home computing, it is increasingly common to find peer-to-peer networks in private houses. These are often set up to allow every computer in the home to share a connection to the Internet or printer.

Summary
Questions

3 What is the purpose of a bridge?

4 Explain how the CSMA/CD protocol is used to ensure high-speed transmission around Ethernet networks.

Study Questions

1. Identify appropriate uses for the following cable types:

(a) coaxial;

(b) twisted pair;

(c) fibre optic.

2. Give one example of an application that requires a client–server network.

3. Give an example where a peer-to-peer network might be used.

4. What is the purpose of the CAT standard used for twisted pair cabling?

Examination Questions

1. The figure below shows the physical layout of a small local area network consisting of three workstations and one file server interconnected via a hub. The network is Ethernet-based.

   (a) The network in the figure behaves as a bus network. Draw a carefully labelled diagram of the bus equivalent of the hub-based network of the figure. [2]

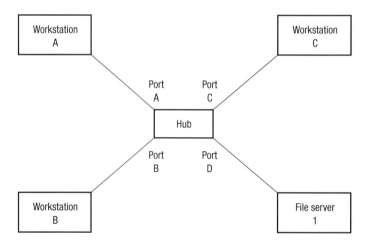

   (b) (i) Three more workstations (D, E, F) and another file server (File Server 2) are added but network users complain that the performance of the network is now very slow. In terms of the operation of this network, what is the most likely cause for the slowing of the network, assuming there are no hardware faults? [2]

   (ii) To overcome this problem the network is split into two segments and bridged by a bridge with two ports, Port 1 and Port 2. Draw a carefully labelled diagram of the physical configuration of this new network. [2]

(c)   The second figure shows another way that the computers in the local area network can be connected. The network uses switched Ethernet.

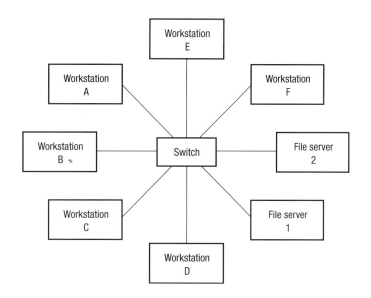

(i)   Explain how the operation of switched Ethernet differs from that of hub-based Ethernet.   [2]

(ii)   What is the advantage of the switch-based network in this figure compared with the hub-based network in the previous figure for the same number of computers?   [1]

AQA January 2003 Paper 5

2   The diagram below shows part of the logical layout of an Ethernet-based local area network consisting of several desktop PCs connected using a bus topology.
The network is split into two *segments* linked by a bridge.

(a)   Why is it necessary sometimes to split local area networks based on a bus topology into two or more segments?   [1]

(b)   Describe the involvement of the bridge in the diagram in traffic management on the Ethernet segments.   [2]

(c)   The network in the diagram is physically realised using two hubs, a bridge and twisted-pair cabling to interconnect the desktop PCs. Draw a labelled diagram of the layout of the network that uses these components.   [2]

(d)   The network in the diagram is operated as a peer-to-peer network. Explain peer-to-peer networking.   [2]

AQA June 2003 Module 5

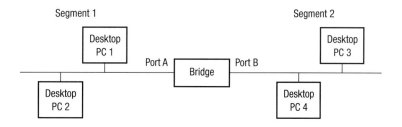

Electronic data interchange

Electronic Data Interchange, or EDI, is a standard format for transmitting business documents around a wide area network. Large businesses tend to have many common documents which are used extensively and regularly. For example, invoices, orders and other financial documents will all have a standard format.

EDI allows these documents to be transferred quickly and reliably around workstations on a WAN. The use of EDI means that the standard format of the document is understood and interpreted correctly on receipt.

EDI sends data in a 'transaction set' that contains a segment of data, for example, the contents of one form. In addition to the data, a header and footer are transmitted. This is similar to the concept of 'packets' explained in Chapter 22. The difference is that each transaction set will typically contain one entire document and the person receiving the data, known as a 'trading partner', will know the format of each set.

EDI is becoming the standard method for sending out exam results from the exam boards to individual schools and colleges. A feature of EDI is the ability to encrypt the information so that hackers cannot view the information even if they are able to intercept the transmission. This feature is particularly useful when sending exam results or other sensitive information, such as business sales figures or individuals' health information.

Value Added Networks (VANs)

A VAN is any privately owned network that is hired out to other users. Essentially it is a WAN owned by one business, that allows other businesses to use their network. Businesses that want to use a VAN will pay a fixed monthly fee and charges based on how much data they send around the network. In addition to access to the network, VAN providers will also offer EDI, encryption services, secure e-mail and other services.

Businesses that use VAN providers may do so because it is cheaper than the cost of installing and maintaining their own WAN. It may be that they simply don't have the expertise to set up their own network and prefer to use a service provided by a third party.

VAN providers are now having to compete with the Internet as many businesses can use the infrastructure it provides rather than relying on a VAN provider. However, VAN providers may have many clients using their network allowing them to reduce the costs to each individual client.

Summary Questions

1 Give two examples of the typical uses of EDI.

2 List four services typically offered by a VAN.

3 Identify two reasons why an organisation would use a VAN as opposed to setting up their own WAN or using the Internet.

4 A large engineering company has several offices located throughout the world. It has an ongoing requirement to send detailed engineering drawings between offices. The files are typically around 10 Mb and they send around 20 per day. Discuss whether a WAN, a VAN or using the Internet would be the most suitable way of meeting their requirements.

Cable modem

A cable modem is a device that enables data to be transmitted along the same cable that delivers cable TV into the home. Cable TV is carried down high-speed coaxial cable. The cable enters the home through a 'splitter'. One of the connections goes to the TV and the other goes to the cable modem. There is a connection between the cable modem and the computer. Typically, the cable plugs in directly to an Ethernet network card.

Cable modems can deliver higher transmission rates than standard modems and telephone lines. Typical transmission rates at the time of writing are 1.5 Mbps, though in theory it could be closer to 25 Mbps.

Cable therefore provides users with a 'broadband' connection although it is only available in areas that provide cable television. The modems are usually supplied by the cable company as part of an integrated package of TV, telephone and Internet access.

Integrated Services Digital Network (ISDN)

ISDN is a method of creating high-speed data transmission using the standard telephone system. ISDN does not need to convert data from digital to analogue as it sends data over the telephone wires in digital form. It does this through an 'ISDN adapter' working like a switch. It is often referred to as an ISDN modem although it is not actually modulating or demodulating the signal.

An ISDN adapter is needed at either end in order to send and receive the data in digital form. ISDN does not rely on the power supplied by the telephone

company but has its own electricity supply to send the signals.

There are different types of ISDN line. Domestic users have access to Basic Rate Interface (BRI) which uses three channels (2B+D), two B channels which send and receive data, and one D channel which is used for signalling information. The B channels typically operate at 64 Kbps which means that you could have one channel for sending and one for receiving, or you could combine the two to create one 128 Kbps channel.

The Primary Rate Interface (PRI) is available for business users and has 30 B channels for sending and receiving data and one D channel for signalling. As with BRI, the channels are used to send both voice data and digital data at the same time allowing simultaneous use of the telephone and the Internet.

Asymmetric Digital Subscriber Line (ADSL)

ADSL is another method of providing high rates of transmission using the standard telephone network. The concept is very similar to ISDN in that an 'adapter' is required at either end of the transmission. In common with ISDN, data is transmitted digitally so no conversion is needed.

The difference with ADSL is that it splits the frequencies available on the telephone cables into three channels of different bandwidths. Asymmetric means 'not balanced' and refers to the fact that the bandwidth of each channel is set according to how much data will be transmitted through it. It does this because transmitting voice data does not require the same amount of bandwidth as downloading from the Internet.

Therefore, one channel is set up to send and receive voice data for telephone conversations, one channel

Photograph 24.1 **Cable modem**

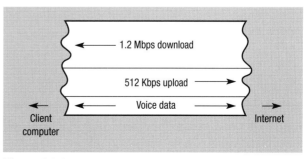

Figure 24.1 **ADSL**

is set up to upload to the Internet and the third channel is set up to download from the Internet.

Different bandwidths have been allocated to each channel. The channel for downloading is the largest as the volume of data travelling in this direction is the greatest. This is because a web site will typically contain graphics, photographs or video and sound. Most data that is uploaded to the Internet is likely to be quite small in volume as it will probably be text based, for example, an Internet address or a search within a search engine. It is possible to adjust the bandwidth of the three channels according to the data that is being transmitted.

Summary Question

5 Explain why ADSLs allocate more bandwidth to downloading from than uploading to the Internet.

The limitation of ADSL is that you need to be located within a certain distance of the telephone company's ADSL adapter. As you move further away from the adapter, the transmission rates reduce significantly. For example, if you are within 2.7 km of the adapter, you could achieve transmission rates of over 8 Mbps. If you double the distance, the transmission rates can fall by approximately 75 per cent.

CODEC

CODEC refers to any technology, hardware or software, that COdes and DECodes data. It can refer to a device that converts analogue to digital and vice versa, for example, a modem. However, a CODEC can also be used to compress and decompress data which otherwise would take up a large amount of disk space. Combining the ability to convert and compress at the same time, CODECs are commonly used when converting analogue video into a compressed video format such as MPEG, or when converting analogue audio into digitised sound such as WAV.

CODECs therefore are used for a variety of multimedia applications such as downloadable movies and audio tracks, video conferencing, television broadcasting and video messaging on mobile phones.

CODECs can be implemented using software or hardware or a combination of both. MPEG, for example, can be decoded using either hardware or software. The advantage of using software is that the user will not need to buy and install specialised

hardware in order to handle coded or compressed data files. It is also easier to add new functionality to a software-based CODEC. Software-based CODECs generally result in smaller file sizes than a hardware-only implemention.

However, hardware CODECs enable the conversion and compression in real time. This is essential for some applications such as video conferencing or live TV broadcasting where a delay would be unacceptable. Hardware CODECs can provide better picture quality particularly from a computer with a less powerful processor, as the CODEC is carrying out most of the conversion rather than the processor. Hardware CODECs also have a low power consumption which makes them ideal for portable devices such as PDAs and mobile phones.

Video conferencing

Video conferencing is a facility that links at least two computers together with digital video cameras. Its purpose is to allow people to talk and see each other at the same time through their computer. In order to video conference, you need what is now commonly known as a 'web cam' which is in fact a digital camera capable of transmitting moving images. There is also a piece of software that is supplied with the camera that enables you to establish the connections and view the person at the other end through their camera.

Video conferencing was available long before the explosion of the Internet. It was initially developed to allow business people to communicate without

Photograph 24.2 **Video conferencing**

the need to travel to see each other. Educational establishments also used it in some cases to deliver lectures to a number of people at the same time. Students living in remote geographical areas in countries such as Scotland and Australia have been using 'remote learning' techniques such as this for a number of years.

Since the increase in use of the Internet, the price of video conferencing has reduced to the point where it would be feasible to set it up in your own home. The limiting factor is the rate at which data can be transmitted along communication channels. Digital video images generate very large files as they are made up of a large series of frames. In order to receive good quality images in real time, a high-speed transmission channel is needed. If you have viewed digital video you will see that the image is somewhat 'jerky' as the frames refresh. Video conferencing is usually achieved using broadband techniques such as ISDN or ADSL.

Inter-networking

'Inter means 'between'. Therefore, inter-networking refers to the ability to transmit data between networks. Hence the term Internet, which is described as a network of networks.

Although this sounds simple, the practicalities of connecting millions of computers and tens of thousands of networks are very complex. To understand inter-networking fully you must appreciate all of the physical connections that need to be made, all of the devices that are used to connect networks, how data is transmitted and how protocols are used to allow data to be transmitted and received correctly. In fact, you need to read Chapters 20 to 26 to fully appreciate how many different aspects there are to inter-networking.

Summary Questions

6 Identify two advantages and two disadvantages of video conferencing for a business.

7 Describe the hardware and software needed to video conference.

Study Questions

1. What is the typical transmission rate of:

(a) a cable modem;

(b) an ISDN line;

(c) an ADSL.

2. Give two examples where a home user might want to increase the amount of bandwidth for uploading to the Internet.

3. Internet access can be made through ISDN, ADSL, cable modem or traditional modem. Compare these four methods in terms of cost, availability and transmission rates.

4. What is 'broadband satellite'?

5. What is MPEG and why has it become popular?

6. Video conferencing has not been as popular as many people predicted a few years ago. Why do you think this is the case?

Examination Questions

1. (a)   What is the function of a modem?   [2]

    (b)   State three forms of communication, other than text, that can be transmitted
          through an Integrated Services Digital Network (ISDN).   [3]

    (c)   Why does using an ISDN telephone line to connect a computer into a wide
          area network eliminate the need for a modem?   [1]

2. A CODEC (Coder-Decoder) is often used to compress (and decompress)
    video and audio data.

    (a) On some video-capture and editing systems the CODEC is entirely
         software-based whereas in others the CODEC is implemented in hardware
         and software on a plug-in board. Why is the hardware and software CODEC
         preferred to the software only CODEC?   [1]

    (b) Why must a CODEC be used if a movie from a video camera is to be
         stored on DVD-R?   [1]

    AQA June 2003 Module 5

3. Give one advantage and one disadvantage of using an ADSL connection to connect to the
    Internet compared to a standard modem.   [2]

The Internet is described as a network of networks. It is a global interconnection of computers and networks.

We are in the middle of an information revolution. The Internet has had an enormous impact on society. It is changing the way we communicate, work, socialise, shop and bank. The Internet has grown exponentially over the last 10 years and now has an estimated 600 million users worldwide.

The Internet started life as ARPANET in the late 1960s. ARPANET was a collection of connected computers set up by the American military as a secure way of transferring sensitive data during the Cold War with Russia.

During the 1980s the network expanded and was used by a much wider community including universities and research centres. The Internet as we know it now started to take shape in the mid-1980s when Tim Berners-Lee, a British scientist working in Switzerland, created the World Wide Web (WWW). Berners-Lee had been using the Internet to transmit and receive research documents but had found the interface very clumsy. As a result he developed the concept of an organised browser to allow people to navigate and search the Internet more easily. As a consequence, the WWW is perceived as being the same as the Internet. In fact, the WWW is a service provided on the Internet albeit one used by millions of people. It is possible to use the Internet without using the WWW.

After this, many other organisations began to use the WWW to offer services to users. During the 1990s there was an explosion in the range of services on offer from Internet Service Providers, to search engines to e-mail. This coincided with a massive increase in the number of people who were buying PCs for home use. Manufacturers of home PCs began to supply computers with pre-installed browsers and modems ready to be connected to the Web.

Internet service providers (ISP) and on-line service providers

The communications technology involved in connecting your computer to the Internet is similar to (but much more complex than) a standard telephone connection. When you make a standard telephone call, you will be connected via a 'telephone exchange' to the person that you are phoning. When you connect to the Internet, a similar thing happens in that you must first be connected to an Internet Service Provider (ISP). The ISP provides your computer with a 'gateway' to all the other computers on the Internet.

ISPs therefore act like telephone companies – they provide you with access to the network and the software needed, and you pay them for the connection. There are many ISPs to choose from and the market has become very competitive. One of the key factors in choosing an ISP is the price that they charge. There are two main connection methods provided by ISPs.

Dial-up: Like telephone calls, you are charged for the amount of time that you are connected to the Internet. When you want to log on, your computer connects to the ISP. You then pay a charge for every minute that you spend on-line until you log off. Call charges for home users in the UK are currently around 1p per minute so this method can work well for occasional users.

Leased line: A permanent connection between the user and the ISP is made. This is becoming the preferred method for home users of the Internet as it provides an 'always on' service at a fixed price. The newer broadband service providers insist that their customer use a leased line, usually ADSL or ISDN.

As the Internet grew in popularity during the 1990s, a number of businesses called 'on-line service providers' started to operate. For a fee, these companies offered various services to their Internet users such as e-mail provision, search engines, chat rooms, news, TV listings and local information. More recently, the ISPs have also offered these services in addition to providing access to the Internet. By definition, this makes them 'on-line service providers' as well. There are still some companies who act only as on-line service providers but these days, most ISPs have to offer other services in order to compete.

ISPs come and go. They are better known by their brand names and some of the most well known at the time of writing are Freeserve, AOL, VirginNet and Tiscali.

Uniform Resource Locator (URL)

A URL is the full address used to find files on the Internet. For example:

http://www.awebsite.co.uk/index.html

The contents of the file that a URL locates will vary depending on the Internet protocol being used. In this example, hypertext transfer protocol (HTTP) is being used. The file it points to is an html file called index.html which contains 'hyperlinks' to further pages. HTTP indicates that the file can be accessed using a browser. Consequently, most URLs start with HTTP although it is not always necessary to type it in the address line.

The address is made up of several parts:

- **The protocol being used, which could be http or ftp.**

Summary Questions

1 Explain why a modem may no longer be needed in order to connect to the Internet.
2 Identify four reasons why you would choose one ISP over another.
3 List four services typically offered by an ISP.
4 Identify two scenarios where it would not be necessary to type http:// when inputting a URL into the address bar of a browser.

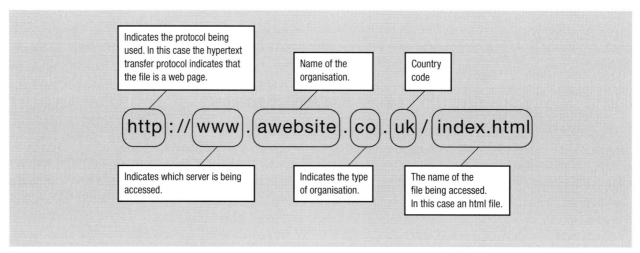

Figure 25.1 **Uniform Resource Locator**

- The 'domain name' which is the location that contains the file.

- A pathname to locate the file needed.

Domain name

The domain name identifies organisations or groups on the Internet. For example:

www.bbc.co.uk

- **www** indicates the host server. Often the www does not need to be typed as most commonly used web sites are accessed via www.

- **bbc** is the name of the organisation. Domain names have to be unique so organisations had to act quickly to secure a domain name that is the same as the name of their organisation. All domain names are registered with a central agency called ICANN to ensure uniqueness.

- **co** indicates that it is a company. This part of the name is referred to as the top-level domain name. It indicates the type of organisation. There are some commonly used top-level domains which you should be aware of.

  - **.com** indicates that the organisation is commercial, that is, a business;
  - **.gov** indicates that the organisation is part of the government;
  - **.ac** indicates that the organisation is an academic institution, usually a college or university;
  - **.sch** indicates that the organisation is a school;
  - **.org** indicates an organisation other than a commercial business, for example, a charity or trade union;

  - **.net** indicates a company providing internet services.

- **uk** indicates that the web site is based in the UK. There are a number of two letter country codes and new ones are being added all the time. Country codes are abbreviated using their own language as follows in these examples:

  - **.au** is Australia;
  - **.de** is Germany (Deutschland);
  - **.it** is Italy (Italia);
  - **.es** is Spain (Espania).

IP address

An Internet Protocol (IP) address is a number that uniquely identifies every computer that sends or receives data on the Internet. An IP address is a 32-bit code made up of four numbers separated by dots as follows: 234.233.32.123. This makes little sense to us as users which is why we use the domain name. Domain names are designed to be easy to remember and relevant to the organisations.

However, the protocol used to transmit data (TCP/IP) can only work with numbers. Therefore, every domain name is 'mapped' to a number. This number is the real Internet address and uniquely identifies the computer that is transmitting or receiving data. It is called an IP address because it uses the Internet Protocol.

A domain name is sometimes described as a 'proxy' for the IP address which means that the user types in a domain name which is transferred to a name server which then translates the name into the IP address. An analogy could be the ability to store numbers on a mobile phone. The user selects a name from the list which is then looked at to find and dial the actual telephone number.

Summary Questions

5 Write out a URL and label each part.

6 Explain the relationship between a domain name and an IP address.

7 There is a one-to-one relationship between an IP address and a domain name. Why are both needed?

126

Intranet

An intranet is an internal Internet. Many organisations including businesses and schools will set up an intranet containing information specific to the organisation. An intranet looks like the www and works in the same way. Users will use browsers and search engines to find pages on specific topics. However, the users will not be connecting to the Internet. Instead they will only be connecting with other work-stations and servers within their local area network. The content of the intranet is therefore limited to whatever the organisation decides to put on it.

Many schools use intranets and set up different pages for each of the subject areas in the school. It is common to have an area specifically to show student work and there may be chat rooms specifically for students of that school. Businesses use them to disseminate information to their employees. They may also have an internal e-mail system which uses the server to route the mail to the appropriate mail boxes.

The advantage of an intranet is that it only contains relevant data so users do not suffer from information overload. Access to information is also faster and more secure than an Internet connection. However, the information may be so limited that users prefer to go on the Internet. There is also a large cost in terms of time and human resources to set up the intranet and keep it up to date.

Summary Questions

8 What is an intranet and how might it be used within an organisation?

9 Identify one advantage and one disadvantage of an intranet to an organisation.

Study Questions

1. Intranets are often used within schools and colleges.

(a) Identify three advantages of using an intranet in a school environment.

(b) Identify three disadvantages.

2. IP addresses are 32-bit numbers made up of four groups of numbers: ###.###.###.###. What are the first and last IP addresses available using this format?

3. Which ISP currently has the highest number of users? Identify all the factors that have led to their success.

Examination Questions

1. An example of a domain name is:
    www.bodasoft.co.uk

    (a) Using this example, explain each part of the address:
    (i)   www
    (ii) bodasoft
    (iii) co
    (iv) uk

    (b) The domain name is referred to as a proxy for the IP address. What does this mean? [1]

    (c) Why don't users use an IP address rather than the domain name? [1]

2. (a) Once connected to the Internet, the user can access a whole range of
        information, including the World Wide Web. What type of application
        software is required to access a web site?   [1]

    (b) A Uniform Resource Locator (URL) is the address for data on the Internet.
        For example, http://www.bbc.co.uk is the address to find the BBC home page.
        Explain the two different parts of this address.
        (i)   http://   [1]
        (ii) www.bbc.co.uk   [1]

3. The Internet is one example of a WAN (Wide Area Network).
    (a) Describe a WAN.   [1]
    (b) Why is a protocol needed?   [1]

AQA June 2001 Module 1

CHAPTER: 26
Advanced Internet

The World Wide Web (WWW)

It is a common misconception that the Internet and the World Wide Web are the same thing. In fact, the Internet is the infrastructure, that is, the connection of all the networks and the telecommunication links between them. The WWW is available via the Internet.

The World Wide Web is a global collection of web sites and pages that may contain text, graphics, sound and video. A common feature of web sites is the use of 'hyperlinks' which allow users to click on an item on a web page which links directly to another web page. There are virtually no regulations regarding the content of the WWW, so anyone with the appropriate software and hardware can create a web site on any topic. Consequently there are now millions of pages of information covering every conceivable topic.

Web browsers

In order to view the World Wide Web, you need a 'web browser' which is a special piece of software designed to allow you to access and view web pages. Common features of browser software are:

- **An address bar to type in domain names to take you directly to a site.**

- **Navigation buttons to move forward and backward between pages and a home button to take you back to your start-up page.**

- **A print button.**

- **A 'favourites' section where you can 'bookmark' (store) the addresses of web pages that you want to access on a regular basis.**

- **A 'history' folder that contains a list of web sites that have been accessed previously.**

- **A built-in search engine for searching the entire WWW.**

- **A link to e-mail.**

Perhaps the most popular web browsers are Internet Explorer and Netscape Navigator which have very similar features but are provided by different companies.

Summary Questions

1 The terms 'Internet' and 'World Wide Web' are often used to mean the same thing. Describe these terms making the difference between the two clear.

2 List four features you would expect to find in a browser and, for each, explain why it is needed.

Search Engines

A search engine is a piece of software that allows you to search for web pages on the World Wide Web by typing in key words relating to the topic that you are searching for. If you know the domain name of the web site or page that you want to access then it is much quicker to type this into your web browser. However, there will be many occasions when you do not know the name and this is where a search engine is vital.

It is an enormous task to search every single page on the Web and no one search engine covers the entire Web. Exact figures are impossible to calculate, but even the best search engine probably covers only around 35% of the web. Search engines work in different ways to try to produce the best results in terms of coverage and relevance. Common approaches are:

- **Web 'crawlers' or 'spiders'. The search engine looks for every reference to the key word in the web pages that it searches. Some crawlers only look at the 'meta-tags' which are special header files attached to every web page that contain key words.**

- **Meta Search Engine. This is a search engine that passes the query to several other search engines and shows the results of all the searches.**

- **Directories. Some search engines manually categorise the web-sites rather than relying on automated systems based on counting key words. When you use Yahoo you will follow a series of categories until you find the web site that you want.**

- **Natural Language. Ask Jeeves is the best example of this where the user types in a question or phrase in the way that they might speak it. For example: 'Where can I find out how to wire a plug'.**

- **Relevancy formulas. These are search engines that use a mathematical formula to calculate how relevant they think each web site is based on the key words.**

Some search engines use a variety of these techniques to produce the best results. There are many search engines available and they are almost always provided as a free service on the Web.

Internet registries and registrars

The WWW is not owned by any single organisation. There are a number of organisations that ensure that we can get access to it. We have already looked at the importance of the ISP in providing us with a gateway to the WWW. ISPs and other businesses also offer 'web hosting' services which means that if you want your own web site, they will store the web site on their servers for others to access. The web hosting company will store your web site under its domain name.

Every web site must have its own unique domain name which in turn has its own IP address. It is the job of an 'Internet Registrar' to maintain the records of all of these names in an 'Internet Registry'.

There is one organisation, set up by the American Government, that is in overall charge of all the domain names in use across the world. This organisation is called ICANN (Internet Corporation for Assigned Names and Numbers). ICANN is an independent non-profit making organisation which is made up of a number of elected individuals from business, technical, academic and user communities who only serve for short periods of time to ensure that the domain names are allocated fairly.

ICANN license other registrars around the world who then register domain names at different geographical levels. For example, '.co.uk' businesses are registered with an organisation called Nominet which acts as the registrar for the UK.

Hypertext Transfer Protocol (HTTP)

HTTP is the set of rules that govern how multimedia files are transmitted around the Internet. The content of the WWW is such that text, graphics, video and sound can all be transferred as part of a web page. HTTP ensures that the files are transferred and received in a common format.

Summary Question

3 What is the purpose of an Internet Registry?

You will have noticed that most URLs contain a HTTP prefix:

http://www.awebsite.co.uk/index.htm

HTTP indicates the use of the hypertext transfer protocol which means that the file that the URL is pointing to (index.htm) is a multimedia file to be viewed through a web browser.

Hypertext refers to the fact that the web pages will have hyperlinks to other files. When you select a URL either by typing it in, or by clicking on a hyperlink, the HTTP on your computer sends a request to the IP address of the computer that contains the web page. The HTTP on this computer than handles the request and sends back the web page in the appropriate format.

This uses the 'client–server' model which means that your web browser acts as a 'client', requesting the services of the computer that contains the web page, the 'server'. Both client and server computers must use the same protocols so that the files can be sent and received in the same format.

File Transfer Protocol (FTP)

FTP is another set of rules relating to the transfer of files around the Internet. It is commonly used when a web page is uploaded from the computer of the person who created the site to the web hosting server. It is also used when software is downloaded from web sites. When FTP is being used for this purpose, it will be shown as the prefix in the URL, for example:

ftp://www.gamesdownload.com/blocker.exe

It is similar to HTTP in that it works using the standard layers of TCP/IP. However, HTTP tends to be used to transfer viewable content (web pages) whereas FTP is commonly used to transfer program files, in this case, a free game.

Telnet

Telnet is an Internet resource that allows remote access to computers connected on the Internet. This means that using one computer, you can access another computer and all the information and resources on that computer as if you were sitting at it. This uses the client–server model whereby the computer that you use acts as the client and the computer that you control is the server. The server computer is more commonly referred to as the host.

Telnet is a combination of software and protocols. The software provides an interface with which to connect to the host and the Telnet protocol dictates how the computers will communicate. Telnet uses 'terminal emulation', which means that one computer emulates or copies the other. For example, when you type on the keyboard of the client computer, what you type is emulated on the host.

There are a number of scenarios where Telnet is useful. For example, if you want to connect to the school or college intranet, you could use Telnet to provide you with access to it even when you are on your home computer.

Usenet

Usenet is a facility on the Internet on which you can post and read electronic messages. The messages are stored on Usenet servers and are organised by topic into 'newsgroups'. ISPs usually provide free software which allows anyone with Internet access to take part in any newsgroup that is running on the Internet. Usenet was one of the first applications of the Internet and as a consequence it is now enormous. There are millions of users taking part in thousands of newsgroups, posting messages, reading and replying to them. Ongoing discussions are referred to as 'threads'.

Newgroups are identified by their address which is similar to a web address. For example 'rec.arts.books'. Newsgroups are organised in a hierarchical structure in order to manage the sheer volume of groups. There are around 20 major categories which are identified by their prefix, in this case Recreation. The sub-category here is Arts and a further categorisation gives us Books. Within this there may be hundreds of newsgroups on different books. Other major categories include 'comp' for computing and 'alt' for alternative which tends to include some of the more undesirable content.

Summary Questions

4 What is meant by multimedia?

5 Explain the need for protocols such as FTP and HTTP.

Study Questions

1. Describe the process that Nominet use to allocate domain names.

2. The WWW is one service available via the Internet. Identify two other services that are available.

3. Identify three browsers that are available and explain why you might choose to use one rather than the others.

4. Identify other ways in which information can be downloaded from the Internet without accessing the WWW.

5. What is HTTPS?

6. Give two examples where it would be useful to gain remote access to a computer network using Telnet.

7. Telnet is sometimes associated with hacking. Why is this the case, and what security measures could prevent its use for unauthorised purposes?

8. Identify four common topics for a newsgroup.

9. There are some concerns about the use of newsgroups as many of them are completely unregulated and users are able to send any type of information in any format. What could be done to prevent the misuse of newsgroups?

Examination Questions

1. Port A of a router in the diagram below is assigned the IP address 192.168.1.1. Port B is assigned the IP address 213.208.10.146. Which of these IP addresses needs to be registered with the Internet Registrar and why? [2]

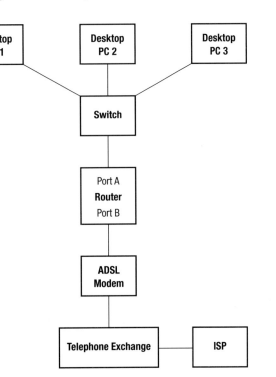

CHAPTER:27
Advanced web sites

Web page construction and HTML

HTML (hypertext mark-up language) is the language used to program how information will be displayed on a web page. It is similar to a programming language in that the designer types in lines of code. The code has to be input using the correct key words and syntax. This code is then converted by the browser into a finished web page. HTML has become one of the standard mark-up languages although there are other mark-up languages available, such as XML.

It is possible to create web pages without any knowledge of HTML. Some software such as Dreamweaver and FrontPage will allow the user to create web pages graphically and will automatically write the HTML. It is also common to find HTML under the 'save as' option of most word processing and desktop publishing packages, which means that files created in these packages can be converted to be displayed as web pages. Most HTML designers use basic text editors such as 'Notepad' to write their code.

The code describes the layout of the page, the colours and the font styles to be used, and will also contain links to web resources and other files such as movie or sound files. The following basic HTML code has been commented. The following screenshot shows how the page will be displayed in a browser.

Code	Comment
`<HTML>`	Start of HTML code
`<Head>`	Open the header
`<Title> Basic HTML example </title>`	Title text is displayed at the top of the browser
`</head>`	Close the header
`<body bgcolor = "yellow">`	Set background colour to yellow
`<font face = "Arial" align = "center" size = 10>`	Set font to Arial size 10
`<p> Welcome to the page`	Text for a paragraph
`</font>`	End of font
`<hr>`	Horizontal line
`<font face = "Times" size = 4>`	Set font to Times size 4
`<p> This is a very basic example of some html code`	Text for a paragraph

` It has been produced using a` `<b> text editor </b> </p>`	Creates a line break and displays 'text editor' in bold
`<p> Html is a mark up language: </p>`	Paragraph of text
`<li> It controls the way` `information is displayed on the page`	Bullet point
`<li> It is <b> not </b> a` `programming language`	Bullet point
`<li> It allows you to insert` `<u> hyperlinks </u> </li>`	Bullet point with 'hyperlinks' underlined
`<p> Click <a href =` `"http://www.bbc.co.uk">here` `</a> to go to the BBC web site </p>`	Hyperlink to the BBC web site. Could contain links to other services
`<p><img src = "horse.bmp" align =` `"middle"></p>`	Inserts an image file
`</font>`	End of font
`</body>`	End of the body of text
`</HTML>`	End of HTML page

1 Draw a labelled diagram to show the appearence off the web page using the following HTML code writing comments on the design where the meaning may not be clear:

```
<HTML>
<Head>
<Title> Welcome to Lincolnshire </title>
</head>

<body bgcolor = "white">

<font face = "Arial" size = 10>
<p> Welcome to Lincolnshire
</font>

<font face = "Times" size = 4>
<p> Lincolnshire is a wonderful county which is flat
<br>It is the birthplace of <b> Sir Isaac Newton </b> </p>

<p> It borders: </p>
<li> Yorkshire
<li> Nottinghamshire
<li> Cambridgeshire

<p> Click <a href = "http://www. lincolnshire.gov.uk">here </a> to go to the local web site
   </p>

<p><img src =  "lincolncathedral.bmp" align = "middle"></p>
</font>
</body>
</HTML>
```

Organisation of web pages on a web site

A web site is a collection of web pages and these pages are connected via hyperlinks. There is no limit to the number of web pages that can be stored on a site. The BBC web site for example has hundreds of thousands of pages. At the root of all these pages is the 'home page' which is the main page that will load when you type in a standard domain name.

The home page introduces the site and will provide key links. Most home pages contain a logo, an introduction to the site, a site map, a search facility and links to the main pages. As the site gets bigger, the organisation of the pages and the links between them becomes more and more complicated. Consequently it is important both as a web designer and as a user, to have a clear idea of the structure of a site.

There are three main models of organisation:

Tree structure. Each page will contain a number of hierarchical links to a set of related pages. Each of these will connect to another set of related pages and so on. This would work well on larger sites where the information being shown has a clear structure. Schools, colleges and businesses could use this. For

example, a computer retailer could use a tree structure to organise a site as shown in Figure 27.2.

Linear structure. Pages are organised in a line which means that one page follows another which follows another and so on. This is suited to sites where the user must access every page in sequence, for example, completing on-line application forms or ordering products from on-line retailers.

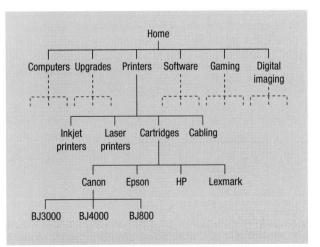

Figure 27.2 **Tree structure showing the design of a web site for computer retailer**

Random structure. There is no apparent logic to the organisation of the pages. Instead there are hyperlinks from one page to the next as deemed appropriate by the designer. On-line dictionaries and encyclopaedias might use this method as there may be several routes of enquiry that the user may want to follow having searched for a key word.

Java and applets

Java is a programming language which is used extensively to create content within web pages. It is assumed that Java was written for the WWW, though in fact it was developed in the mid-1980s by Sun Microsystems as a generic language for programming chips within consumer electronic devices.

It was designed to be 'portable' which means that code written for one microprocessor could also be used on other makes of microprocessors. It is an object-oriented language which has become popular as programmers are able to create self-running programs called 'applets'.

An applet is a small application or program. A Java applet runs inside a web page. The Java applet will run on any computer with a Java-friendly browser and is self-executing which means that it does not need any additional software to run it. This is a useful feature on web pages as content can be created in a Java applet that might otherwise need a specialised piece of software. For example, to use an Access database you will need a copy of Access on your computer. Using a Java applet, a database can be accessed without the need for any other software.

Java is used on web pages to create animations and can also be used to create content that requires interaction from the user, for example, filling in an on-line form.

Active Server Pages (ASP)

An ASP is an HTML page that contains one or more small executable programs within it. It was developed by Microsoft to enable web pages with dynamic content to be updated within a web page without having to go back to software stored on the server. The program may be written in Visual Basic or Microsoft's version of Java, which is called Jscript. A common example would be a Java applet as described in the previous section.

A typical example of an ASP would be an on-line membership database where the contents of the database are constantly changing as new members join and old members leave. Rather than accessing the database software itself, the user can update details using the ASP. Another example would be an on-line product catalogue that is changed as the products change, or an on-line auction where the bids are constantly changing.

With reference to the client–server model, the program is usually stored on the server that contains the web page. When the HTML is viewed using a browser, the program will run. An ASP stored on the server allows the program to run regardless of the browser software being used. Some browsers may not be able to open ASPs that are stored on the client side.

Summary Questions

2 State the most appropriate structure for organising web sites for the following organisations. For each, explain why you think it is appropriate.
 (a) The police force.
 (b) University (application form).
 (c) On-line atlas.

3 Identify two advantages of an applet over a standard application.

4 Identify two advantages of an ASP compared to a standard web page.

Study Questions

1. HTML is a mark-up language. Explain two ways in which a mark-up language differs from a programming language.

2. Give two examples of web sites that would benefit from using ASPs, explaining why in each case.

3. What other mark-up languages are available and how do they differ from HTML?

4. Look at three different web sites and identify whether they are organised in a tree, linear or random structure.

Examination Questions

1.   Example.htm

```
<HTML>
  <HEAD>
    <TITLE>Two Ways of Sending Data</TITLE>
  <HEAD>

  <BODY
    <a HREF="Process.asp?myname=Fred">Click here</a>
    <p>
    <FORM method="POST" ACTION="Process.asp">
      Please enter your name:
      <INPUT name="myname" size=10>
      <p>
      <INPUT type"submit" value="SEND">
    </FORM>
  </BODY>
</HTML>
```

(a)   With reference to the figure draw a labelled diagram to show the appearance of
the web page when viewed through a web browser.   [5]
A server-side script, Process.asp, processes the data posted by the web browser.
Process.asp is shown in the second figure.

```
<HTML>
  <HEAD>
    <TITLE>Form and Query String processing</TITLE>
  </HEAD>
  <BODY>
    <%
      Avariable=Request ("myname")
      Response Write Avariable
    %>
  </BODY>
</HTML>
```

(b) What is the value assigned to the variable Avariable when this script executes if the user:

    (i)   clicks the hyperlink in the first figure;   [1]

    (ii)   clicks the SEND button after typing the name James?   [1]

(c) What value is sent to the user's browser when the user:

    (i)   clicks the hyperlink in the first figure;   [1]

    (ii)   clicks the SEND button after typing the name James?   [1]

(d) Both Example.htm and Process.asp were created on a client computer and then uploaded to a folder D:\AQA\WWWRoot on a web server. The web server has been configured to present this folder to the World Wide Web as the web site with domain name www.example.co.uk.

    (i)   What protocol would have been used to upload the files Example.htm and Process.asp?   [1]

    (ii)   What URL was used in the browser's address line for the browser to load the web page Example.htm?   [3]

    (iii)   What other service should the web server support to allow the owner of the web site to access the web server from a remote location in order to create a subfolder ASPScripts in D:\AQA\WWWRoot?   [1]

AQA January 2003 Paper 5

2. A company advertises its HTML courses on the Internet.

(a) What is the Internet?   [2]

This figure shows the HTML form of a web page advertising HTML courses.

(b) With reference to the contents of the figure, draw a labelled diagram to show the appearance of the web page when viewed through a web browser.   [5]

(c) The link in the HTML contains the Uniform Resource Locator (URL) of another web page. Explain the four parts of this URL.   [4]

```
<HTML>
<HEAD>
 <TITLE>
  ECS Ltd
 </TITLE>
</HEAD>

<BODY>

 <H1> HTML Courses </H1>
 <P>1. Introduction to HTML
 <P>2. Basic HTML
 <P>3. Advanced HTML
 <A HREF=http://www.ecs.co.uk/main/page.html>more info</A>
</BODY>
</HTML>
```

AQA June 2002 Module 5

CHAPTER:28
Advanced uses of the World Wide Web

E-mail

E-mail, or electronic mail, is a message that can be sent from one computer to others. The messages are primarily text-based but graphics, sound and video can be incorporated or attached. E-mail is considered to be one of the 'killer applications' on the Internet, that is, one of the main reasons that the Internet has become so popular. In fact, the ability to send e-mails pre-dates the invention of the World Wide Web.

Assuming you have the appropriate hardware and software the benefits of e-mail are:

- The cost of sending a message is very small compared to more traditional methods such as normal mail or fax machine.

- E-mail messages are usually sent and received within a few seconds which compares favourably with other methods of communication.

- E-mail has become a favoured method of communication for personal and business messages.

- The ability to send attachments has made it a common way of transmitting other files as well.

- Copies of the same message can be sent to many people at the same time.

- They are easy to reply to as the software automatically inputs the address of the sender.

The disadvantages of e-mail are:

- You cannot be sure that your message has been received at the other end.

- It is not 100 per cent secure. Therefore, some organisations may choose not to use e-mail for important communications.

- There is a large volume of unsolicited e-mails, called 'spam'. Most e-mail software will offer some filtering which will block some, but not all spam.

- E-mail is often misused by employees within organisations. This means that they are not working when they should be and may be offending others with the material that they are sending. There have been many high profile cases of well-known

businesses who have sacked workers for misusing e-mail.

- **E-mail can only be used for electronic messages and media. For example, you could not send a parcel via e-mail.**
- **Most viruses are spread via e-mail.**
- **Many people do not have access to e-mail.**

In order to send and receive e-mail your computer must have the following hardware and software:

E-mail software: This is the application itself. There are a number of free e-mail providers who will allow you to download their software from the Internet. Perhaps the best known is Hotmail which allows you to access your e-mail messages from any computer with Internet access. In addition to the software, you are given access to their servers where all the messages are stored. Another Microsoft product, Outlook Express, is perhaps the most popular e-mail software among business users, although this is not provided free of charge. It is usually provided as part of a software suite.

Modem: You must have a physical connection to the Internet which is usually made through a modem. Recently, broadband techniques have become more popular allowing faster Internet access. Broadband access is achieved through a cable modem, or an ISDN or ADSL adapter.

Internet Service Provider (ISP): The ISP acts as a gateway to the Internet giving you access to the Internet. Some ISPs also offer free e-mail software.

Common features of e-mail software are:

Security: All e-mail providers require you to have an e-mail address that is unique and a password to prevent unauthorised access. They may also have filters that prevent 'spam' and use encryption techniques to reduce the chances of important information being read by unauthorised users.

Compose: This is where you type your message. You must include the e-mail address of the person or people you are sending the message to. The first part of the address is the e-mail name chosen by the recipient. The last part (after the @ sign) indicates who is providing the e-mail facility.

yourname@hotmail.com

Address book: An area to store e-mail addresses for future use. You can normally store the addresses along with the real names of the recipient. When composing, you click on a name in the address book rather than having to type it in. Some e-mail software allows you to set up groups of addresses to allow you to send bulk e-mails.

Inbox: Where all incoming messages are stored and can be viewed. They will be listed showing the name of the person who sent you the message and the date it was sent. Free e-mail providers tend to limit the amount of space available in your Inbox. This is because they are storing everyone's messages on their own servers and they tend to get full.

Outbox/Sent messages: Stores copies of any messages that you are ready to send or you have sent respectively. This may be particularly useful for more formal e-mails such as business correspondence.

Attachments: Any type of file can be attached to an e-mail. This is a particularly useful facility and is used to send graphics and sound files, to send business documents, or to send coursework from your college computer to your home computer. Some of the free e-mail providers will limit the size of the file that can be sent. Hotmail, for example, only allows attachments of up to 1 Mb. Attached files are automatically scanned for viruses as this is a common method of spreading them.

Internet Relay Chat (IRC)

Internet Relay Chat is a text-based communication system that allows you to enter 'chat rooms'. Within these rooms you send messages in 'real time' to anyone else in the same chat room. This means that your message will appear on the screen for anyone in the chat room to see, almost as you type it. Each room will have a different name which usually indicates the nature of the 'chat' taking place.

IRC is provided by commercial businesses that have their own servers. All you need is the appropriate software to access the chat rooms. The software is supplied either by your browser, or you can download it from the Internet. Once the software is installed, your message will be routed to the server of the IRC provider. You effectively become a part of their network.

Summary Question

1 Identify the hardware and software needed to send and receive e-mails.

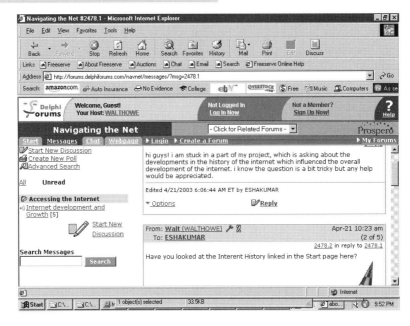

2 Newsgroups and IRC both use a client–server model. Explain this concept in relation to IRC.

3 How might an IRC chat room be 'moderated'?

Features of chat rooms include:

Rooms: An IRC provider will usually have a range of rooms that cover different topics. You can switch between rooms at any time and view the users who are active in each room at the current time. Some providers allow you to create your own rooms.

Security: You will be provided with a unique user name and password. Many chat rooms are filtered either by keywords, or by manual supervision. This prevents messages becoming offensive or inappropriate. Some rooms are completely unfiltered.

Private chat: Most IRC rooms have the facility to have a one-to-one chat with another user. If this is selected then you do not see all the other messages that are appearing in the chat room. Effectively, you go into your own separate room.

Attachments: IRC allows you to send and receive files via the chat room. This works in a similar way to attachments with e-mail.

Address book: You can store lists of names and their contact details and contact them by their user name via the chat room.

On-line shopping and banking

There has been an enormous growth in the number of people undertaking their shopping and banking on the Internet. Some experts thought that people would not be prepared to shop and bank on the Internet due to the fear of fraud. However, recent improvements in security, as outlined in the next chapter, have increased consumer confidence and it appears that a sizeable number of people are prepared to do business on the Internet. All the major banks and retailers now have web sites where on-line transactions and purchases can be made, respectively. In addition, there are a number of new and successful businesses that only operate on the Internet. The generic term for businesses operating on the Internet is 'e-commerce'.

The advantages to the business are:

- **Overheads are reduced as there is no need for retail premises, that is, shops.**

- **Businesses can attract new customers through the Internet who might not have come into their shops.**

- **The number of employees can be reduced which reduces costs.**

- **Customers have access to information 24-hours-a-day increasing the chances of making sales.**

- Businesses do not have to carry all items in stock as they can source them after the customer has placed an order.

- Businesses are able to collect information about their customers that they wouldn't be able to do normally.

- There is no money to handle. It can all be done through electronic funds transfer (EFT).

- It eliminates the need for an intermediary agent, for example, insurance can be bought direct rather than via a broker, airline flights can be booked direct rather than through a travel agent.

The disadvantages to the business are:

- Many businesses have to run traditional retail businesses alongside their Internet operation which increases costs, for example, Tesco still have all their stores and they operate a home delivery service on the Internet as well.

- Sales may be reduced as customers are unable to see and try the products before they buy them.

- The web site may be hacked and money could be stolen.

- The web site may be hacked in order to cause embarrassment to the business.

The advantages to the customer are:

- Reduced travel time and costs as they do not need to visit the shops.

- Prices may be reduced as the businesses can offer lower prices if they have lower overheads.

- Customers can place orders 24-hours-a-day, every day.

- The customer may be able to sample the product on-line, for example, view movie clips or listen to music before buying.

The disadvantages to the customer are:

- You cannot see the real product before you buy it.

- Many people enjoy the social aspects of shopping.

- Some financial transactions may be very personal and customers may prefer to do these face-to-face.

- A customer could be the victim of fraud if a site was hacked.

- Products may take a while to be delivered.

Case study

Music downloads

The WWW has had an enormous impact on the way music is sold and distributed. Traditional CD sales have been hit by free download sites such as Napster and Kazaa. These sites offer a peer-to-peer network whereby users can locate music files held on the computers of anyone else connected through the site. It has become an ongoing legal battle to try to close these sites down as it is technically illegal to download copyrighted material.

However, the large record companies and music retailers are taking a new approach. EMI and over 20 on-line music retailers have signed up to an agreement to offer 140 000 tracks on-line. Users will make a 'micro-payment' of between 5p and £5 to download individual tracks or whole albums.

The computer company Apple launched iTunes in April 2003 and sold more than five million tracks in eight weeks. Microsoft, Yahoo and AOL are also planning to offer a downloading service to cash in on what many consider to be the main growth area for the WWW over the next few years.

There are a number of issues:

- **Many different companies and individuals own the rights to music. This means that if the owner does not sign up, then many tracks will be inaccessible in legal form.**

- **If the free sites still exist then many users may continue to download for free. However, many users appear to be happy to pay for legal copies judging by the iTunes experience.**

- **It may not be profitable to sell downloads for only a few pence as the cost of handling the transaction is likely to be much larger than this. However, there are a number of e-businesses who already offer this service.**

- **Once a track has been downloaded legally, it may be difficult to stop that user selling the track on to other users. A number of systems are being introduced to prevent this.**

Study Questions

1. Why might an e-mail provider:

(a) limit the size of your inbox to 1 Mb;
(b) limit the size of an attachment to 1 Mb?

2. On what basis might you choose one e-mail provider over another.

3. Describe two ways in which an e-mail can be made secure from hackers.

4. Internet shopping will mean the end of high-street shops. To what extent do you think this might be true?

5. Some people will never use the WWW for e-banking or e-shopping. Give reasons why this might be the case.

6. Many parents are becoming increasingly concerned about their children's use of chat rooms. Why might parents be concerned and what can be done to prevent possible problems?

Examination Questions

1. Briefly describe two benefits of shopping via the Internet over telephone shopping, and for each give a feature of the Internet that supports this benefit. [4]

AEB Summer 1999 Paper 2

CHAPTER:**29**
Advanced issues on the Internet

Threats on the Internet

There are some inherent risks when using the Internet. These often relate to the potential threat of someone discovering personal or sensitive information about individuals and organisations and the information being misused. There is also an increasing risk from viruses, file corruption and denial of service attacks.

Case study

Unemployed man cripples the Port of Houston, Texas

An unemployed man from Dorset was arrested following a joint investigation by the FBI and the Metropolitan Police Computer Crime Unit. Aaron Caffrey carried out a 'denial of service' attack in September 2001 when he allegedly bombarded the port's web server with thousands of electronic messages from his home in Dorset. This effectively 'clogged up' the server so that it was unable to carry out its routine tasks including providing navigation and mooring information for hundreds of ships in the 25 mile long port.

In October 2003, Caffrey was found not guilty, claiming that although the attack came from his computer, he had been hacked, and the hacker had used his computer to carry out the attack.

Programmer hacks payroll system

Stephen Widdowson, a computer programmer, hacked into the payroll system of his own company during 2002 and redirected thousands of pounds every month into his own bank account. He fled to South Africa but was tracked down and sentenced to 3 years' imprisonment.

HACKERS

Hackers are individuals or groups that gain or attempt to gain unauthorised access to individual computers or the networks of organisations. Hackers' motives vary enormously. At one end of the scale there is the amateur hacker who views hacking as a game and simply enjoys breaking into other people's systems. When they get in, they rarely do any damage. At the other end of the scale, there are professional hackers who can make a living by carrying out fraudulent acts.

There are also groups of 'ethical hackers' who enjoy the notoriety that hacking brings. These people tend to target large organisations such as Microsoft in order to expose weaknesses in their security measures. Their justification for this is to make big businesses take a more serious approach to Internet security. Other hackers have political or religious motivations and may target the web sites of government agencies or religious groups in order to get their own views across.

VIRUSES

A virus is a small program which loads itself onto a computer with the aim of 'infecting' the computer or network in some way. The severity of viruses varies from ones that simply display messages through to viruses that destroy the contents of your hard drive. New viruses come out every day and the motivation of the authors is usually malicious. Virus checking software is used to identify and kill viruses.

Firewall

A firewall describes the technique used to protect an organisation's network from unauthorised use by users outside the network. Its main purpose is to prevent hacking. A firewall is constructed using hardware and software.

An organisation that has a local area network will have a number of computers linked together which will all have access to internal information. Commonly, an organisation will use an intranet as a means of distributing this information. The LAN may also allow users access to the Internet and this is where their own LAN becomes vulnerable. By establishing a connection to the Internet, it is possible for hackers to use this connection to access information stored on the LAN.

Case study

Melissa

The Melissa virus was launched in March 1999 and was one of the first high-profile viruses spread around the Internet. Named after a Florida stripper, it spread to an estimated one million computers and caused £50 million worth of damage to computer systems and data.

The virus was spread via e-mail as an attachment. When the user opened the attachment it launched the virus which deleted computer files. At the same time, it sent the original e-mail and attachment to the first 50 contacts in the computer's address book. In turn this attached to 50 contacts in each of these 50 and so on. This is why it was able to spread so quickly.

The man who wrote the virus, David Smith, was fined $5 000 and only escaped prison by helping the authorities to track down and eliminate other viruses. He described the virus as a 'colossal mistake'.

Case study

I love you

On 4 May 2000, a computer school student from the Philippines launched the virus which he claims to have written as a school project. It was similar to the Melissa virus in that it was sent as an e-mail attachment and replicated itself to the e-mail addresses in the address books of the recipients. Once launched, the 'love bug' destroyed computer files. Estimates of the damage were in billions of pounds.

The student, Onel de Guzman, was charged under Philippine legislation usually used to prosecute credit card fraud. The student's college project was part of the evidence used to convict him.

There are a number of ways of creating a firewall. One method is to have two network interface cards (NICs) in the server – one for the LAN and one for the Internet. When data packets are received through the Internet NIC, they can be examined before being passed around internally via the LAN NIC. Firewall software is used to examine the packets to ensure that they do not contain any unauthorised data. At a basic level, the header of each packet can be examined to check that it has come from a recognised source. If it has then it can be routed around the LAN. If it hasn't then that packet can be rejected.

Firewall software may also have a facility that keeps a log of all the data being transmitted so that it can be traced. The IP address of the computer sending each packet can be recorded. It may also generate automatic warnings if it identifies that the server is being attacked by hackers.

Encryption

Encryption is the process of turning data into a form that cannot be understood without being deciphered. It is a security measure that prevents data being readable if it were to be intercepted when being transmitted around the Internet. Encryption techniques can be applied to any data and are not unique to the Internet. However, encryption has become more important with the increased use of the Internet for shopping and banking. Wireless communications are the easiest to intercept and as the Internet makes extensive use of satellite links, encryption has become more important.

There is a great deal of sensitive and personal information being transmitted: credit card details, personal financial information, business information regarding new product developments, business sales figures and so on. Organisations must decide on the level of risk and how damaging it would be if information was discovered by someone outside their organisation. For example, if one of the main banks could be easily hacked and a customer's account details discovered, then this would be very damaging to their business.

The level of encryption put onto any file can vary. Encryption can be weak or strong depending on the risk. Strong encryption takes much longer to hack, but the costs are higher. The mechanics and methods of encrypting files are covered in more detail in Chapter 36.

Digital certificates

A digital certificate is a means of proving who you are when dealing with people and organisations on the Internet. It is usually used by businesses to authenticate that they are genuine and that any transactions you undertake with them will be honoured.

**Summary
Question**

1 Explain how hardware and software can be used to create a firewall.

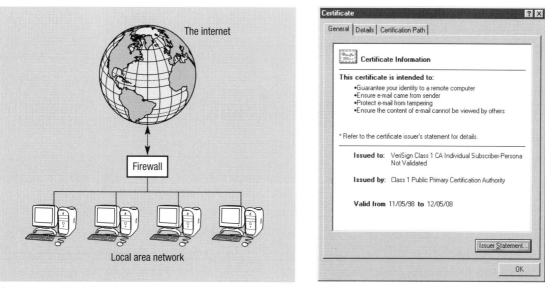

Photograph 29.1 **Firewall**

Photograph 29.2 **Digital certificate**

Certificates are also used by some government agencies such as the Inland Revenue. The certificate contains the name of the organisation and a serial number which is registered with a Certification Authority who issue the certificates. Digital certificates will also contain information about the encryption method employed by the organisation.

Digital certificates were introduced to encourage people to do business on the Internet as many consumers are concerned about fraud. If a hacker discovers your credit card number, then they could purchase items from the Internet using your card.

Web sites using digital certificates usually advertise the fact prominently on the site using the logo of the Certification Authority. Examples of digital certificates are Thawte and VeriSign.

Moral, ethical, social and cultural issues

The explosion in the use of the Internet has thrown up a number of moral, social and cultural issues, and opinion is divided as to whether it is fundamentally a good or bad thing. Whole books have been written discussing the influence of the Internet on modern society and you do need to be aware of some of the issues raised. The intention of this section is not to express a particular opinion but to identify that there are two sides to any moral, social or cultural issue. As A Level students you are expected to view both sides of the argument and be able to express an opinion.

FREEDOM OF SPEECH

The Internet has provided a forum for anyone (with the right equipment) to express their views freely. This can be viewed as good or bad. On the one hand it provides people with a voice that they didn't have before. This is referred to as 'empowerment'. People can broadcast their opinions to a large audience. Prior to the Internet this could only be done through TV or the newspapers, so now we have a much more diverse range of opinions being expressed. On the other hand, this means that

people and organisations with extreme views can also express their opinions. This could include incitement to racism, violence or terrorism.

PORNOGRAPHY

Figures vary, but it is claimed that 30 per cent of all Internet traffic is to view pornography. Images that are banned in any other medium can now be viewed over the Internet and opinions on this vary. Why should we be able to view something on the Internet that is banned on TV, in the cinema or in printed media? On the other hand, why shouldn't consenting adults be allowed to look at what they like?

NATIONAL SECURITY

There is evidence to suggest that terrorist groups use the Internet to spread their message and to plan terrorist activities. Often they will use strong encryption techniques to ensure that government agencies cannot find out what they are doing. Should they be allowed to use the Internet in this way or do they have a right to express their views?

REGULATION

Every other form of media is subject to some regulations. Films, TV programmes, books, magazines, and newspapers all adhere to rules relating to their content. Could the Internet be regulated? Should the Internet be regulated? Who would be in charge of regulation?

There is a fundamental problem in that the Internet is an international network. Even if it was decided by one country that it should be regulated, it may not be possible to enforce the regulations on web sites from other countries. See the case study at the end of this chapter.

INFORMATION 'UNDERCLASS'

A large number of people in this country and across the world do not have access to the Internet. At the time this book was written, an estimated 600 million people have access to the Internet. There are six billion people in the world so only 10 per cent have access. The reasons for this are varied. In some developing countries it may be that the infrastructure, such as electricity and telephone lines, does not exist. In developed countries such as ours, it

Summary Questions

2 Describe three measures that can be taken to prevent unauthorised access to computer systems.

3 Describe three ways in which a computer system can be protected against viruses.

4 Discuss the following techniques, considering how effective they are against hackers:
(a) encryption;
(b) digital certificates.

could be lack of money or lack of training or simply that people do not want it. Either way, there is a concern that these people may be disadvantaged in some ways by not getting access to vital information. For example, many government departments publish information over the Internet that may not be available elsewhere. More businesses are using the Internet to advertise jobs and this disadvantages people who may not see the advert without access.

UNEMPLOYMENT

The rise of Internet shopping and banking has meant that some businesses have changed the way they are structured and this has lead to the loss of some jobs. For example, some banks are reducing the number of branches that they have as more people carry out transactions on the Internet. Therefore, the employees at the branches lose their jobs. On the other hand, the Internet has created many jobs for people who create and support web sites.

SUMMARY

There are many other factors that could be taken into account in this section and these topics are a small selection of the issues raised. Remember that you are the first generation to grow up with the Internet and also remember that there is a sizeable percentage of the population who have never used it and don't want to use it.

As is clear from the topics discussed above, ethical and moral issues become a matter of debate. In an attempt to provide some guidance, The British Computer Society (BCS) have produced a code of conduct and a code of ethics which guide individuals and organisations on the ethical use of computer systems in general, including Internet usage. Observing the code is a condition of membership to the society and although it is not legally enforceable, any breaches of the code could lead to dismissal of an employee, or a student being asked to leave a college.

The main principles of the code of conduct are that members should:

- **always operate in the public interest;**
- **have a duty to the organisation that they work for, or the college they attend;**
- **have a duty to the profession;**
- **maintain professional competence and integrity.**

Case study

Self-regulation on the Internet

In 1996, several UK ISPs set up the Internet Watch Foundation (IWF) to combat criminal activity carried out on the Internet. It has no legal powers and is not funded by the government. Its primary role is to operate a telephone hotline so that Internet users can report any web sites where they consider the content to be illegal. Primarily this relates to child pornography but also includes adult pornography, e-commerce frauds and offensive activity such as abusive communications.

When suspected illegal activity is reported, the Foundation will look at the site and if it is considered illegal they will issue a 'notice and take down' which means that the ISP will remove it from their server. In the five year period from 1996 to 2001 they claim to have removed 30,000 images of child pornography. However, 90 per cent of the sites that are reported on the hotline are not based in the UK and, therefore, the ISPs can not remove the sites.

Another aspect of the work of the Foundation is to educate users about the dangers of the Internet, to promote the use of filtering software and to encourage the adoption of the Internet Content Rating Association (ICRA) rating for web content.

In some countries, the government has attempted to control the content of the Internet. Australia passed the Broadcasting Service Amendment (Online Services) Act in 1999 to regulate online content. In Saudi Arabia, all ISPs have to go through a government-controlled server where the content is regulated. In the USA any attempts to control the Internet are rejected due to the First Amendment of the Constitution which enshrines the freedom of speech.

Study Questions

1. Should the Internet be censored?

2. Explain whether you think it is technically possible to censor the Internet.

3. Some countries do censor the Internet. Find a country that does impose censorship and describe how they do it.

4. New viruses come out every day. Identify a recent virus. What does the virus do? What was the intention of the person who wrote it?

5. "No system is 100 per cent safe". Discuss this statement considering all the methods available to an organisation to protect their computer systems and data.

6. Identify an organization that provides digital certificates. Explain the level of security they provide for users.

CHAPTER:**30**
Generic packages

Introduction

Generic packages comprise programs that are designed to be used for a variety of purposes. This means that users can use the same package to carry out a wide variety of different tasks. Some software is designed for specific tasks, for example, accountancy software can only be used for that purpose. On the other hand, generic packages such as word processing software, could be used for creating letters, reports and other documents, or even web pages.

Strict definitions of what constitutes a generic package vary. Commonly, it refers to word processing, spreadsheets, databases, desktop publishing and presentation packages but could be extended to include graphics and web design tools.

As an A Level student, you should make sure that you have practical experience of using each of the generic packages. In addition to needing these packages for coursework, you may also be asked to answer theoretical questions on aspects of their use in an exam. You should also be aware that there are a number of competing packages available. In your exam you should **never** use brand names in your answers – always refer to software using the generic terms. The table below shows the generic name of each of the main general purpose packages and some examples of the brand named products that are currently available.

Generic name	Brand names
Database	Microsoft Access
	Lotus Approach
	Logotron PinPoint
Spreadsheet	Microsoft Excel
	Lotus 1-2-3
	Eureka
Word processing	Microsoft Word
	Lotus Word Pro
	Corel WordPerfect
Desktop publishing	Microsoft Publisher
	Adobe PageMaker
	Adobe InDesign
	Corel Ventura
	Quark XPress
Presentation software	Microsoft Powerpoint
	Lotus Freelance Graphics
	Corel Presentations

Summary
Question

1 Apart from cost, what are the advantages of buying software as part of a suite?

Generic packages are often 'bundled' together to form a 'software suite'. Standard office applications are usually sold in this way and include some or all of the packages listed in the table and possibly some form of 'personal organiser' software such as Microsoft Outlook or Lotus Organizer.

Microsoft Office dominates the 'office suite' market but there are alternatives, such as Lotus SmartSuite or Corel Office. Software sold as a suite is cheaper than the sum of its parts and also provides better integration between packages allowing the user to link objects from one application to another.

There are some common features within all generic packages and some which are unique or particularly relevant to certain packages. The next section describes each package and identifies the most common or pertinent features of each.

Databases

Database software allows the creation, maintenance and interrogation of a database. A database is a collection of data on a related theme. The purpose of a database is to store data, allow editing and updating of that data, and enable the user to carry out searches. There are several packages available for the PC ranging from simple flat-file databases such as PinPoint through to sophisticated relational database systems such as Microsoft Access or Lotus Approach.

Large businesses and organisations are likely to have thousands or even millions of records to store and PC-based solutions are not sufficient for this purpose. Specialist database software, such as Oracle, is available. It is designed to run on networks and is able to cope with large volumes of data and produce rapid searches. For example, the Police National Computer (PNC) stores millions of records on people and vehicles. This database is constantly being updated and queried and the response time needs to be a matter of seconds.

Common features of database software are:

- **Add, edit and delete records – The contents of any database will constantly change. New records will be added, old records deleted and changes to existing records will need to be made.**

- **Data dictionary – This describes the contents of a database including a definition of all the field types and sizes, use of primary keys and validation checks being used.**

- **Queries – The facility that allows data to be analysed in different ways. A query at a basic level is simply a search.**

- **Forms – A user interface that enables the user to input information and to view information already stored.**

- **Reports – The output from the database. Reports are designed to be printed out.**

Spreadsheets

Spreadsheets are designed for users who work primarily with numerical data or data that is best presented and manipulated as a table. It was one of the first applications written for computers and is considered to be a 'killer application' in the sense that it encouraged people to use computers for this purpose. Spreadsheets are used extensively to handle financial information for businesses, manage personal finances, create invoices and generate quotes.

They can be very powerful when used for 'modelling' purposes. A model is where real-life factors can be re-created using the spreadsheet and then different scenarios can be created. These are referred to as 'what if' scenarios. For example, an architect may use a spreadsheet to calculate the cost of constructing a building. The architect could then 'model' different scenarios to look at the effect on costs: 'what if' we build a six storey building instead of seven?; 'what if' we increase the floor space by 200 sq m?

Spreadsheets are made up of cells into which the user can type text, numbers or formulae. The power of a spreadsheet lies in the fact that it has hundreds of different formulae that can be used and that the data in the cells can be linked so that it automatically updates when changes are made. In addition, there are a number of ways in which data can be presented including tables, graphs and charts.

Common features of spreadsheet software are:

- **Rows, columns and cells: All data is entered into cells which can be uniquely identified using the column** identifier which is a letter and the row identifier which is a number. For example, E2 is the cell where column E and row 2 intersect.

- **Sheets:** Spreadsheets can be constructed using any number of different sheets which can contain links between them.

- **Formulae:** Users can enter standard mathematical functions and use functions covering statistics and trigonometry, finance and date and time. There is also a range of look up functions.

- **Absolute and relative cell referencing:** When copying from one cell to a range of cells, the spreadsheet will automatically adjust the cell references for you. This is known as relative addressing. There are occasions when you would not want the automatic adjustment and this is when absolute addressing should be used (see the example below).

- **Formatting:** In addition to the standard handling of font styles and sizes, spreadsheets also have styles for ranges of cells and standard formats for displaying numbers such as currency and percentage.

- **Macros:** A macro is a facility where routine tasks can be recorded and then run automatically. For example, if you needed to create a chart each month based on sales figures, a macro could be written which would generate the chart when the user clicks on a control button.

- **Graphs:** Bar charts, pie charts, line graphs and scatter plots can be produced.

The extract below is from a spreadsheet set up by a photocopying shop which carries out regular copying for a number of clients. It shows the account for one of these businesses. As you can see, the cost per copy varies depending on the number of copies per month – once the company goes over 3000 in any one month, they pay a reduced rate per copy.

The formula for cell C4 is shown. It uses an IF statement to identify whether the number of copies has exceeded 3000. If it has then the number in cell B4 is multiplied by the value in cell E5. If it does not exceed 3000, then the value in cell B4 is multiplied by the value in cell E4.

The use of a $ sign fixes the references to cells E5 and E4. This is absolute cell referencing. When the formula in cell C4 is copied, it will still reference cells E4 and E5. However, the B4 reference will change to B5 as it needs to reference the next row. This is relative cell referencing.

Also notice that the figures in column C are shown incorrectly. The actual answer in cell C4 should be £127.75 but it has been rounded to 128 as the format of the cell has not been set to currency with two decimal places.

Word processors

Word processing software is used to create and edit text-based documents. Common uses are for creating letters, reports, memos, coursework and books. Most word processors can now be used for creating web pages. Modern word processing software also contains facilities to handle graphics which makes the distinction between word processing and desktop publishing rather blurred.

Common features of word processing software are:

- **Text input and editing:** The main feature of a word processor is the ability to input text from the keyboard or via scanning techniques and to manipulate the text.

- **Formatting:** There are many options for formatting font sizes, styles and colours. Whole paragraphs can be justified left, centre or right, and line spacing can be adjusted. Text can be wrapped.

- **Styles:** These are collections of formatting options. For example you may want all headings in your document to be Arial Bold Font Size 14 centred. This can be set as a style which can then be applied to any block of text.

- **Multimedia:** Modern word processors can handle any type of digital data including graphics, animations, video and sound.

- **Save As options:** Most word processors allow the user to save the file in a number of formats. This is useful for transferring files from one package to another. For example, you could save as a 'txt' file to transfer the text from one type of word processor to another, or save the file as 'html' so that it can be accessed by a browser.

- **Mail Merge:** Most word processors include a facility to write a standard letter and then merge in name and addresses from a file – usually a database or spreadsheet file will be used. This means that the letter can be created for multiple recipients but it only needs typing once.

- **Spell and grammar check:** Spell checkers will compare every word in a document against a dictionary file that contains acceptable words. Users can add their own words to this dictionary. A common mistake is to rely on the spell-checker, but they can make mistakes and they will not pick up errors in grammar. Grammar checkers aim to identify poor English but are less reliable at picking up errors than spell-checkers.

Desktop publishing (DTP)

Desktop publishing software is used to create documents and publications. It is similar to word processing in that it handles text and graphics. Desktop publishing differs in that the software is focused on the manipulation of the layout and will contain predefined templates for a range of publications including magazines, business stationery, cards, newsletters, banners and web sites.

Most DTP packages use frames to construct the document. The user will place a frame on a document positioning and sizing it to the appropriate dimensions. They will then put text or graphics into this frame before moving onto the next frame and so on. Text is handled as a continuous flow which means that when one text frame is full you can set it to flow into another text frame. DTP allows much greater flexibility over the overall design of a document and is used extensively by businesses who publish magazines, books and other printed media.

Common features of DTP software are:

- **Templates:** Predefined layouts are available including business forms, newsletters, calendars, brochures and web sites.

- **Wizards:** Wizards are a feature of most general purpose packages and are particularly useful when creating publications. Used in conjunction with the templates, they guide the user through the

Summary Question

2 Describe three differences between word processing and desktop publishing.

set-up procedures saving time and reducing the technical complexity.

- **Frames:** Text, pictures, graphics and tables are positioned on the publication inside frames.

- **Import options:** As DTP is a multimedia package, the software will include the facility to import text, tables, graphics and images from a variety of sources.

Presentation packages

Presentation packages are designed to create presentations usually in the form of a slide show that can be played on a PC or projected onto a bigger screen. They combine text and graphical information and may also include sound. Like DTP packages, they will include a number of predefined templates into which the user types their information.

Presentation software is being used in educational establishments to allow teachers to present to students and for the students to present to each other. Businesses also use them when presenting information to their employees or clients. Their purpose is to enhance the quality and impact of any presentation so many of the features are purely visual. In some cases, presentation software replaces a human presenter as slide shows can be left to run with the slides changing at timed intervals.

Common features of presentation software are:

- **Templates:** Standard layouts for slides including title screens, text and graphics boxes and a range of background themes.

- **Transitions:** As the user moves from one slide to the next, there are a number of styles in which this transition can be made, for example, sweeping in from the sides. Transitions can be timed automatically or prompted by the user.

- **Animations:** These control the way in which objects are displayed on the slides. For example, text can be presented one letter at a time, or a paragraph at a time. Graphics can

sweep in from the side or animated graphics can run continuously as the slide is being displayed.

- **Hyperlinks:** Many presentations are linear in nature which means that one slide logically follows on from the next. However, there may be occasions when the presenter wishes to branch off in a different direction before returning to the main theme. The use of hyperlinks allows this.

- **Import options:** As presentation software supports different media such as video and sound, the software will include the facility to import resources from a number of sources.

WHAT MAKES A GOOD PRESENTATION?

As part of your A level course, you will probably be asked to use presentation software. The definition of what makes a good presentation varies from one person to another. However, there are some 'rules of thumb':

- **Be consistent:** Use the same theme for every slide in the show. Use the same background colour and style.

- **Make it appropriate for the audience:** A different style is needed for presenting to your class colleagues than might be needed for a formal presentation to your teacher/lecturer.

- **Use colour carefully:** There are 16 777 216 colours available. Don't try and use them all! The use of colour should assist the audience in understanding your point. If it doesn't help then change it. Make sure there is a good contrast between the foreground and background colours.

- **Use appropriate font styles:** You probably only need to use two or three different fonts in your presentation. Use one for headings and another for the body of the text.

- **Graphics:** Do not use irrelevant graphics and animations. 'Clip art' is often overused and many of the images have lost their impact.

- **Use the appropriate font size:** Remember that your slide show will probably be projected on to a screen which could be 2m by 1m. Anything

under font size 20 could be difficult to read.

- **Don't put too much on each slide:** There is a danger of writing a small essay on each slide and the audience will probably not read it. Use bullet points that prompt your speech.

- **Don't over use transitions:** there are two elements to this. Each slide will have a transition style and each block of text or graphics can also be controlled. This is usually referred to as animation. Be consistent and don't use too many different styles.

Summary Questions

3 Identify a suitable application for each of the generic packages listed:
(a) word processor;
(b) spreadsheet;
(c) database;
(d) desktop publisher;
(e) presentation software.

4 Describe how hyperlinks might be used in a presentation package.

5 Describe four features of a bad computer-based presentation.

Study Questions

1. Describe three features of database software that could be useful for a doctor's surgery.

2. Describe three features of spreadsheet software that could be useful for an accountant.

3. State three advantages and one disadvantage of buying software as part of a suite.

4. Some people suggest that individual general purpose applications such as word processing and spreadsheets will be replaced by a single package that combines the functionality of all these applications. Comment on how likely you think this is.

Examination Questions

1. The following is an extract from an old spreadsheet which shows how many dollars would be obtained for different amounts of English money and the commission that would be paid on converting pounds into dollars.

	C	D	E	F
1	Exchange Rate			Commission in Pounds
2	3	Pounds	Dollars	
3				
4	Commission When pounds < 50			
5	2%	1	3	0.02
6	Commission When pounds >=50	5	15	0.10
7	1.5%	10	30	0.20
8		15	45	0.30
:	:	:	:	:
:	:	:	:	:
20		75	225	1.13
21		80	240	1.20
22		85	255	1.28

(a) The formula in cell E5 is D5 * C2 where $ denotes absolute cell referencing. What is the formula in cell E8? [3]

(b) The value in cell F20 is calculated from 1.5 × 75 / 100 which equals 1.125. However, the value displayed in cell F20 is 1.13. How might this happen? [1]

(c) Write the formula that was entered in cell F5 and copied to cells F6 to F22. Your formula should perform an automatic recalculation if the value in cell C5 or the value in cell C7 is changed. [6]

AQA June 2001 Module 2

CHAPTER:31
Advanced applications and effects

Applications of computers in a variety of contexts

Computing has thousands of applications and the average user probably only uses a few of them. In an exam you will be expected to comment on the use and application of computers in any situation where they are used. Therefore, it is important that you realise that using a PC is only one small part of computing. Computers are used in science, education, manufacturing, data processing, publishing, leisure, design, communication, embedded systems, information systems, the Internet, artificial intelligence and expert systems to name but a few.

As students the exam board expect you to:

- **Consider the purpose of an application.**
- **Discuss the application in the chosen context.**
- **Consider the user interface.**
- **Understand the communication requirements of an application.**
- **Discuss how well the application meets the needs of the organisation.**
- **Discuss the social, legal, and ethical consequences of the application.**

Case study

The National Strategy for Police Information Systems (NSPIS)

NSPIS was introduced in 1994 and was designed to provide a standard approach to the use of software across all UK police forces. Its objectives are to ensure that all police forces have a standard way of carrying out routine tasks and communicating with each other over their individual networks. It comprises a number of applications:

- Vehicle Procedures Fixed Penalty Notice (VP/FPO) – software that tracks and enforces the payment of parking fines.

- Home Office Large Major Enquiry System (HOLMES) – software designed to analyse evidence and investigate crimes.

- National Legal Database – software that provides advice and wording for local regulations and by-laws.

- Case Preparation – software that records all the documentation used by the police and the courts during legal trials.

- Custody – software that assists custody officers in recording information on people detained by the police.

- Command and Control – software that supplies real-time support for police incidents.

- National Management Information System (NMIS) – software that provides reporting functions for managers within the police force, for example, to report on overall crime statistics.

- Human Resources – software for career development, recruitment and other personnel issues.

Case study

Congestion charging in the city of London

On 17 February 2003, Ken Livingstone, the Mayor of London, introduced congestion charges for cars entering the streets of central London. Drivers are required to pay a daily £5 charge or face a fine of £80 when they enter the charging 'zone'.

- Payment can be made by SMS texting, online payment systems, swipe card, telephone or kiosk.

- A network of cameras cover every entrance to the zone. The cameras each take four pictures a second and up to 1.5 million photographs are taken each day of over 250 000 different vehicles.

- OCR software is used to convert registration number on the images into text. This is automatically encrypted to prevent misuse by hackers.

- Every registration number is entered into a database that already contains the registration numbers of every car where the driver has paid the charge. Where there is a match, the number is automatically deleted. Where there is no match, the registration number is fed into the Driver Vehicle Licensing Agency (DVLA) database to identify the owner of the vehicle. The DVLA register every driver and vehicle in the country.

- Manual checkers then look at the photographs of the non-payers to verify the details and fines are mailed to their home addresses.

- The data centres that handle all these processes have fail-safe systems which mean that in the event of a system crash, a back-up system will be used.

The two case studies included here have been chosen to allow group or class discussions based around the bulleted points above. These are just two examples from thousands that could have been chosen and it is very important that you keep up to date with the latest applications of computing. See the Resources list in Appendix 2.

Expert systems

An expert system, or knowledge-based system (KBS), is an application that allows the user to benefit from the knowledge of an expert or group of experts. They are designed to solve problems in areas where it would normally require a large amount of human expertise. For example, in medicine, doctors input details about a patient's condition and their expert system will make a diagnosis and suggest suitable treatments. Expert systems tend to be very specific in terms of the problems they are designed to solve. Therefore, one system can vary significantly from another. However, they all have four main components:

- **Data: Also known as a knowledge base, the data is provided by human experts. New data may be added at regular intervals. For example, a medical expert system will need updating as medical knowledge changes. New medical case studies will be added and the effect of new drugs needs to be recorded. It is worth noting that data on its own is meaningless. It becomes knowledge when it can be used to infer other information.**

- **Rules: The rules that will be applied to the data are also provided by the human experts. When an expert system is first produced it is likely to contain some inaccuracies. Therefore, the rules will need adjusting to ensure that the outputs from the system are realistic.**

- **Inference engine:** This is a piece of software used to search the knowledge base. It is separate from the data itself.

- **Interface:** A programmer will create an appropriate human–computer interface (HCI) to allow the user to use the rules that interrogate the data. The interface must also provide some explanation to the user of the outcome produced from the system. It is important to note that expert systems are not designed to replace humans – they are used to help the user make a decision.

Expert systems use declarative programming languages such as Prolog which was covered in Chapter 11. Prolog enables a programmer to construct the rules and data on which the system will be based. A declarative program is needed because the outcome of the program is not known – instead, there are many possible outcomes depending on how the user interrogates the system. Expert systems belong to a branch of computing called Artificial Intelligence (AI) in that they try to mimic the responses of a human expert.

A typical expert system for fault diagnosis on a car engine would work like this:

```
IF the car will not start
   AND the starter motor is
   functioning correctly
      AND the battery is charged
         THEN it is likely that
There is no petrol in the car
The alternator is broken
```

The expert system will examine its knowledge base in order to suggest possible faults. In this case it has a 'goal' which is that the car won't start. It starts by examining the rules and data. As it discounts each possibility it leads to a number of suggestions. This small example also demonstrates how much knowledge needs building in to the system. There are hundreds of reasons why a car might not start and the expert system needs to consider all of them. In this case, the car might not start because the driver hasn't turned the key.

The first expert system was called MYCIN and was developed in the 1970s in order to assist doctors with the diagnosis and treatment of infectious blood diseases. Since then a large number of expert systems have been developed covering various medical fields.

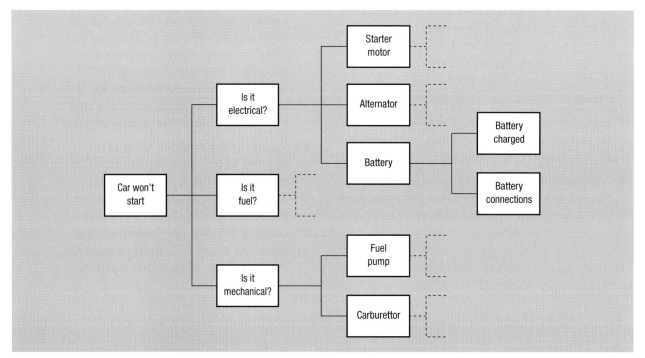

Figure 31.1 **Decision tree for an expert sytem**

Hundreds of expert systems have been written covering a range of specialist fields:

- Fault diagnosis on equipment such as computers, audio equipment, engines and central heating systems.

- Prospecting for oil using geological data.

- Analysing tax returns for large businesses.

- Modelling military situations for the army.

- Identifying appropriate judicial sentences for criminals.

- Supplying solutions for computer help-desk problems.

- Providing financial advice to businesses and private investors.

- Helping social security benefit claimants.

- Identifying poisonous leaves and berries – used by GPs/and Accident and Emergency departments in the treatment of suspected poisoning.

Summary Questions

1 What are the four main components of any expert system?

2 'The first version of any expert system will probably not work'. Why do you think this might be the case?

3 How can the effectiveness of an expert system be assessed?

4 Identify three problems that may arise with an expert system.

Study Questions

1. Identify a problem that would benefit from an expert system. Identify four possible data items and three possible rules.

2. How might an expert system be used by a student to select a suitable university course?

Examination Questions

1.   A GP surgery introduces a new system that automatically produces prescriptions and then emails them to the pharmacist. The email is sent while the patient is being seen by the Doctor so that by the time the patient arrives at the pharmacists, the prescription is ready.

   (a)   Describe two advantages to the patient of this system.   [2]

   (b)   Describe two disadvantages to the surgery.   [2]

   (c)   How could the patient reliably prove their identity to the pharmacist when picking up the prescription?   [2]

2. Some people in this country would like to introduce a national identity card. It has been suggested that a 'smart card' could be used in conjunction with biometric techniques.

   (a) Explain two methods of using biometric techniques to prove someone's identity [2]

   (b) Give one advantage of using this method compared to a photo ID [1]

   (c) Give one reason why a law-abiding citizen may not want to carry a national identity card [1]

Introduction

There are very few Acts of Parliament that are specific to the world of computing. The two main ones are the Data Protection Act 1998 and the Computer Misuse Act 1990. In addition there have been two recent Acts that are related to computers although not specific to them. These are the Freedom of Information Act 2000 and the Regulation of Investigatory Powers Act 2000. The Copyright, Designs and Patents Act 1988 is also of particular relevance to computing.

In addition to these, using a computer does not exempt you from all the other laws of the land. For example, someone who carries out an act of fraud on the Internet can be prosecuted under a Fraud Act. Someone who steals computer data can be prosecuted under a Theft Act. Someone who makes false allegations about someone else in an e-mail can be prosecuted for libel.

Data Protection Act 1998

The Data Protection Act was introduced in 1984 as a result of public concerns about the increasing use of computers to store personal information. It was updated in 1998 to reflect the enormous changes in the use of information during the 1990s. It places controls on organisations and individuals that store 'personal data' electronically. The definition of personal data is any data on an individual where the person (known as the 'data subject') is alive and can be individually identified.

Therefore, any data that contains a name and address is automatically covered by the law even if there are only a few records and the information is not particularly private. This has an impact on a wide range of organisations including banks, shops, doctors, dentists, local councils, governments agencies, schools and credit card companies.

The Act states that with a few exemptions, any person or organisation storing personal data must register with the Information Commissioner. 'Information Commissioner' is a confusing term in that it relates to an actual person and the organisation that they run. The organisation itself is independent but was set up by the Government to oversee Data Protection and Freedom of Information. The commissioner's mission is:

We shall develop respect for the private lives of individuals and encourage the openness and accountability of public authorities.

– by promoting good information handling practice and enforcing data protection and freedom of information legislation; and

– by seeking to influence national and international thinking on privacy and information access issues.

162

There are eight main principles behind the Data Protection Act. Anyone processing personal data must comply with the eight enforceable principles of good practice. They say that data must be:

- **Fairly and lawfully processed.**

- **Processed for limited purposes.**

- **Adequate, relevant and not excessive.**

- **Accurate.**

- **Not kept longer than necessary.**

- **Processed in accordance with the data subject's rights.**

- **Secure.**

- **Not transferred to countries without adequate data protection.**

Another feature of the Act is that data subjects have the right to know what data is stored about them by any particular individual or organisation. These are known as 'subject access rights'. If this information is incorrect then the data subject has the right to have it corrected. The organisation must be given notice and may charge a small fee to the data subject. There are a few exemptions to this, for example, data may not be disclosed if it is against issues of national security. The other main exemptions are:

- **Staff administration of businesses and organisations including payroll.**

- **Advertising, marketing and public relations within a business.**

- **Accounts and records of some 'Not For Profit' Organisations.**

- **Accounts and records for personal, family or household affairs (including recreational purposes).**

Summary Questions

1 Define the following terms from the Data Protection Act:
   (a) data subject;
   (b) personal data;
   (c) subject access rights.

2 A large bank uses data collected from customers with personal loans to provide a car manufacturer with a list of people who have bought new cars using their loans. Which of the eight data protection principles have been breached?

3 What rights does an individual have in relation to personal data stored about them?

Case study

The Inland Revenue

The Inland Revenue is the government department responsible for holding the income tax and national insurance records of 60 million people in the UK. They have around 60 000 staff who have access to these records. In January 2003 they reported that a number of their staff had been accessing the records of their family, friends, and even famous people. In some cases it was out of 'idle curiosity' but in other cases the information was either sold or used maliciously.

The Inland Revenue is bound by the Data Protection Act 1998 DPA which states that the data that they hold must be held securely and not used for any unauthorised purposes. 226 staff have been disciplined, with some staff being dismissed. All 226 staff could be prosecuted under the DPA.

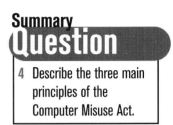

Freedom of Information Act 2000

The Freedom of Information Act 2000 extends the 'subject access rights' of the Data Protection Act and gives general rights of access to information held by public authorities such as hospitals, doctors, dentists, the police, schools and colleges. Both Acts are overseen by the Information Commissioner.

The Act gives individuals access to both personal and non-personal data held by public authorities. The idea behind the Act was to provide more openness between the public and government agencies. Therefore, the agencies are obliged to give the public access to information and to respond to individual requests for information. Much of this is done through web sites and e-mail communications.

Computer Misuse Act 1990

The Computer Misuse Act 1990 was introduced primarily to prevent hacking and contains three specific offences relating to computer usage:

- **Unauthorised access to computer programs or data: This includes some forms of hacking including breaking through password protection and firewalls, decrypting files and stealing another user's identity.**

- **Unauthorised access with further criminal intent: An extension of the first offence where there is a clear intention to carry out a further criminal act such as an act of fraud or a copyright breach.**

- **Unauthorised modification of computer material: This includes falsifying bank details or exam grades, spreading viruses designed to corrupt data and programs and interfering with system files.**

The Act was introduced before the widespread use of the Internet, which has led to problems with enforcement. Prior to the Internet, hacking did take place, but not on the scale that it does today. There are now millions of computers and networks connected to the Internet and the opportunities for hackers have increased enormously. The National Hi-Tech Crime Unit reported in 2000 that every UK business was attacked, on average, three times a month by 'cyber criminals'. Despite this, there were only fifteen convictions under the Act in that year.

A common defence that has been used successfully in court is that because organisations and individuals choose to create web sites and invite other users to access the site, any hacking cannot be considered 'unauthorised' in the eyes of the law. Therefore, the hackers are not breaking the law. Virus spreading is also a common misuse but the police find it difficult to track down the perpetrators. Another common misuse is a 'denial of service' attack where an organisation will receive thousands of 'hits' to its web site or e-mail server which clogs up their system so much that no one else can access the site. Again, this specific offence is not covered by the Act.

Summary
Question

4 Describe the three main principles of the Computer Misuse Act.

There is a lot of pressure on the Government from the computer industry and other businesses operating on the Internet, to introduce new laws to reflect the current activities of the cyber-criminal. The European Commission are also introducing proposals that cover cyber-crime across the European Union and there is a cyber-crime convention attended by the governments of 32 nations who are committed to the on-going introduction of new laws.

Regulation of Investigatory Powers (RIP) Act 2000

The RIP Act 2000 was introduced to clarify the powers that government agencies have when investigating crime or suspected crime. It is not specific to the world of computing but was introduced partly to take account of changes in communication technology and the widespread use of the Internet.

There are five main parts to the Act. The most relevant to computing are Part 1 which relates to the interception of communications, including electronic data, and Part 3 which covers the investigation of electronic data protected by encryption. In simple terms, it gives the police and other law enforcement agencies the right to intercept communications where there is suspicion of criminal activity. They also have the right to decipher this data if it is encrypted even if this means that the user must tell the police how to decrypt the data.

It also allows employers to monitor the computer activity of their employees, for example, by monitoring their e-mail traffic or tracking which web sites they visit during work time. This raises a number of issues relating to civil liberties, which were discussed in Chapter 29.

Copyright, Designs and Patents Act 1988

Copyright gives rights to the creators of certain kinds of material allowing them control over the way in which the material is used. The law covers the copying, adapting and renting of materials.

The law covers all types of materials but of particular relevance to computing are:

- **Original works including instruction manuals, computer programs and some types of databases.**

- **Original musical works.**
- **Sound recordings.**
- **Films and videos.**

Copyright applies to all works regardless of the format. Consequently, work produced on the Internet is also covered by copyright. It is illegal to produce 'pirate' copies of software or run more versions on a network than have been paid for. It is an offence to adapt existing versions of software without permission. It is also an offence to download music or films without the permission of the copyright holder.

Study Questions

1. Explain why the Computer Misuse Act is inadequate as a measure for preventing hacking.

2. There is currently a lot of pressure on the government to update the laws relating to computer misuse. Why is the current legislation considered by some to be ineffective and what could be done to improve it?

3. Do you consider the RIP Act to be an infringement of civil liberties?

4. How effective is the DPA in preventing the misuse of data?

Examination Questions

1. In some countries government agencies routinely monitor the content of e-mail routed over the Internet.
    (a) Give two reasons why some governments may allow this to happen. [2]
    (b) Suggest one way in which an individual may make it difficult for any such agency to read the contents of a particular e-mail sent over the Internet. [1]

    AQA January 2002 Module 2

2. A student on work experience in the payroll department of Widgets plc, when left alone, successfully logged into the company's computer system by guessing the administrator's user id and password. The student changed the hourly rate of several employees by accessing the company's payroll file.
    (a) The Computer Misuse Act defines three types of offence. What two offences did the student commit according to this Act? [2]
    (b) Given that the student was left alone in the computer room, the company should have prevented or detected what happened. Describe briefly three methods of security that the company could have used. [3]

    AQA January 2001 Module 2

3. (a) The growing level of public concern over data stored in computer systems led the government to pass the Data Protection Act 1984. The Act was introduced to protect the right of individuals to privacy. Give three reasons relating to the nature of computing systems that give rise to this concern. [3]

    (b) Name two other Acts that relate to computer systems. [2]

    AQA January 2003 Module 2

4. Computer software is now covered by the Copyright, Designs and Patents Act 1988. State three provisions of the Act that apply to copyrighted software. [3]

    AQA June 2002 Module 2

CHAPTER:**33**
Social and economic consequences

Social consequences

The impact of computers over recent years has been enormous. Computers are now critical to most organisations including multi-national businesses, government agencies, and schools and colleges. It is difficult to find any business or organisation in the developed world nowadays that does not rely on their computer systems. In addition to this the rise in the number of home users means that millions of people now have access to computers and conduct many everyday activities on them.

Alongside these developments, microprocessors and embedded computer systems have become an intrinsic part of modern life. Consider how many times you come across a 'computer' during the average day: mobile phone, microwave oven, CD and DVD player, cash point (ATM), EPOS systems in shops, and so on. It is fair to say that most of us have become completely reliant on this technology.

Case study

National Air Traffic Services (NATS)

In January 2002, National Air Traffic Control Services (NATS) opened a £623 million air traffic control centre at Swanwick near Southampton. The computerised centre handles thousands of flights every day and is responsible for ensuring that all flights take off and land safely and follow the correct routes in UK airspace.

It is a critical application and its activities are closely monitored by the Civil Aviation Authority (CAA) and the Health and Safety Executive (HSE) both of which are government organisations.

Flights used to be handled from West Drayton near Heathrow Airport, but the system there was becoming out of date, hence the move to Swanwick. This represents a major change for the organisation mostly due to a brand new IT system being installed. However, since its launch there have been a number of alleged problems:

● Operators had trouble reading the new screens confusing the code EGPF (Glasgow) for EGFF (Cardiff) directing flights to the wrong airport.

● Operators could not clearly make out the number 6 on the display. As a result, some altitude readings were out by 6000 feet.

● One workstation failed causing a further 100 to fail.

● A near miss between two passenger jets was caused due to an operator moving the text label on his screen that indicated the location of one of the jets.

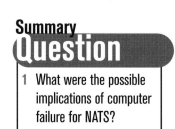

Summary
Question

1 What were the possible implications of computer failure for NATS?

In most cases, the use of computers improves the quality of our lives: mobile phones allow us to keep in touch wherever we are and cash point machines give us access to money 24 hours a day. Many processes are much quicker when computers are involved: booking a holiday or banking online save us time. Computer-controlled systems can also make the world safer: aeroplanes use 'automatic pilots' and smoke alarms save lives.

There is, however, an inherent danger when we rely so completely on technology. Computer systems do fail. With critical systems such as an automatic pilot, this failure could be catastrophic and may even lead to death. With other applications the problem may simply be an inconvenience such as an error on a bank's computer records.

Economic consequences in the UK

Computers have a direct impact on a number of UK industries. There are a number of ways in which the impact of the computer industry on the UK economy can be measured. It is important to realise that the state of the economy changes so quickly that the figures quoted in this section are already out of date. It is also difficult to provide exact figures as definitions of the 'computer industry' vary. The figures quoted here are based on a 2002 policy document produced by the Office of Science and Technology, in which the government classed electronics, communications and computer services as the three main components of the computer industry.

As A Level students, it is important that you keep up to date with the latest developments in new technologies and understand how these may impact on the UK economy as a whole. For example, web-based businesses are still relatively new and adoption of the Internet is still not universal throughout the country; the mobile phone revolution has just entered a new phase with the introduction of video messaging; web TV and radio are still in their infancy, and wireless networking is just starting to be adopted. Any one of these developments could have an effect on the economy as a whole. See Appendix 2 for useful publications and web sites.

Production: The government measures the amount of money from profits and wages that are made in the computer industry. Recent statistics from the Office of Science and Technology suggest that the industry is currently growing by 10 per cent per year and contributes 8 per cent of all production in the country.

Employment: The rate of employment varies between different parts of the industry. Employment in electronics and communications is currently stable. The main area of growth is in computer services which are those jobs involved with selling and maintaining computer systems. These jobs account for 4 per cent of total employment in the UK.

Many people are worried that computers have been replacing people and that this will lead to unemployment. However, it would appear that computers have created more jobs than they have replaced. Many workers have been displaced by computers and have had to retrain as a consequence. For example, automation and the use of robots in factories has led to unemployment in some areas of manufacturing, such as car production.

Exports: Another government measure of success is how many products and services the UK can sell to other countries. In 1998 £32.6 billion worth of computing related products and services were sold to foreign countries. At the same time, the UK bought £35.2 billion worth from other countries so we actually bought in more than we sold.

Impact on other industries: It is difficult to measure the impact that computers have had on other industries. For example, banks and retailers rely heavily on computers and in turn these businesses contribute to the UK economy. There have been some notable shifts in trends recently, not least the move from traditional banking and shopping to e-banking and e-shopping. There are many other businesses which are closely linked to computing such as aerospace, pharmaceuticals and insurance and their use of computers makes them more efficient and profitable.

Lower prices: The cost of electronic equipment has been falling in recent years. This means that consumers can buy them more cheaply which increases demand. This is good for the economy as it means that people are spending more money, which in turn creates more jobs.

Summary Questions

2 Identify three ways in which society as a whole has benefited from computer technology.

3 How can the economic impact of computing be measured?

4 What impact has computer technology had on employment?

Study Questions

1. Describe three effects that computers have had on the economy of this country.

2. Explain how the use of computers has impacted on the following industries:

(a) tourism;

(b) banking;

(c) shopping.

3. Robots have replaced humans in some aspect of manufacturing, for example, in car production. Explain the impact of automation on:

(a) car workers;

(b) the car manufacturer.

4. Describe the dangers of relying on computers within a hospital environment.

5. Identify three scenarios where the reliance on computers could have critical consequences.

Examination Questions

1. Explain why a large scale system government system designed to prevent fraud:
   (a) might not work at all [1]
   (b) might not work as expected [1]
   (c) might not be completed on time [1]

2. A new computerised system is used to allocate pupils to schools in their area. Explain how this will benefit the following groups of people (each benefit must be different):
   (a) Parents [1]
   (b) Schools [1]
   (c) the government [1]
   (d) pupils [1]

Files and file types

At one time the term file meant a store of related data and was linked almost entirely with database applications. The definition has become increasingly fuzzy so that now more or less anything you save on a computer is called a 'file'. If you use this 'new' definition then all applications store data in files of one sort or another and some are more organised than others. How the data is organised in a file is therefore dependent on the file type.

Some file types are very important because they allow data to be transferred between different applications. For example, data saved as a text file could be loaded into a word processor, a desktop publishing package or presentation software, whilst data saved in a CSV (comma separated variable) file could be used in a database, spreadsheet or word processor.

A text file consists entirely of text with the words 'delimited', or separated, with spaces. Files generated by application software, such as a word processor, are larger than you would expect. This is because they contain much more than the text you have typed in – they must store details such as page layout, font size and tab settings as well.

Your PC probably recognises a wide range of file types, which are shown as an extension to the filename. It can use the extension to decide which software can work with which files. Some common file types are:

- txt – text
- csv – comma separated variable
- bmp – bitmap graphics
- jpg – Joint Photographic Experts Group (JPEG, another graphics format)
- mp3 – sound file
- wav – sound file
- doc – document produced by MS Word
- exe – a file that can be 'executed' (in other words, it is a program).

Files, records and fields

Using the more formal definition of a file as a store of related data you can break the structure down further. A file is made up of a number of records. Each record

Summary Question

1 Why is the file type (also known as the file extension) an important part of the file name?

stores all the data about one person or thing, so a file that contains data about students at a college will contain a record for each student, and the files being used at a supermarket will hold all the details about each product it sells, each in its own record.

Field names

	Name	Age	Height (m)	Gender
	Georgina	19	1.80	F
	Jerome	18	1.85	M
Records	Kevin	20	1.74	M
	Nathan	21	1.87	M
	Sophie	21	1.76	F

Each record in turn holds individual items of data. In the case of the students this might be their age or their gender, and in the case of the supermarket it might be the description that is printed on your till receipt or the cost of the item. All the records contain the same collection of fields, though it might be that some of the fields are empty – there will probably be a field that stores the date that a student leaves the college, but they haven't all left yet.

Key fields

The main reason for storing data in a file is so that the data can be easily extracted. In order to allow this to happen, each record needs to have something that makes it unique. Imagine carrying out a search for 'Chris Walker' on the student database. No name is unique and it might be that there are two or more Chris Walkers on the student file. The only way to make sure you have the right details is to have some way of uniquely identifying each Chris Walker.

The way to do this is give each student some sort of identifier – perhaps an admissions number. In a file system this is known as a primary or key field. Like it or not we all have a large number of keys attached to us – we all have National Insurance num-

bers and NHS numbers, and most of us have bank accounts, driving licences and library cards. In fact we are surrounded by keys – a video recorder has a serial number, a car has a VIN (Vehicle Identification Number), even this book has a primary key – its ISBN (International Standard Book Number).

This key is actually different to all the other keys mentioned in this section. In all the other cases the key identifies one unique thing or person, but the ISBN identifies a publication. There will be lots of other books with the same ISBN as this one, what the ISBN is identifying is a publication not an individual copy of a book. The bar code on a tin of beans works in much the same way – it is identifying a particular make and size, not an individual tin.

Sometimes you might not want to identify one unique item, but you may want to find all the records that share a common feature. For example, you want to carry out a search for all the students in your Computing group. In this case, the field 'Subject' is called a secondary key – it links records together, but it is not unique.

Fixed and variable length fields

The amount of memory or storage space needed to store these fields and records depends on the field types and sometimes the data they are storing. Some field types always take the same amount of memory regardless of the data that is stored in them. For example if you want to store the number of pupils in a school then you are most likely to use an integer (whole number). Visual Basic allocates four bytes to integers, so no matter how big or small each school is they will be allocated four bytes.

If you have access to Visual Basic you might want to look at how many bytes are used for each of the data types Visual Basic supports and try to work out how those bytes are used. You can view them by searching for 'Data Type Summary' under the Help option.

The most common variable length field is used to store text. Whilst you need the same number of bytes to store every school's 'roll', the number of spaces needed to store the name of the school varies considerably. For example, John Port School only needs 16 characters including spaces, whereas Queen Elizabeth's High School needs 29.

Summary Questions

2 Explain why it is important that a record structure contains a key field.

3 Explain the difference between a primary and a secondary key.

Using variable length fields means that you minimise the amount of space your file will need, but it will make the file harder to use or maintain. We will be considering these problems in the next chapter.

When memory and hard disk space were at a premium programmers went to great lengths to keep the size of the records and files down to a minimum which is one reason why so much data was coded in one form or another. Now that memory and hard disks are so much cheaper this is less of an issue.

File size

To calculate the size of a file you need to add the number of bytes needed for each field and then multiply this by the number of records.

For example, the secretary of a club might set up a database. She might decide to store the member's forename (15 bytes), surname (30 bytes), gender (1 byte) and membership number. The membership number could be stored as an integer and so would take four bytes. This means that each record needs 50 bytes, so if the secretary wanted to store 200 names, she would need $200 \times 50 = 10\,000$ bytes – about 10 Kb.

If your file contains text fields then you may need to consider the 'worst possible case'. For example, if you want to store the first name of a person in your file, you will need to try and find out what the longest name is that you are likely to want to store. You could plan for nine spaces to accommodate Francesca, Alexander and Elizabeth, but all you need is one Christopher-Robin and all your plans are ruined. In this case it would probably be sensible to allow yourself 20 spaces, but even then there is no guarantee that this will be enough. Other non-numeric fields such as postcodes or car registrations are more predictable.

Using this fixed length field system means that files will inevitably contain wasted space as few names would need the space set aside for the 'worst possible case'. The real benefit of using fixed length fields is that it is much easier to maintain the file. This includes adding, amending, deleting and searching. We will be looking at these processes in more detail in the next chapter.

Summary Question

4 Each record in a file contains four fields – a six character product reference code, space for up to 40 characters of description, a current stock level and the unit cost (cost per item). An integer needs four bytes of memory and a real needs five.
   (a) How much space will be needed to store each record?
   (b) What is the theoretical maximum number of records that could be stored on a standard 1.44Mb floppy disk?

Study Questions

1. Explain why it is generally not a good idea to use people's names as a primary key.

2. Explain the benefits and drawbacks of using:

   (a) fixed length fields;

   (b) variable length fields.

Examination Questions

1. A file of 80 records has the following record structure:

    ProductID, ProductDescription, QuantityInStock

    ProductID is a four-byte integer, ProductDescription is a fifty-six byte fixed length string, Quantity In Stock is a four-byte integer.

    (a) What is the size of this file in bytes? Show your working. [2]

    (b) Suggest a suitable primary key for this file. Justify your choice. [2]

    On closer examination, it is found that 30 per cent of the file storage space is wasted.

    (c) Explain why this may occur with the current record structure. [1]

    (d) How could the record structure be changed whilst retaining three fields per record so that this problem is overcome? [1]

    (e) Give one disadvantage of the restructured solution. [1]

    AQA June 2002 Module 2

In Chapter 34 you were introduced to the concept of a file as a collection of related data and we looked at the relationship between files, records and fields. Now it is time to see how the file and its contents might be organised.

There are a number of routine processes that you need to be able to carry out on a file. The main processes are adding, amending or deleting records and you will almost certainly want to interrogate the file in some way, and you may want to be able to sort the data as well. The way in which you organise your files can have a dramatic effect on how easy or hard these processes will be.

Serial files

The simplest way to store data is in a serial file. In its crudest form a serial file can be seen as a disorganised list because there is no logical order to it. As new items of data arrive they are added to the end of the file – a process known as 'appending'. An important feature of 'appending' is that the data will probably be stored in variable length fields.

SEARCHING A SERIAL FILE

Data in a serial file can only be searched using a linear search. This means you will have to start from record one and check each record in turn until you either find the record you want or you run out of records to check.

MAINTAINING A SERIAL FILE

Maintaining a file means carrying out work such as adding new records, deleting unwanted records, and amending existing details. Carrying out any sort of file maintenance on a serial file can be very time consuming. Each time you perform even the simplest task you will have to create a whole new file. This is because there is no way of maintaining the data where it is. This is rather like trying to change the details in an important list of names. You can't add new details in the right place – there won't be any room left, you can't easily amend an entry without making a mess, and if you decide to delete a name you will have to cross it out. Often the only sensible thing to do is to rewrite the whole list.

DELETING FROM A SERIAL FILE

The process for deleting a record is easy to describe – you read each record from the file in turn and if you want to keep it you write it to a new file and if you don't want to keep it you don't.

```
Repeat

   Read next record from the file

   If this is the record to delete Then

      Do nothing

   Else

      Save the record to a new file

   End If

Until there are no more records to read
from the old file
```

AMENDING A SERIAL FILE

The process for amending an existing record is only a little more complex than deleting. You read each record in turn, and when you find the record you want to amend you replace the incorrect data and save the amended record to the new file.

This might seem like a very simple process, but in fact this can be a very long process, as every record in the original file has to be read and, in most cases, written unchanged to a new file.

```
Repeat

   Read next record from the file

   If this is the record to amend Then

      Save the amended details to a new file

   Else

      Save the record to a new file

   End If

Until there are no more records to read
from the old file
```

Both of these processes creates a new 'generation' of the file – every time you run them they create a whole new file; a new generation. In most cases there is no point in keeping all the old versions, and common practice dictates that you keep three generations – the so-called Grandfather/Father/Son principle.

There is another problem with using serial access files to store data. Imagine that a serial file consists of the names

George, Thomas, Hassan, Jill, Adam

and you want to change Jill to become Jillian and then Thomas to become Tom. You will remember that the amend process reads each record in turn and saves either the original or the amended version to a new file. In this case the names George, Thomas, Hassan will all have been copied

to the new file before the name Jill is encountered. The new version of Jill is now used and finally Adam is copied across. The resulting file now looks like this:

George, Thomas, Hassan, Jillian, Adam

However, you haven't dealt with changing Thomas to Tom so you will have to go through the whole process all over again and create a whole new file just to cope with the second change.

With only five records this a fairly straightforward process, but most files contain thousands or even millions or records, and each record could contain many bytes of data. This makes the whole process very time consuming. The big catch is that the user has no control over how many times the 'generation' process is carried out and for this reason serial files are only used to store either very simple data sets, or where it is unlikely that you will need to amend the data.

A simple example of this is used in a till in a shop. When you pay for goods you are given one copy of the till receipt and the shop keeps another. The shop keeps a copy in case they want to check their sales for the day. Keeping records of the day's transactions on till receipts is cheap and it is highly unlikely that the shop will want to look through the receipts anyway so storing them in a serial file is ideal.

Sequential files

A sequential file is a serial file that has been organised in some way. The organisation is usually by some sort of key. A sequential file version of our original list of names could be sorted into alphabetical order:

Adam, George, Hassan, Jill, Thomas

Amending and deleting records in a sequential file uses exactly the same technique as the serial file – read in each record from the old file and save, amend or delete as necessary – but before you start the process you must make sure that these transactions are sorted in the same way as the main file.

Now suppose that you want to carry out the same amendments to this sequential file – change Thomas to Tom and Jill to Jillian. Before you start you would need to 'sort' the names so that they are in the same order as the master file, so that Jill is now first in the list and Thomas second.

The amending process is now exactly the same as before. Adam, George and Hassan are all transferred to the new file then Jill is changed to Jillian and saved to the new file then Thomas is read from the master, changed to Tom and saved to the new master. The difference between this and the serial method mentioned above is that as long as the transaction file is in the same order as the master it should only take one run through the process to carry out all the changes.

ADDING TO A SEQUENTIAL FILE

Adding new records to a sequential file involves identifying whereabouts in the file the new record should be inserted (see code box below). So opting for a sequential file means that file maintenance is much more efficient. As long as the transaction file is sorted in the same way as the master, you will only need to create one new generation of the file.

```
Repeat
   Read next record from the old file
   If new record comes after this old record Then
      Save old record to new file
   Else
      Insert new record in new file
      Save old record to new file
      Copy the rest of the old file across to the new file
   End if
Until there are no more records to read from old file
```

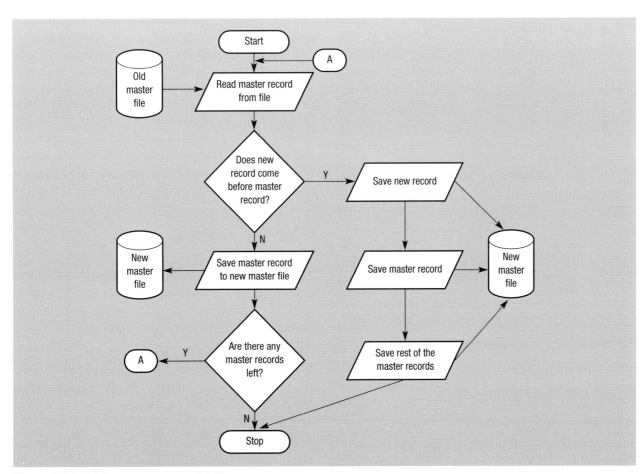

Figure 35.1 **Adding to a sequential file**

The one process that does not change is searching – you are still restricted to using a linear search. Because of this sequential files tend to be used in situations where the data on the file only needs updating occasionally. A typical use for sequential files is a payroll package where updates will probably only take place once every week. Because of the way data is accessed on a serial or sequential file, the file might be stored on tape, though it works equally well on random access media such as floppy or hard disk.

The 'grandfather/father/son' principle

As we have seen above, the process of merging a transaction file with a master file creates a whole new generation – a new master file. If the new master file becomes corrupted in any way it is possible to recreate it by re-merging the old master file and the transaction file.

It is common practice to keep past generations of master files and transaction files because they act as a backup system. This builds up the 'grandfather/father/son' process as older versions of the file can be recycled.

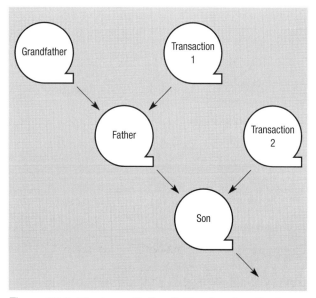

Figure 35.2 **The 'grandfather/father/son' method**

Direct (random) access files

One of the best ways to describe a direct access file is a computerised version of a card index system. The amount of data you put on each card will vary from card to card. Some cards might have only a word or two whilst others will be full, but in the end you have a finite amount of space to write in. This is therefore a fixed field length system. The benefits of using a card index approach is that searching can be much more efficient than with a sequential file.

The most important feature of a direct access file is that each record takes up exactly the same amount of space in the file. This means the physical location of each record can be determined from its key. For example, if each record takes up 40 bytes then record number 1 would start at byte number 1 in the file, record number 2 would start at byte 41, record 3 at byte 81, and so on.

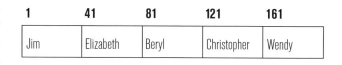

This makes the processes involved in maintaining a direct access file very different from those needed to support a serial or sequential file.

SEARCHING A DIRECT ACCESS FILE

There are three techniques that you might be able to use to search through a direct access file.

METHOD 1 – BINARY CHOP

You could use the binary chop technique described in Chapter 14. Because all the records in a direct access file take up exactly same amount of space you can calculate where each record will start. This will only work if the cards or records are sorted in some way, and the search you are carrying out is based on that order.

METHOD 2 – HASHING ALGORITHMS

The second method uses a process called hashing. This idea is based on the fact that most databases have a key of some sort in each record. The system works by taking the key and passing it through a hashing algorithm to generate an address.

If the records have keys that are sequential – 1, 2, 3, 4, and so on – then you can take the key and multiply it by the record length. So if each record is 200 bytes long and you want to access record number 6 you can calculate the record will start at byte number 1200 in the file. But this is rarely the case – for example, a company might use the employee's National Insurance number as the key to calculate the address. A National Insurance number looks like this YZ750119A, so this NI number would be used to access record number 750119, but unless the company actually employs a million people the system of using the NI number directly is not going to be very viable because you would need one million corresponding addresses.

To cut down on the addresses the algorithm generates, the company might opt to take just the first three digits from the NI number of its staff. So Z750119A would go to address 750. This system would only need 1000 records.

The problem with this method is that it is almost inevitable that some staff will have the same first three numbers in their National Insurance number. In this case both numbers would generate the same address and so cause a 'clash'. In these circumstances one record uses the address and the other is put elsewhere in the file. The original record would then have to have a system of pointers set up to show where the program should look for other records with the same address.

The two NI numbers YZ750119A and TY750123D would both point to location 750. Only one can actually be using this location so a simplified version of the record might read

NI number   YZ750119A
Name   Mr F. Hill
Other numbers   TY750123D–751

This means that when the NI number TY750123D accesses this record it will be pointed at record 751 instead.

Taking the first three numbers of the NI number is simple but it is important to achieve an even spread of addresses from the hashing algorithm so the computer could carry out more complex calculations such as using squares and only counting every other number to achieve a more even spread.

There are therefore two guiding principles to consider when writing a hashing algorithm. They are that you need ensure that the addresses generated are spread as evenly as possible across the whole file, and that you minimise the number of clashes.

METHOD 3 – SERIAL SEARCH

The third method of searching through a direct access file is to use a serial search – look at every record until you find the one you want. This is the crudest method of searching, but unless the data is organised in such a way that you can use either the binary chop or hashing algorithm methods you will have to fall back on a serial search.

The obvious storage media for a direct access file is some form of random access system – either floppy or hard disk. There is little point in using a serial access system such as magnetic tape because this would automatically force you to use a serial search. You can read more about random access media in Chapter 49.

MAINTAINING A DIRECT ACCESS FILE

The method for adding a record to a direct access file depends on how the key is used. If the system uses a hashing algorithm to locate a record then that same algorithm can be used to find the address within the file for the record that you want to access. The other alternative is to allocate the next key in the sequence and append it to the file. In either case there is no need to create a whole new file – you alter the content of the existing file in some way instead.

Amending an existing record in a direct access file is very straightforward. Once you have located the record the details you want to alter overwrite the data that is already there. The only possible problem is if the data you are trying to store exceeds the space allocated to it. If you have put 10 spaces aside to store a person's first name, you will not be able to store Christopher or Bartholomew.

The method for deleting a record depends on how the record is stored. The simplest method is to leave the record where it is in the file structure but set a field to indicate that the record space is empty.

Because a direct access file is updated as it stands you would need to make sure you took regular copies of the file. As with the serial file structure you would still need to keep copies of the transaction files just in case the latest version of your file develops a fault.

Examination Questions

**Summary
Questions**

1 Why is it important to keep a copy of all the transactions as well as previous generations of a master file?

2 Explain the difference between a serial and a sequential file.

3 Explain the difference between inserting and appending a record.

4 Two files are to be merged to create a third. What is merging?

5 Explain how a linear search works.

6 Explain why it is important that the records in a transaction file are ordered in the same way as those in the master file it is to be merged with.

7 Explain how the 'grandfather/father/son' principle works.

8 A direct access file can be searched using a binary chop method. Explain how this system works.

1. The construction of an electronic English–French dictionary is trialled by creating a simpler version using one hundred English–French word pairs stored line-by-line in a text file, A.

    (a) (i)   What is a text file? [1]

         (ii) Name the most suitable type of software for a typist to use to create the contents of file A. [1]

         (iii) What hardware could have been used to enter the word pairs, printed on paper, directly into the computer system? [1]

    (b) A computer program reads word pairs, one line at a time, from file A. It stores each word pair in a sequentially organised file of records, file B, by English word.

         (i)   State two characteristics of a sequentially organised file. [2]

         (ii) Give the field names for two essential fields of file B. [2]

File B is read sequentially and its records are stored in file C, on a direct access medium, by applying the following hashing function to each English word in file B.

(Sum of ASCII codes of all letters in the English word) Mod 150

For example, applying the hashing function to the word BAD using ASCII codes A = 65, B = 66, D = 68 produces

$$(66 + 65 + 68) \text{ Mod } 150 = 49$$

(Mod gives the remainder after integer division.)

    (c) File C consists of 150 records initially empty.

         (i)   What use is made of the number produced by the hashing function when storing each word-pair record in file C? [1]

         (ii) Why is Mod 150 used? [1]

         (iii) Give two properties that this hashing function should have. [2]

    (d) Using only file C, list the main steps that a computer program must follow to display on a VDU the French equivalent of an English word entered at the keyboard. Your solution must take account of the case when the English–French word pair is not present in file C. [5]

AQA January 2003 Module 2

2.   The file, CurrentUserIds, has the following record structure.

UserId, Password, NoOf DaysSincePasswordLastChanged

UserId is a 17-byte fixed length string, Password is a two-byte integer, NoOfDaysSincePasswordLastChanged is a single byte integer.

(a)   What is the size of this file, in bytes, when the file CurrentUserIds contains 1500 records?   [1]

(b)   The file CurrentUserIds is used by a computer system to authenticate (check) a user's UserId and password typed at a keyboard when the user logs onto the system.
The logon program collects a user's password as an alphanumeric string, e.g. 'AQA5511CPT2' and converts it to a two-byte integer using a one-way hashing function or algorithm before sending it across a network for authentication (checking).

(i)   Give two reasons why the system converts passwords to two-byte integers.   [2]

(ii)   Outline three major steps that a typical hashing function/ algorithm would use to convert an alphanumeric string to a two-byte integer.   [3]

(iii)   Why is the hashing function used for the passwords a one-way (irreversible) function?   [1]

AQA June 2003 Module 2

3.   A stock master file is updated by a transaction file using sequential file access. A purpose of the stock master file is to ensure that the levels of stock will meet demand.

(a)   (i)   Give four essential fields for the stock master file.   [4]

(ii)   Give three essential fields for the transaction file.   [3]

(b)   Why should the transaction file be sorted, and in what order, prior to updating the master file?   [2]

AQA January 2001 Module 2

4.   A hashing algorithm is used to store and access records on a backing store.

(a)   Define the term hashing algorithm.   [2]

(b)   Give two features of a good hashing algorithm.   [2]

Summary Questions

9   Explain how the details in a record in a direct access file are updated.

10 The integrity of the data in a sequential file is maintained by creating transaction files and using the 'grandfather/father/son' method. Explain how the integrity of the data in a direct access file can be maintained.

11 A company gives each of its 40 employees a five-digit reference number. Their computer uses a hashing algorithm that adds the five digits together to generate an address for an employee's details.
   (a) How many addresses can be generated using this method?
   (b) Do you think this is a suitable hashing algorithm? Explain your answer.

CHAPTER:36
File security and integrity

Data is very valuable – even the data you keep on your home computer has probably taken many hours to create and may be irreplaceable. Imagine how long it would take you to re-enter it all, then try to imagine what would happen if your local bank suddenly found all its data had been rendered unusable. Replacing hardware or software that has been damaged might be expensive, but data is much more valuable than any computer or program.

Security

Security is the process of ensuring that data is kept safe. There are a number of ways of looking at security. Users need to make sure that data is not accidentally changed or deleted. They also need to guard against others trying to gain access to their data. As long as you have a well-thought-out recovery plan in place and you save your work regularly then having someone else amending or deleting your work is not a huge problem. What is a big problem is that they can access and therefore use your data.

Back-up copies

One way to safeguard data is to take a copy of it. A back-up copy should be made at regular intervals. This might be based on a set time interval, for example a school would probably back-up all its data every 24 hours, or it might be more appropriate to create a back-up copy after each major change to the data. This process is called an incremental back-up and is certainly the best method to use when you are working on a word-processed document. If you intend to keep previous copies of a file it is common practice to add either a date and time stamp or a version number to the file.

Back-up copies are kept on secondary storage such as disk or magnetic tape. It is important that the back-up copies are kept apart from the computer system that has generated them. In the early days of computing one university kept their back-up copies in the same building as their computers – that was until the building burnt down.

Copying files to tape is a slow process, and as a result the back-up process is normally carried out when the system is quiet, typically overnight. In situations where it is important that no data is lost at all, details of the changes made to the data are also stored in a transaction file. This is so that if the master files crash sometime during the day, the situation can be recovered by merging the back-up copy made the previous night and the transaction file that stores details of all the transactions made so far.

On a much smaller scale it is important that users save their files as they are working – there is nothing more frustrating than losing two hours' worth of work because you turn the computer off without thinking or there is a power failure. Most programs will prompt to remind you to save.

Archiving

Keeping large amounts of data can be counter-productive – it will take longer to locate the details you want, and you will need ever increasing storage capacity to store all the details.

Details or records that are no longer needed either immediately or in the long term can be archived. This process involves storing a copy of the details on a different storage medium such as magnetic tape, and then deleting the details from the 'live' or active file. It is unlikely that data that has been archived will ever be needed again, but if need be it could be retrieved from the long-term storage media though obviously this may take some time to do.

This means that archiving is not the same as creating a back-up. A back-up is a copy of an entire file, whilst an archive stores a copy of data that is no longer on the 'master' file.

Physical security

A simple security measure is to keep data off-line – storing it on a separate secondary storage system such as floppy disk, CD-RW disk or some form of magnetic tape so that it will only be accessible when the user loads the data up. However this is generally too slow and cumbersome in most situations. In order to prevent the accidental deletion of data you can put some sort of physical block on the media it is stored on. There is a 'write protect' hole in a floppy disk and once data is written to a CD-R disk it cannot be altered.

Other physical methods include limiting access by keeping the computers that can access the data in a secure area and insisting users log off the network whenever they leave their workstations. Some computers will log a user off after a set time has elapsed or if the computer has been inactive for a set period of time. Some computers are kept in secure areas with access controlled either by key, password entered via a keypad or a swipe card.

Photograph 36.1 **Swipe card**

Passwords

Password protection is a common feature on many computer systems and there are many ways that it can be controlled. Forcing users to change passwords regularly does not stop someone else 'guessing' a user's password but it does limit how long that person has unauthorised access to the data.

Locking a user out after a set number of attempts at entering a password will stop someone taking repeated guesses at someone else's password. Banks use this system in their Automated Teller Machines – if you get your PIN wrong three times in a row then the ATM will keep your card. Some car stereo systems use a similar technique – you can have three attempts at a password before the unit shuts down for an extended period of time.

Short passwords are easy to work out, so setting a minimum number of characters could make guessing the password that much harder, and asking users not to use familiar words such as family names or dates of birth also gives the opportunist less chance of guessing. Forcing users to include digits or nonsensical words in their passwords will stop so called 'dictionary attacks'. A dictionary attack is where someone

Summary Question

1 It is a common misconception that changing your password will make it harder for someone to guess what it is. Why is it important that passwords are changed regularly?

trying to break into a computer sets up a program that tries all the words in a dictionary.

The only complication with using passwords is what to do if you forget the password. There was a case some years ago where a scientist had protected his research with a password that only he knew. Unfortunately the scientist died and left no clue about the password he had used and so all the valuable data he had been working on was effectively lost. One way round this is to create a 'back door'. This is a password known only to the creators of the software or possibly the systems manager. This means that if all else fails someone can gain access to the data.

Some computer manufacturers are now starting to use biometric password systems such as fingerprints. This should help to overcome the problem of the user that cannot remember their password.

Access rights

It is possible to set the attributes of a file so that is either 'Read/Write', which allows you to change the contents of the file, or 'Read Only' which means you can 'see' the data but you cannot alter it. Some computer systems also allow their users to 'hide' the file so that an unauthorised user will not be aware that the file is present on the computer.

Summary Question

2 Use examples to explain what is meant by the term 'access rights'.

Passwords can also be used to control access to networks. An administrator will have so called 'god rights' or 'universal rights'. This means they can see all aspects of the network – they can access other users' work areas and change those other users' access rights.

Other users might be restricted to accessing specific sections of the network and only be allowed to carry out specific functions with the data they can see.

Encryption

Despite all the best efforts some unauthorised users will gain access to files, so the final 'fall back' method is to encrypt your data. Encryption is the name given to the process of altering the data in such a way that even if someone can gain access to it they will not be able to make any sense of what they find.

Encryption works by taking each byte of data and passing it through a process that changes it in some way. The simplest way to do this would be to shift all the characters up one place in the alphabet so that 'hello mum' becomes 'ifmmp nvn'. To decrypt the message you shift the letters back one place in the alphabet. The problem with this example is that it is not very secure. Anyone accessing the data could analyse the frequency with which each letter occurs or look for patterns, and so work out what process has been carried out and then decrypt the message.

A more complex system would be to add different numbers to each character, depending on the character's position in the text. The device that is used to alter the data is called a key. In this example the word 'computer' has been used as the key.

Original message:
the meeting has been cancelled

Add the key:
computercomputercomputercomput

Encrypted message:
wwrphyjllctpcuxretrduwffftybzx

This particular example works by taking the place value of each letter in the alphabet to generate the new letter. So the first letter, t, is the 20th letter in the alphabet, c is the 3rd so this creates the 23rd letter – w. The place value of the letters in the alphabet have been added to create the new character in the message.

A more complex process might carry out some other arithmetic operation on the original character and the corresponding character in the key.

The more complex the key or the process that is used, the harder it will be to break the code, and some modern keys are hundreds of characters long.

PUBLIC/PRIVATE KEYS

The symmetric key system described above is easy to overcome, so a much more popular option is to use public/private key technology. In order to use this system you need two keys. Your computer sends out the public key to anyone that wants to communicate with you. They use your public key to modify their message before it is sent. The only way to decrypt the messages that get sent is to have a different, private key. This means that even if someone has the public key your computer is using they will not be able to decrypt your message.

Verification and validation

It is important to make sure that data being entered into a computer system is as accurate as possible. There is an acronym, GIGO, which stands for garbage in garbage out, meaning that if you put incorrect data into a computer you cannot expect anything meaningful back out of it.

Verification is the process of making sure that the data is entered accurately into a system from an external source, such as a questionnaire. It does not matter, at least at this stage, if the data on the questionnaire is incorrect, what is important is that it is entered as it appears on the source document.

The simplest way to do this is by visually checking the copy on the screen against the source document. This is knows as 'visual verification'. However, this is prone to operator error. It might be possible to send a copy of the data stored in the system to the originator of the data for checking. A more complex method is called 'double-entry verification'. Two operators enter the same data and the computer then compares the two sets of data and identifies any discrepancies.

Validation can be described as checking the data as it is entered against a set of rules. Common examples are:

- **Range check: To ensure data falls within set limits, for example, an age field may be set between 0 and 120.**

- **Format check: To ensure that data is entered in a set format, for example, a date field may be set to DD/MM/YY.**

- **Type check: To ensure that data is entered as a specific data type, for** example, a name field must be text, an age field must be numeric.

- **Presence check: To ensure that the data field is not left blank. This is often referred to as a 'required field'.**

- **Look-up check: To ensure that data that can be entered into a field only if it appears in a predefined list, for example, a gender field would have a look-up of M and F only.**

Integrity

Despite all your efforts to keep your data secure there is always the chance that the data might become corrupted in some way. The problem now is that you might never know the data you are using has been changed. Keeping the data in its original, uncorrupted state is also known as maintaining the integrity of the data.

Whilst security systems are visible to the user the processes that maintain the integrity of the data will only become obvious if they detect a fault with the data.

A lot of the processes detailed below are also used when data is being entered into a system or moved from one place to another within the system.

PARITY CHECK

Parity checks have been around for a long time; you can trace their roots back to the days when computer programs were stored on paper tape. As a result this is a relatively low-level integrity check.

A byte consists of a series of bits. A parity bit is an extra bit that is tagged on to a byte. The value of the parity bit is determined by the number of ones in the original byte. Parity can be either odd or even. The odd or even refers to the number of ones that are found in the original byte.

Summary Questions

3 Give four steps you can take to ensure your data is kept secure.

4 When data is sent between two computers on a wide area network it is encrypted. Explain why this is necessary.

5 Explain how an encryption key works.

6 Explain the public/private encryption key mechanism.

If a system was using even parity and a particular byte contained the bit pattern 0110100 then the parity bit would be set as a 1. The byte with its parity bit now becomes 10110100. There are now an even number (4) of ones and so this byte has 'even' parity. When the byte is processed the number of ones is recalculated to make sure there is still an even number of ones.

The big problem is with this system is that it is crude – it doesn't matter how badly the byte is altered, as long as there are an even number of ones it will pass.

CHECK DIGITS

Check digits are a common way of checking data that is being entered into a computer. For example they are used on the bar codes printed on goods at a supermarket. Like a parity bit a check digit is a value that is added to the end of a number to try and ensure that the number is not corrupted in any way.

The check digit is created by taking the digits that make up the number itself and using them in some way to create a single digit. The simplest, but most error prone method is to add the digits of the number together, and keep on adding the digits until you have only a single digit remaining. So the digits of 123456 add up to 21 and 2 and 1 in turn add up to 3, so the number with its check digit becomes 1234563. When the data is being processed the check digit is recalculated and compared with the digit that has been transmitted.

The problem with this system is that if two numbers are transposed (swapped round) the check digit will be the same. For example, the numbers 1234 and 4321 both add up to 10. In order to overcome this, each number in the pattern is given a weighting. This means that each number is multiplied by a different 'weight' or scaling factor. A common method for calculating a check digit is known as a modulus-11 and is shown below.

BATCH TOTAL

A batch total indicates how many records or items of data are being sent. For example, if a business were sending in their yearly trading figures and the figures were broken down by months then the batch total would be 12, and if a school was sending the exam results of a class the batch total would be the number of students in a class.

HASH TOTAL

A hash total is a total that has no use other than as a check on the integrity of data. For example, you might want to transmit the details of the size of a parcel, so you send the dimensions and a hash total that is based on all three dimensions added together. A parcel that is 10 cm by 15 cm by 20 cm would make a hash total of 45. The 45 has no use apart from as a check.

CHECKSUM

A checksum is a specific type of hash total. A checksum works by adding together the values of all the bytes that are held in a block or file. So the checksum of the password 3431 would be 3 + 4 + 3 + 1 = 11 and the data item 'FISH' might generate a checksum of

Summary

Questions

7 The bit sequence 0101101 is to be sent between two computers. A parity bit is to be added to this bit pattern. What will the parity bit be if the system is using even parity?

8 A mail order company gives each of its 'members' a six-digit reference number. A check digit is added to the end of this number.
(a) Use the modulus-11 system to calculate the check digit for the member code 325421.
(b) Is the member number 0127345 a valid code?

Calculating a modulus-11 check digit					
Original number	2	3	0	4	5
Weighting	6	5	4	3	2	(this starts from 2, not 1)
Multiply by weight	12	15	0	12	10
Add together	12	+15	+0	+12	+10	=49

divide by 11 $49 \div 11 = 4$ remainder 5

subtract the remainder from 11 $11 - 5 = 6$

so the check digit is 6 and this makes the number 230456

298 because the ASCII values if the letters in FISH are 70, 73, 83 and 72, and these add up to 298.

CONTROL TOTAL

A control total is the total of a set of values. For example if you were sending a set of exam marks then a control total might be the total of all of the marks gained by all of the students. A salesperson might submit two control totals when they send in their monthly report – the total number of sales they have made and the total value of those sales.

Summary Questions

9 Explain the difference between the security and integrity of data.

10 Give two steps you can take to maintain the integrity of your data.

11 The table below shows the sales figures of the number of photocopiers sold by a salesperson over a period of 12 months. Use this table to explain the difference between hash total, checksum and control totals.

Month	1	2	3	4	5	6	7	8	9	10	11	12
Sales	12	23	34	43	12	52	23	12	17	19	21	34

Study Questions

1 A junior school is keen to start using passwords so that their pupils can have their own, private work area. Create a set of rules about passwords suitable for this age group.

2 Some password systems force you to change your passwords regularly and they will not allow you to use the same password twice. Why is this?

Examination Questions

1. (a) What is meant by data security? [1]
   (b) Explain one technique for ensuring the security of data. [2]
   (c) What is meant by data integrity? [1]
   (d) Explain one technique for ensuring the integrity of data. [2]

2. (a) Describe two measures that could be taken to prevent unauthorised access to data stored in a database. [2]
   (b) Describe two methods that could be used to ensure the integrity of data stored in a database. [2]

AQA June 2001 Module 2

3. A large insurance agency suffered a major disk failure late one Friday afternoon. The system had to be recovered from the back-up taken over Thursday night.
    (a) What would be the immediate result of this failure on the routine daily running of the business? [1]
    (b) What procedures needed to have been followed to ensure that a full recovery was possible? [4]
    (c) If the insurance agency had not been able to recover all the lost data, what aspect of current legislation would it have been breaking? [2]

    AEB Summer 2001 Paper 2

4. A school or college network has to have arrangements in place for the safety of the programs and data stored on it. These include the network operating system, various application programs and students' individual work. Suggest three techniques which could be employed to ensure the safety of this material, briefly explaining or justifying each technique. [6]

    AEB Summer 2000 Paper 2

5. The transaction file in a company's payroll process includes employee number, hours worked, department number and week number. State briefly how each of the following validation checks might be applied to the data when the transaction file is created.
    (a) Control total. [2]
    (b) Range check. [3]
    (c) Check digit. [2]

    AEB Summer 2000 Paper 3

CHAPTER:37
Database concepts

A database is a collection of related data stored in a file or a set of related files. The file is made up of fields and records and is organised in way that allows data to be searched and accessed efficiently. Databases tend to be used where large volumes of data need to be stored. For example, a typical bank database might have several million records and several hundred fields of data contained in each record. Due to the size of most databases and the fact that there may be many users with different requirements from it, the organisation of the file can become very complex.

The flat file approach

A flat file consists of any number of records each of which contains a set of fields. Throughout the next four chapters we will be using a video shop database as an example. A video shop would use a database to record data on all of its customers, videos and rentals made.

The following extract shows the database stored as a flat file:

Customer Name	Customer Address	Date of Birth	Video	Date out	Date due
John Smith	1 High Street	30/03/67	Matrix	19/03/03	20/03/03
Mary Jones	14 Acacia Ave	23/04/78	Training Day	19/03/03	20/03/03
Brian Harris	3 Main Street	15/04/84	Titanic	19/03/03	20/03/03
Helen Moore	11 High Street	20/04/82	Star Wars	20/03/03	21/03/03

This extract shows four records (rows) and six fields (columns). Each record holds the details of the loan of a video identifying which customers have borrowed which videos.

This method works well for small databases where the data being stored is relatively simple. For example, if a market research survey were carried out, a flat file could be used where each record represents one set of answers, and each field represents a question asked. The extract from the video shop above is rather unrealistic in that each customer is different and each video is different. In real life, this would be more complex. For example:

● **one customer may rent several videos on the same night;**

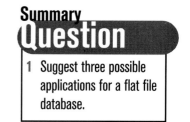

Summary
Question

1 Suggest three possible applications for a flat file database.

- different copies of the same video may be rented to different customers on the same night;

- one customer may rent the same video on more than one occasion.

In fact, there are likely to be a number of relationships that exist within the data. This presents a number of problems with the flat file approach.

Problems with the flat file approach

Consider the video shop example again (at the bottom of the page) but this time a couple more records have been added.

- **Data inconsistency:** John Smith has rented two videos on different days. When his details were typed in on the second occasion, the address has been input as 10 High Street rather than 1 High Street. Therefore, there is a problem with the consistency of the data.

- **Data redundancy:** The details for John Smith and Mary Jones have been typed in twice. This means that their addresses and dates of birth are repeated. Every time they rent a video, their details will be entered again. This leads to a large amount of redundant data which is a waste of storage space.

- **Inefficiency:** Inputting the customer's details every time they rent a video is also time consuming.

It would be impractical to collect and record these details every time a video was rented. Also, if John Smith were to change his address then it would be necessary to go back and amend every record that contained his details. Failing this the file would contain different addresses for John Smith and the video shop would not know which one was correct.

- **Difficult to analyse:** As the number of rentals grows the file will get very large and more difficult to manage. A great deal of processing may be required to extract relevant data from it when it is needed.

- **Program – data dependence:** Different users may have different requirements for the data. For example, one department may use the data to keep track of overdue videos while another uses the data to calculate the financial accounts of the business. In large organisations this problem is magnified. It is common for different departments to use their own programs to manage and extract the data. With a flat file, this means that every department would have to re-write their programs every time the data changed. This is known as 'unproductive maintenance'.

Customer Name	Customer Address	Date of Birth	Video	Date out	Date due
John Smith	1 High Street	30/03/67	Matrix	19/03/03	20/03/03
Mary Jones	14 Acacia Ave	23/04/78	Training Day	19/03/03	20/03/03
Brian Harris	3 Main Street	15/04/84	Titanic	19/03/03	20/03/03
Helen Moore	11 High Street	20/04/82	Star Wars	20/03/03	21/03/03
John Smith	10 High Street	30/03/67	Mr Bean	20/03/03	21/03/03
Mary Jones	14 Acacia Ave	23/04/78	Pearl Harbour	21/03/03	22/03/03

In view of the problems associated with the flat file approach new techniques were developed. These are explained in the next four chapters:

- **Relational databases – Chapters 38 to 40.**

- **Database Management Systems (DBMS) – Chapter 41.**

Study Questions

1. Identify four different databases that your details are stored on at the moment.

2. A large bank may use a number of different databases to help run the organisation. Identify three different databases that they might have.

Examination Questions

Examination questions on flat files are usually part of a question on DBMS – see Chapter 41.

Summary Questions

2 Describe three problems with the flat file approach.

3 Using an example other than the video database, give examples of the following:
   (a) data redundancy;
   (b) data inconsistency.

4 Suggest three reasons why the information that we store about John Smith could be incorrect.

CHAPTER:**38**
Relational databases

A flat file database can be viewed as one file that contains records and fields. A relational database is made up of several inter-related files. Relational databases were devised in response to the needs of businesses and other organisations to store large and complex databases. As you saw in the previous chapter, the flat file approach is inefficient, prone to error and usually only suitable for small databases.

The relational database approach recognises that when databases are created there are a number of relationships that exist within the data. For example, if you were to set up a database for a video shop you may create one file to store customers, one to store videos and one to store rental details. There are some in-built relationships between these three files. For example:

- **one customer may hire many videos;**
- **one video title may be hired by many customers over a period of time;**
- **one customer may have many rentals.**

Entities

In a relational database, the data is not stored in three different files. Instead it is all stored in one file, but the file is divided into separate tables which are called entities. In this example there are three entities: CUSTOMER, VIDEO and RENTAL. It is common practice to identify entities with capital letters and this has been adopted in this book.

One of the first tasks when creating a relational database is to decide on how many entities are needed to solve the problem. To do this, you must use a technique called 'normalisation' which ensures that databases are truly relational. This technique is explained in more detail in the next chapter.

Attributes

An attribute is a field in a relational database. With the video shop database example, we will store different items of data relating to each entity. Typical attributes could be:

CUSTOMER: Customer Name, Address, Phone Number, Date of Birth
VIDEO: Video Name, Age Classification, Genre
RENTAL: Date of Rental, Date Due Back, Price, Overdue Y/N

Summary Questions

1 Describe three problems associated with the flat file approach to databases.
2 What is a relational database?

Relationships and entity relationship diagrams

A relationship is the link created between two entities. Each entity will be related to at least one of the other entities. If there is no relationship between the entities then by definition it would not be a relational database. There are three types, or degrees, of relationship:

One-to-one: one video will be rented to one customer.
One-to-many: one customer will have many rentals.
Many-to-many: many customers could have many videos.

Entity relationship diagrams are used to show these relationships as follows:

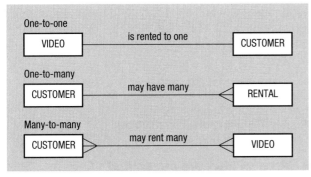

Figure 38.1 **Entity relationship diagram**

Notice that the name of the entity is shown in the box with the lines indicating the nature of the relationship. Labels are usually added above the lines to clarify the relationship.

The nature of relationships are sometimes hard to define. You should choose the one that best describes the relationship in logical terms. In our example you could say that the relationship between CUSTOMER and RENTAL could be any one of the three:

● **One customer has one rental.**

● **One customer has many rentals.**

● **Many customers have many rentals.**

However, the most accurate way to describe it is that one customer could have many rentals because this best describes the nature of the relationship in a real-life context.

When creating a relational database, you should replace any many-to-many relationships with one-

to-many relationships. In the example, we replace the many customers to many videos relationship setting up the RENTAL entity as a link as shown:

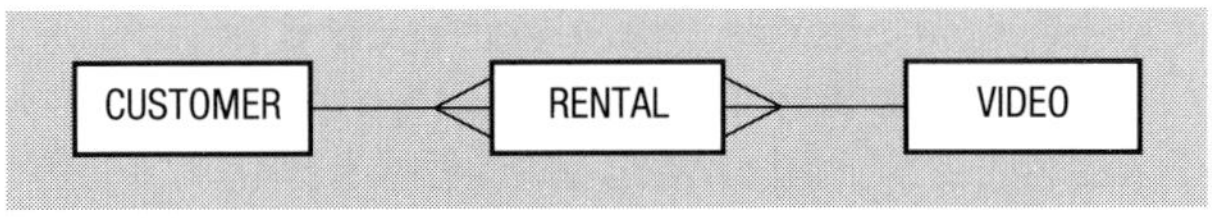

CUSTOMER ◁ RENTAL ▷ VIDEO

Figure 38.2 **Resolving a many-to-many relationship**

Primary key

The primary key is the attribute in each table that uniquely identifies each record. There must be a way of ensuring that every record in each entity can be identified individually, otherwise the relationships cannot be made. For example, in the CUSTOMER entity we will need to store hundreds of names and addresses. We could use the customer's name as the primary key but if there were two customers with the same name, then we would not be able to tell one from the other. There are three possible solutions:

● **Use a unique attribute:** Sometimes there is an attribute that is already unique. For example, if you were storing personal details you could use the National Insurance number as this is unique to every person in the country. If you were storing data about cars, you could use the registration number as this is unique to a particular car.

● **Create a unique attribute:** we could invent a unique code or identifier (ID) for each customer. Then if two people had the same name, the ID would be used so that you knew which was which. This could be used in our example as we could create a Customer ID. Some relational database programs such as Microsoft Access have a facility called 'AutoNumber' which automatically allocates a unique number to each record.

Summary Question

3 Explain the following terms:
(a) entity;
(b) attribute;
(c) relationship.

- **Use a compound key:** Two or more attributes could be used in combination. For example, using name and address as a compound key may ensure that each record is unique as it is unlikely that you will have two customers with the same name at the same address. However, it is still possible, for example, a father and son who are both called John Smith who live at the same address.

Foreign key

A foreign key is an attribute that appears in more than one entity and is used to create the relationship between entities. For example, if one customer can have more than one rental, how do we create the one-to-many relationship between the CUSTOMER entity and the RENTAL entity? The answer is to put the Customer ID in the RENTAL entity as a foreign key. The relationships in our video shop case study could be shown as in Figure 38.3:

- Primary keys have been added for each entity in the form of unique IDs.

- Customer ID appears on the CUSTOMER table as the primary key and on the RENTAL table as a foreign key.

Summary Question

4 Describe how primary keys and foreign keys are used to create relationships between entities.

- Video ID appears on the VIDEO table as the primary key and on the RENTAL table as a foreign key.

Now that the relationships have been created, the three entities become one database. Users of the database will be unaware of the structure in the background. As far as they are concerned they are dealing with one database that contains all the information they need. It is common practice to write out the details of relational databases in standard database notation as shown:

CUSTOMER (<u>Customer ID</u>, Customer Name, Address, Phone Number, Date of Birth)

VIDEO (<u>Video ID</u>, Video Name, Age Classification, Genre)

RENTAL (<u>Rental ID</u>, Date of Rental, Date Due Back, Price, Overdue Y/N, *Customer ID*, *Video ID*)

Note:

- **The name of the entity is shown in capitals.**

- **All the attributes are placed between brackets.**

- **Primary keys are underlined.**

- **Foreign keys are shown in italics.**

Secondary key

A secondary key is any attribute that the user may set up in order to identify, search or sort the records in a relational database. For example, Customer ID is needed as the primary key, but a user may find it

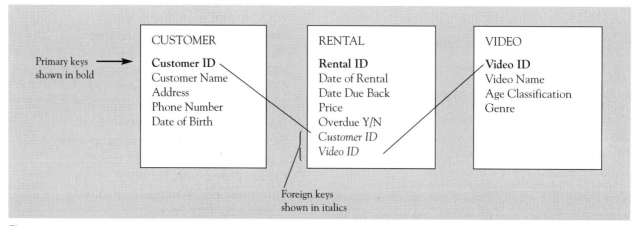

Figure 38.3 **Primary and foreign keys (the video shop database)**

more useful to use the Customer Name as the main attribute for searching and sorting the database. In this case Customer Name is set as the secondary key and it will be indexed.

Indexing

An index in a relational database works in the same way as an index in a book. If you want to find a particular topic in a book you could scan through until you find it or you could look in the index which will have all the topics listed in alphabetical order. A page reference will then be given. Primary and secondary keys will be indexed and the database will use these indexes to speed up the searching process on the database. This becomes more critical as the database grows larger.

Query by example (QBE)

A query is a means of extracting information from a database. In the video shop example, a query could be created to identify all customers with overdue videos, or all the videos that are rated 15+. It is very similar to a search in that the user inputs the criteria for the query, for example, Video.Age Classification >=15. A query may have to extract information from several entities within

the relational database and will store or display all records it finds that match the query.

Query by example (QBE) is one method of performing a query whereby the user inputs an 'example' of the type of query they want to do. Within Microsoft Access a QBE is performed by inputting the criteria for a selected attribute or attributes and listing all the other attributes that are needed.

In the screenshot below:

- **Overdue Y/N = Yes is used as the query criteria and this will return all records where the video has not been returned.**

- **Customer Name and Address are included from the CUSTOMER entity.**

- **Video Name is included from the VIDEO entity.**

- **Rental ID, Date Hired, Date Due Back, Price, Customer ID and Video ID are included from the RENTAL entity.**

The records that meet the criteria could be displayed on screen, saved into a separate table or printed out in the form of a report depending on how the user wants the information.

Summary Question

5 Identify one advantage and one disadvantage of using indexes in a relational database.

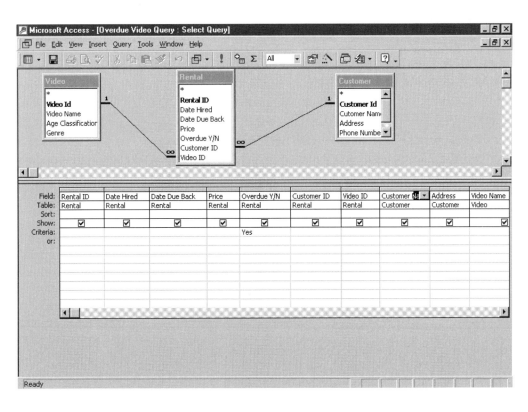

Study Questions

1. Give an example of QBE that might be carried out on a college database.

2. A database is used to store details of students, teachers, classes and subjects. Identify at least three relationships that exist between each of these entities. Show your answer in the form of an entity relationship diagram.

Examination Questions

1. (a) Explain how data inconsistency may arise in an application based on a separate file approach. [3]

   (b) How does the database approach prevent data inconsistency arising? [1]

   (c) Name two typical validation controls used in a database system. [2]

   AQA January 2003 Module 2

2. A newspaper publisher uses a relational database to record details of advertisements placed by businesses and members of the general public.

   Two relations (tables) CUSTOMER and ADVERTISEMENT are used for this database:

   CUSTOMER (CustomerId, Name, Address, CustomerType)
   ADVERTISEMENT (AdvertId, Content, DateAdvertPlaced, NoOfNights, Classification, CustomerId)
   Each advertisement is assigned a unique Advert Id.

   (a) What is a relational database? [1]

   (b) State a suitable primary key for the CUSTOMER relation. Justify your choice. [2]

   (c) (i) Explain what is meant by foreign key. [3]

   (ii) Name the attribute which is the foreign key in the ADVERTISEMENT relation. [1]

   (iii) State a suitable primary key for the ADVERTISEMENT relation. [1]

   (d) Indexes are created on the Customer Id and Name attributes.

   (i) Why is an index used? [1]

   (ii) Which of the two attribute indexes is a secondary index? [1]

(e)   The following shows a sample of the CUSTOMER table and of the ADVERTISEMENT table.

CustomerId	Name	Address	CustomerType
⋮	⋮	⋮	⋮
⋮	⋮	⋮	⋮
920	Jones	......	Business
868	Smith	......	Non-business
919	Adams	......	Non-business
655	Gregory	......	Business
⋮	⋮	⋮	⋮
⋮	⋮	⋮	⋮

AdvertId	Content	DateAdvertPlaced	NoOfNights	Classification	CustomerId
1	Lawnmower for sale	10/7/2000	3	General Sales	567
2	Child's bicycle	10/7/2000	2	General Sales	868
3	Ford Mondeo, T reg	11/7/2000	5	Cars for Sale	920
4	Ford Fiesta, M reg	12/7/2000	5	Cars for Sale	655
5	Electrician, no job too small	12/7/2000	10	Electricians	800
⋮	⋮	⋮	⋮	⋮	⋮
⋮	⋮	⋮	⋮	⋮	⋮
12021	Fiat Uno, P reg ...	1/12/2000	3	Cars for Sale	868
12022	Study desk for sale	1/12/2000	2	General Sales	919

The following shows a query by example (QBE) applied to the CUSTOMER and ADVERTISEMENT tables.

CustomerId	Name	CustomerType	Classification	DateAdvertPlaced
		Business	Cars for Sale	

(i)   What will be the minimum number of records returned by this QBE?   [1]

(ii)   Complete the QBE to extract the names and addresses of all non-business customers placing an advert after 12/7/2000.   [4]

3. A charity uses a relational database to keep track of donors and their donations. Donations are given weekly, monthly and annually (donation type). Two relations (tables) are used for this database.

DONOR and DONATION
DONOR (DonorId, Name, Address, DonationType)
DONATION (DonationId, AmountGiven, DateDonationGiven, DonorId)

Each donation is assigned a unique DonationId.

(a) What is a relational database? [1]

(b) Select a suitable primary key for the DONOR relation. Justify your choice.

(c) (i) Explain what is meant by the term foreign key. [2]

  (ii) Name the attribute which is the foreign key in the DONATION relation. [1]

  (iii) Select a suitable primary key for the DONATION relation. [1]

(d) Indexes are created on the DonorId and DonationType attributes.

  (i) Why is an index used? [1]

  (ii) Which of the two attribute indexes is a secondary index? [1]

(e) The following are extracts from the DONOR table and the DONATION table.

DonorId	Name	Address	DonationType
:	:	:	:
:	:	:	:
567	Jones	......	Weekly
868	Smith	......	Monthly
919	Adams	......	Weekly
920	Gregory	......	Annually
:	:	:	:
:	:	:	:

DonationId	AmountGiven	DateDonationGiven	DonorId
1	5	10/7/2000	567
2	7	10/7/2000	919
3	200	17/7/2000	920
4	7	17/7/2000	919
5	5	17/7/2000	567
:	:	:	:
:	:	:	:
12021	20	10/7/2001	868
12022	200	17/7/2001	920

The following shows a query by example (QBE) applied to the DONOR and
DONATION tables.

DonorId	Name	AmountGiven	DonationType	DateDonationGiven
			Weekly	10/7/2000

(i)   How many records will be returned by this QBE?   [1]
(ii) Using the result of the QBE, calculate the total amount given.   [1]

AQA January 2001 Module 2

CHAPTER:39
Advanced relational databases

Entity relationship modelling

Entity relationship (ER) modelling is the process of identifying:

- **the entities that are needed to make a relational database;**
- **the nature of the relationship between entities (one-to-one, one-to-many, many-to-many);**
- **the primary and foreign keys;**
- **the other non-key attributes in each entity.**

For the video shop example, Chapter 37 showed it was possible to solve the problem with three entities. You will find that many database problems can be modelled into this standard three entity solution whereby one entity acts as a link between the other two. Here, the RENTAL entity acts as a link between the customers and the videos that they hire.

ER modelling becomes more difficult when it is necessary to have more than three entities. In AQA exam questions, students have been asked to model up to six entities.

Normalisation

Normalisation is the process of ensuring that a relational database conforms to certain rules that ensure that the data within it is stored in the most efficient way. When a database is constructed according to these rules it is said to be in 'normal form'. There are various levels of normal form and the level that a programmer needs to go to depends on the complexity of the database. For A Level, you should be able to develop a database to 'third normal form' (3NF).

Normalisation can be used in two ways:

- **to turn a flat file database into a relational database;**
- **to ensure that a relational database has been created in the most efficient method.**

The three stages of normalisation will use the video shop database introduced in Chapter 37. This will begin with the database in a flat file format.

First normal form (1NF)

Reduce entities to first normal form (1NF) by removing repeating attributes.

In simple terms this means that every record is uniquely identifiable and that every attribute is unique. For example, a first attempt may look like this RENTA version .

There are two main problems with this:

- There is no unique way of identifying each rental or each customer. This is a problem, as many rentals are likely to be made on the same day. You will also notice that there are two John Smiths.

- There are three columns for 'Video hired'. This is a problem because data is being repeated, for example, a copy of Matrix has been hired by two different customers. Also, what happens if a customer wants more than three videos?

To make this into first normal form (1NF) we need to create a new entity which we will call VIDEO and we need to add a primary key to the RENTAL entity:

RENTAL VERSION 1

Date hired	Customer Name	Address	Video hired (1)	Video hired (2)	Video hired (3)
19/03/03	John Smith	1 High Street	Titanic	Matrix	
19/03/03	Mary Jones	14 Acacia Avenue	Matrix	Training Day	Star Wars
19/03/03	John Smith	23 Maple Drive	Pearl Harbour		

RENTAL VERSION 2

Rental ID	Date hired	Customer ID	Customer Name	Address	Video hired
0001	19/03/03	2000	John Smith	1 High Street	1000
0002	19/03/03	2000	John Smith	1 High Street	1001
0003	19/03/03	2001	Mary Jones	14 Acacia Avenue	1001
0004	19/03/03	2001	Mary Jones	14 Acacia Avenue	1002
0005	19/03/03	2001	Mary Jones	14 Acacia Avenue	1003
0006	19/03/03	2002	John Smith	23 Maple Drive	1004

VIDEO

Video ID	Video name	Genre	Age Classification
1000	Titanic	Drama	12
1001	Matrix	Sci-fi	15
1002	Training Day	Action	18
1003	Star Wars	Sci-fi	12
1004	Pearl Harbour	Action	15

- Notice that the repeated attributes Video hired(1) to (3) have been removed and replaced by a single attribute called 'Video Hired'. If a customer hires more than one video then there will be several records for the same customer in the RENTAL table. In the case of Mary Jones, she has three records in the RENTAL table as she has taken out three videos.

- A primary key called Video ID has also been added to the VIDEO entity just in case there are two videos with the same name.

- It is the Video ID that is now used in the RENTAL entity to uniquely identify each video. The Video ID therefore is the foreign key in the RENTAL table.

- Additional attributes have also been included in the VIDEO entity at this stage.

- Note that a Customer ID has been added to ensure each customer can be identified uniquely.

Second normal form (2NF)

Remove attributes that are not wholly dependent on the primary key.

The non-key attributes are all the other attributes which are not primary or foreign keys. For example, address and phone number are non-key attributes. To be in second normal form, any non-key attributes that are not related to the primary key should be removed to another entity. In this example, Customer ID is only partially dependent on the Rental ID. This means that CUSTOMER needs to be set up as a separate entity:

CUSTOMER

Customer ID	Name	Address	Phone Number	Date of Birth
2000	John Smith	1 High Street	01555 354354	30/03/67
2001	Mary Jones	14 Acacia Avenue	01555 564333	23/04/78
2002	John Smith	23 Maple Drive	01555 653535	23/08/72

Third normal form (3NF)

Reduce 2NF entities by removing attributes that depend on the primary key of another entity.

At present the Customer Name and Address are still being stored in the RENTAL entity.

However, we now have a CUSTOMER entity and the name and address of the customer are dependent on the primary key of this entity. Therefore, they should be removed from RENTAL and added to CUSTOMER.

Therefore, all three entities in 3NF are as follows:

CUSTOMER

Customer ID	Name	Address	Phone Number	Date of Birth
2000	John Smith	1 High Street	01555 354354	30/03/67
2001	Mary Jones	14 Acacia Avenue	01555 564333	23/04/78
2002	John Smith	23 Maple Drive	01555 653535	23/08/72

VIDEO

Video ID	Video name	Genre	Age Classification
1000	Titanic	Drama	12
1001	Matrix	Sci-fi	15
1002	Training Day	Action	18
1003	Star Wars	Sci-fi	12
1004	Pearl Harbour	Action	15

RENTAL

Rental ID	Date hired	Customer ID	Video hired
0001	19/03/03	2000	1000
0002	19/03/03	2000	1001
0003	19/03/03	2000	1001
0004	19/03/03	2001	1002
0005	19/03/03	2001	1003
0006	19/03/03	2002	1004

- The Customer ID is the primary key of the CUSTOMER entity and the foreign key on the RENTAL entity.

- The Video ID is the primary key of the VIDEO entity and the foreign key on the RENTAL entity.

- The Rental ID is the primary key on the RENTAL entity.

Boyce–Codd normal form (BCNF)

There are further levels of normalisation including fourth and fifth normal forms. The truest form is considered to be BCNF, named after the people who originally devised the relational database concept. This is very similar to 3NF but involves the use of 'candidate keys' sometimes called 'compound keys'. For a database to be in BCNF all of the primary keys must be derived from the attributes within an entity.

For example, in the CUSTOMER table, it would not be acceptable to use a Customer ID as this has been created purely to use as the primary key. Instead, the other attributes must be combined into a candidate key to create a unique primary key.

In the example we have been using, customer name could not be the primary key as it does not identify each record uniquely – how do you know which John Smith is which? Therefore, name and address could be combined:

John Smith 1 High Street
John Smith 24 Maple Drive

There is still a chance that this will not guarantee uniqueness. For example, some parents name their children after themselves and they live at the same address. By adding the Date of Birth attribute, you have created a 'candidate key' that is almost guaranteed to be unique.

There is not a great deal of difference between 3NF and BCNF. For a commercial application, relational databases may be normalised fully to BCNF. In your coursework, it is necessary to normalise up to 3NF.

Study Questions

1. A company employs engineers to fix faults on photocopiers. The company has 20 engineers and over 200 clients. The engineers will travel to client sites in order to fix their machines and can fix between one and five machines a day. The company employs a 'work controller' who takes the call from the client and then allocates an engineer to the job. She uses a relational database to keep track of all the details relating to the clients, engineers and jobs. Part of the database is shown below in standard notation:

CLIENT (Name, Address)
ENGINEER (Name, Address)
JOB (Date, Nature of Problem)

(a) Suggest a suitable identifier for each entity.

(b) Draw an entity-relationship diagram to show the relationship between the three entities.

(c) Suggest foreign keys that could be used to create the relationships.

(d) Identify four other attributes that the company may store.

(e) Now complete the standard notation.

(f) How could a candidate key be used to create a primary key in the ENGINEER entity?

2. A garage uses a database to store details about its customers, their cars and the repairs that are carried out. The system is currently stored as a flat file, an extract of which is shown below.

(a) Identify three problems with this flat file approach.

(b) A relational database is to be designed using three entities: Customer, Car and Repairs. Normalise the database to 3NF showing your answer in standard notation:

ENTITYNAME (<u>Primary key</u>, attribute 1, attribute 2 ...)

This will involve identifying suitable primary and foreign keys.

Customer	Address	Reg No	Make of car	Date Repaired	Repair carried out
John Brown	1 High Street	M222 HGG	Ford Escort	11/03/03	Replace exhaust
Mary Jones	10 Low Road	K222 HKK	VW Golf	11/03/03	Electrical fault
John Brown	1 High Street	P333 AAA	Citroen Saxo	11/03/03	New tyres
Jane Fox	2 New Lane	J123 AAA	VW Polo	11/03/03	Starter motor

Examination Questions

1. A hospital stores details of its wards, patients and their medical condition in a database in a way that will allow information about these details to be extracted. The data requirements are defined as follows.

   - Each patient is assigned a patient number (unique), surname, forename, address, date of birth and gender.

   - Each ward has a number of beds.

- Each ward is assigned a ward name (unique), name of the nurse in charge and the number of beds it possesses.

- Each medical condition is assigned a medical condition number (unique), name and the recommended standard treatment.

- Each patient may suffer from one or more medical conditions.

- A particular medical condition may be attributed to more than one patient.

- The medical conditions of each patient are recorded.

- Each ward has zero or more patients.

- A patient can be assigned to only one ward at any one time.

- Each ward may have patients with different medical conditions.

Four entities for the hospital database are Ward, Patient, MedicalCondition, PatientMedicalCondition

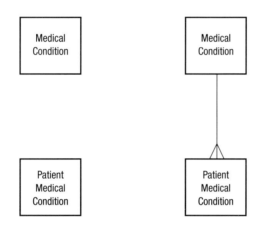

(a) Copy the partially completed entity relationship diagram and, as an aid, show the degree of three more relationships which exist between the given entities. [3]

(b) Using the following format

TableName (PrimaryKey, Non-keyAttribute 1, Non-keyAttribute 2, etc.)

describe tables, stating all attributes, for the following entities underlining the primary key in each case.

(i) Ward [1]
(ii) Patient [2]
(iii) MedicalCondition [1]
(iv) PatientMedicalCondition [2]

AQA January 2003 Module 5

CHAPTER:40
Advanced Structured Query Language (SQL)

Structured Query Language (SQL) is a language that has become the standard method for extracting data from relational databases. It performs exactly the same function as query by example (QBE), which was explained in Chapter 38, in that it allows the user to search and sort data held across several entities or tables. In fact, when you carry out a QBE, the database software such as Microsoft Access, will automatically write corresponding SQL code for you.

When users extract data from a flat file database, they only have one table of data to search. Relational databases are made up of several tables of data which makes searching the data more complex. SQL works by typing in lines of code similar to the code in a programming language. An extract of code is shown below relating to a query that extracts the name and address of all customers called John Smith on the database:

```
SELECT CustomerName, CustomerAddress
FROM Customer
WHERE CustomerName = "John Smith"
ORDER BY CustomerName DESC
```

The structure of the language is:

SELECT: Identifies the columns that you wish to extract. In this example, all the columns are from one table. Where the columns are from more than one table it is necessary to include the name of the table followed by a full stop and then the name of the column. For example, Customer.CustomerName indicates that we wish to extract the CustomerName column from the Customer table.

FROM: Indicates the table or tables that are needed to extract the data. In this example, there is only one table. If there were more, you would have to list them all separating them with commas.

WHERE: Indicates the condition that must be met. In this case, the condition is CustomerName = "John Smith". There may not be any conditions, for example, you may simply want to print a list of customer names. If this is the case, the WHERE statement can be left out altogether.

More complex statements can be used within the WHERE structure including AND and OR statements. For example, the condition could be CustomerName ="John Smith" OR "Mary Jones". To extract all the data for such records, the following SQL would be written:

```
SELECT *
FROM Customer
WHERE CustomerName = "John Smith" OR CustomerName = "Mary Jones"
```

Note that the * is used as a 'wildcard' which means that all attributes are extracted when the query is run.

The BETWEEN command can also be incorporated into the WHERE statement. For example, to extract all videos with a rental value of between £2 and £2.50:

```
SELECT *
FROM Video
WHERE VideoPrice BETWEEN 2 AND 2.50
```

ORDER BY: Indicates the sort order of the extracted data. The default setting is ascending, but the inclusion of DESC sets the sort order to descending.

Example

Suppose we wanted to perform a more useful query which in this case might be to produce the name and address of all customers who have not returned videos along with the name of the video and when it was taken out. The extract should be sorted in ascending order by customer name. This involves querying all three tables.

CUSTOMER

CustomerID	CustomerName	Address	PhoneNumber	DateofBirth
2000	John Smith	1 High Street	01555 354354	30/03/67
2001	Mary Jones	14 Acacia Avenue	01555 564333	23/04/78
2002	John Smith	23 Maple Drive	01555 653535	23/08/72

VIDEO

VideoID	Videoname	Genre	AgeClassification	Price
1000	Titanic	Drama	12	2.00
1001	Matrix	Sci-fi	15	2.50
1002	Training Day	Action	18	3.00
1003	Star Wars	Sci-fi	12	2.00
1004	Pearl Harbour	Action	15	2.50

RENTAL

RentalID	DateHired	CustomerID	VideoHired	OverdueYN
0001	19/03/03	2000	1000	Y
0002	19/03/03	2000	1001	Y
0003	19/03/03	2000	1001	N
0004	19/03/03	2001	1002	Y
0005	19/03/03	2001	1003	N
0006	19/03/03	2002	1004	N

```
SELECT Customer.CustomerName,
Customer.Address, Rental.DateHired,
Rental.VideoHired, Video.VideoName,
Video.Price

FROM Customer, Rental, Video
WHERE Rental.OverdueYN = "Y"
ORDER BY Customer.CustomerName
```

Note that the table names are being shown in the SELECT statement as more than one table is being used to perform the query. This would extract the following data:

CustomerName	Address	DateHired	VideoID	VideoName	Price
John Smith	1 High Street	19/03/03	1000	Titanic	2.00
John Smith	1 High Street	19/03/03	1001	Matrix	2.50
Mary Jones	14 Acacia Avenue	19/03/03	1002	Training Day	3.00

This data may be extracted in the form of a table, or may be compiled directly into a report. In this case, it could be used to create a mail merge which would automatically send reminder letters to all of the customers. You will notice that the SELECT statement can get very long where many attributes need to be extracted. If you need every attribute, one shortcut is that rather than typing them all out individually, you can input SELECT * and all attributes are automatically extracted.

Another useful SQL command is GROUP BY which allows you to group extracted records together. In this example, it may be useful to group the records together on customer name which would then allow a 'total price owing' figure to be calculated as part of the query:

```
SELECT Customer.CustomerName,
SUM(Video.Price),
COUNT(Customer.CustomerName)
FROM Customer, Rental, Video
WHERE Rental.OverdueYN = "Y"
ORDER BY Customer.CustomerName
GROUP BY Customer.CustomerName
```

This query would return the output below:

The price of the two overdue videos for John Smith have been added together by the use of the SUM command. Mary Jones only has one overdue video and the price of that is also shown. The COUNT function has counted the number of records that meet the WHERE criteria which in this example is the number of customers with overdue videos.

Summary Question

1 Write SQL code to create the following queries from the video database example used in this chapter.
   (a) Select all action films.
   (b) Select all customers who have rented action films.
   (c) Select all customers born before 1972.
   (d) Select all customers who hired videos on 19/03/03 ranked in descending order on Customer Name.
   (e) Identify the sum of the prices of all videos hired on 19/03/03.

Customer.CustomerName	SUM(Video.Price)	COUNT(Customer.CustomerName)
John Smith	4.50	2
Mary Jones	3.00	1

Examination Questions

1. Customers placing orders with ABC Ltd for ABC's products have their orders recorded by ABC in a database. The data requirements for the database system are defined as follows.

    - Each product is assigned a unique product code, ProductID, and has a product description.

    - The quantity in stock of a particular product is recorded.

    - Each customer is assigned a unique customer code, CustomerID, and has their name, address and telephone number recorded.

    - An order placed by a customer will be for one or more products.

    - ABC Ltd assigns a unique code to each customer order, ABCOrderNo.

    - A customer placing an order must supply a code, CustomerOrderNo, which the customer uses to identify the particular order.

    - A customer may place one or more orders.

    - Each new order from a particular customer will have a different customer order code but two different customers may use, independently, the same values of customer order code.

    - Whether an order has been despatched or not will be recorded.

    - A particular order will contain one or more lines.

    - Each line is numbered, the first is one, the second is two and so on.

    - Each line will reference a particular product and specify the quantity ordered.

    - A specific product reference will appear only once in any particular order placed with ABS Ltd.

After normalisation the database contains four tables based on the entities

Customer, Product, Order, Orderline

(a) The figure below shows a partially complete entity relationship diagram. Show the degree of three more relationships which exist between the given entities. [3]

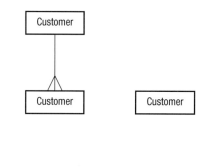

Using the following format TABLENAME (PrimaryKey, Attribute1, Attribute 2, etc) describe tables, stating all attributes, for the following entities underlining the primary key in each case.

(b) Product [2]

(c) Customer [2]

(d) Order [3]

(e) OrderLine [4]

(f) Using SQL commands SELECT, FROM, WHERE and ORDER BY, write an SQL statement to query the database tables for all customer names where the orders have been despatched. The result of the query is to be ordered in ascending order of ABCOrderNo. [6]

AQA June 2002 Module 5

CHAPTER:**41**
Advanced database concepts

Database Management Systems (DBMS)

A DBMS is a program that controls the data that is kept on the database.

One of the biggest benefits of working with a database is that it can be accessed by many different users or programs and the data can in turn be used in many different ways. However this can generate problems – what happens if two programs try to access and update the same item of data at the same time? What happens if a program needs to add a new attribute to an entity, but other programs that access the same dataset don't 'know' about the extra attribute? This process is known as 'unproductive maintenance' – when programs are dependent on the structure of the data.

The answer is to use a DBMS. A DBMS is a program that controls the data that is kept on the database. It also manages how the data is stored, whereabouts in the system it is kept, and it can control access rights as well. The diagram shows how the four departments in a company all access the data files via the DBMS – none of them have direct access to the data.

Summary
Question

1   A sales department decides it needs to add an extra field or attribute to the data it needs to access. Explain how the DBMS will cope with this request.

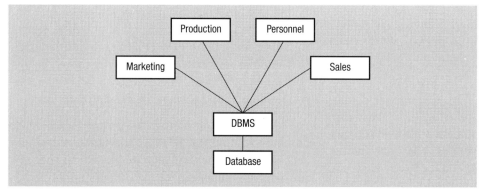

Figure 41.1 **Database Management System**

Data dictionary

The DBMS keeps track of the structure of the files by storing their details in a data dictionary. The data dictionary stores all the background details that tells the DBMS how and where the data is stored. This includes the data types that have been used, any validation routines that have been set up, the relationships between the entities and the file structure used for each table. The data dictionary does not store the data itself – it records how the data will be stored.

If a program wants information from a particular table it sends a request to the DBMS which in turn looks in the data dictionary to identify which table the data is in, and how to find the data within that table. Because all the requests are processed using details stored in the data dictionary it follows that if a new attribute is added to a table the details are updated on the data dictionary – a process hidden from the user. This leads to the concept of program/data independence – the programs and data are not directly linked.

The DBMS also controls just what individual users can and cannot see and do. The manager of a wages department will be able to see all the pay details for all the employees at a company whilst a data entry clerk in the same department might be allowed to see a reference number and name. Both would be totally unaware that the same database stored details of the qualifications held by an employee but this information might be available to the person in charge of staff training. The DBMS will also control what each individual user can do with the data. This might mean the data is read/write or read only or whether or not they have to enter a separate password to be able to alter the data.

There are three different ways of 'seeing' the database. These different views are also known as schema.

1. The external or user schema describes what view each of the different users will 'see'.

2. The conceptual or logical schema describes the structure of the database. This will include details of the relationships between tables and details of the entities and attributes that are being used. This could be seen as a diagrammatic version of the data dictionary.

3. The internal schema describes how the data will actually be stored. It stores details of the file structures that will be used, and how this data will be accessed and updated.

Data integrity on a shared database

One common problem with a database that is accessible to a number of users is what to do if a number of users are trying to access the same data at the same time. As long as the users are only reading the data this is not a problem, but if two or more users want to write data there will be problems.

Imagine two users both want to put some data in the same location. The first person presses the save button and their updated data gets saved to the file. A few seconds later the second presses their save button. Their data now overwrites the first person's data but how do you know which is the most up-to-date version?

One answer is to put a lock on the data. As soon as a user with write access takes an item of data a lock is put on that data item so that no other user can save to that location, and the second person will not be able to save their version of the data without acknowledging that the data may have been altered by another user. You can see a simplified version of this process in use across a network. Two users can both load the same word-processed file, but only the first person to load will be given write access – the other person will see a read-only version of the file.

Data Definition Language (DDL)

A data definition language (DDL) allows a database manager to control a database. It allows the manager to define and create new entities, their attributes, keys and the relationships that link them to existing entities. In other words it allows the manager to control the format and content of the data dictionary.

A DDL also allows the user to control access to the database by maintaining details of users and any access restrictions that may be placed on them by the database manager.

Data Manipulation Language (DML)

Whilst a DDL allows a user to manage the structure of a database, a data manipulation language allows the user to control the data itself. There are four basic functions the user is likely to want to carry out with the data – insert, delete, amend and retrieve – though the DML will allow users to carry out more complex processing of the database. The retrieve section of a DML might be based on SQL (structured query language).

Summary Questions

2 The data managed by a DBMS can be viewed at three different levels or schemas. What are the three schemas and what view do they give of the database?

3 The DBMS uses a data dictionary to control the files. What is a data dictionary?

4 How will the DBMS cope if two users try to read the same data item simultaneously?

5 How will the DBMS cope if two users try to write to the same data item simultaneously?

6 The database manager will use DDL and DML to control the data via a DBMS. Explain the purpose of DDL and DML.

Open Database Connectivity (ODBC)

There are many applications that allow you to create databases, and in turn there are many other applications that can be used to access those databases. ODBC is a kind of protocol. It uses an open standard application program interface (API) to allow different applications such as Access, dBase and Delphi to access a database that has been set up by another application. This process of being able to access the data in a database from different places is called program–data independence.

Database servers

In a conventional network environment the file server acts as a central store – any files that are needed are sent out to the workstations. The user then manipulates the data at the workstation before saving the new version back to the file server.

A database server holds and manages the database itself so that all amendments, searches and so on are carried out at the server. This will help to maintain the integrity of the data as it ensures that there is only ever one version of the data.

Object-oriented databases (OODB)

An object-oriented database offers DBMS facilities linked to an object-oriented data structure. The data is stored in objects which also contain the methods or processes that can be carried out on the data. The concept of object-oriented languages is covered in Chapter 10.

Study Question

1. A database can either be held on a database server or it can be distributed to the users on a local basis. Explain how these two systems work.

Examination Questions

1. (a) Distinguish between a database and a database management system (DBMS). [2]
   (b) Name the three levels in the three level architecture of a DBMS. [3]
   (c) (i) What is meant by unproductive maintenance in the context of a flat file database? [1]
       (ii) Why does a DBMS overcome this problem of unproductive maintenance? [1]

   (d) In a multi-user DBMS concurrent access is allowed to each data item. However, some users are not allowed access to every data item.
       (i) What is meant by concurrent access? [1]
       (ii) Why must concurrent access be controlled in a multi-user DBMS? [3]
       (iii) Explain the role of a Data Definition Language (DDL) in the context of a DBMS including how a DDL is used to specify the data items to which each user has access. [3]

AQA January 2003 Module 5

CHAPTER:42
Operating systems

What does an operating system do?

An operating system is a collection of software designed to act as an interface between the user and the computer. It links together the hardware, the applications and the user, but hides the true complexity of the computer from the user – a so-called 'virtual machine'.

When you are using a computer you are obviously aware of the applications software you are using, whether it is an Internet browser, a spreadsheet or a game of some sort, but you are much less aware of the software that is running in the background. The systems software is dominated by the operating system (OS).

The OS in a modern computer is very large – for example, Microsoft Windows XP needs a minimum of 128 Mb of RAM when the computer is in use. This gives some idea of the complexity of the OS. This is because the OS carries out many tasks. For example:

- It controls the start up configuration of your computer including what icons to put on you desktop and what backdrop to use.

- It recognises when you have pressed a mouse button and then decides what, if any, action to take.

- It sends the signals to the hard disk controller, telling it what program to transfer to memory.

- It decides which sections of memory to allocate to the program you are intending to use.

- It allocates memory to the software to store the text you type in to a word-processed document or the data you put in the cells of a spreadsheet.

- It attempts to cope with errors as and when they occur. For example, if a printer sends an 'out of paper error' or you fail to save a file correctly, it is the operating system that displays the appropriate message.

- It makes sure that your computer shuts down properly when you have finished.

- It manages the memory to ensure all the programs you want to run are allocated the space they need.

- It controls print queues.

- It manages the users on a network – it maintains the lists of user names and passwords and controls which files and resources users have access to.

Summary
Question

1 Explain the purpose of an operating system.

However, it is important to realise that not all computers have an operating system. The microprocessor inside the electronic scales found in many homes only has one simple task to carry out and the input and output routines are predefined so an operating system is not needed.

Classifying operating systems

There are two ways to classify an operating system. One is to look at how many users and how many programs it can cope with at any one moment in time – this will be covered in Chapter 43. The other way is to look at the time the operating system takes to respond to a task.

BATCH OR OFF-LINE PROCESSING

Batch processing involves a user passing a number of tasks or jobs to a computer. The operating system then decides what order to do the jobs in. There is no need for user involvement whilst the jobs are being processed.

Most modern users expect a fast response time from their computer but not all tasks carried out on a computer system need to be processed straight away. For example an electricity company might print out a batch of bills overnight. In this case the time taken between sending the request to print the bills and their actual production might be many hours. In the same way some computer systems are given a batch of jobs to carry out. The operating system then decides what order to do the jobs in and what resources are going to be needed. In both cases it is quite normal to give the computer the jobs to do and then let it get on without any need for interruption.

The main characteristics of batch processing are repetitive processing of large amounts of data, and non-urgency of the results.

INTERACTIVE OR ON-LINE

As the name suggests, interactive processing actively involves the user(s) in some way. This is by far the most common type of operating system you are likely to come across. The computer in your home, at a bank or at your college or school all use this system. The main feature is that you interact with the computer – you enter instructions, the computer responds and you follow on with further instructions. You might say you are having a dialogue with the computer.

REAL-TIME

A real-time operating system is one where there is little or no time delay between the input and the resulting output.

Real-time operating systems can be either 'critical' or 'non-critical'. Critical systems will mostly involve computer-controlled operations where there is little or no human intervention. Examples can include missile control, ABS brakes and industrial processes such as mixing chemicals. Any time delay in these operations could have catastrophic results. In these cases all the inputs come from sensors and the processes being carried out are in a form of a continuous loop as the computer takes a reading from a sensor, decides what, if any, action to take then takes another sensor reading, and so on.

A non-critical real-time operating system might involve a time delay, but here the delay will not cause any real problems. For example, the computer controlling the environment in a greenhouse might take several minutes to open a roof vent or to close a sun blind, but the delay will not adversely effect the plants in the greenhouse.

Another form of real-time operating system involves human interaction. Examples include airline booking systems and supermarkets. In these cases the time taken to complete a task is critical to the efficient operation of the system.

In practice the distinction between interactive and real-time operating systems is often blurred.

NETWORK

The operating system in a network has to cope with the complex task of dealing with multiple users and workstations. It must cope with users logging on with their user names and passwords and then it controls what software, files, workstations and other resources the users are allowed to have access to. It will also control which applications and files can be used at particular workstations as well. This can be very important if the terms of the network licence limits the number of workstations the application can be installed on.

Summary Question

2 Give three examples where each of the following operating system types might be used
(a) batch processing;
(b) interactive;
(c) real time.

Resource management

At one time a home computer was only capable of executing one program at a time. For example, once you had started using a database your computer couldn't be used for anything else until the database program was closed.

A modern home computer is capable of running many programs seemingly at the same time. It is the job of the operating system to make sure that each program is allocated enough memory to operate efficiently. In larger computers that are capable of executing more than one program at one time the operating system will need to control access to other resources such as the CPU, secondary storage and printers.

File management

One of the many tasks the operating system has to deal with is managing files – this includes controlling the structures that are used to store the files.

The hard disk on a home computer is likely to contain many thousands of files and without some sort of logical storage structure it would be impossible to find a specific file amongst so many. The operating system on a home computer uses folders or directories. These allow the user to group similar files together so that, for example, all the files for your Computing course might be kept in one folder whilst all the photos from your digital camera would be kept in another. In the case of the photos it is highly likely that there will be folders in folders. The way folders like these are arranged is known as a hierarchical structure – it looks rather like an inverted tree and indeed the start or base folder is normally referred to as the root folder.

Each file has a filename but because of the folder structure it is possible to use the same filename for different files. In the coursework/photo example there might be a folder called 'miscellaneous' and a file called 'latest' in each area. Obviously this is not particularly good practice, especially if you want to move files between folders and you lose track of which folders you are working with. It is a good practise to use folder and file names that indicate what they are being used for.

As hard disks get larger and larger it is becoming increasingly common to split up or partition a hard disk. This means that although you actually only have one hard disk in your computer, the operating system splits it up into a number of partitions or logical drives. This means your computer seems to be fitted with more than one hard drive. You might use this system to store your applications on one logical drive and your work on another.

The name you give a file is not necessarily unique, but the pathname to the file is. It is rather like the address on a letter addressed to your house – the further on you read the closer you get to the destination. A typical pathname might look like this.

`C:\Windows\Desktop\School\2002GCSE.xls`

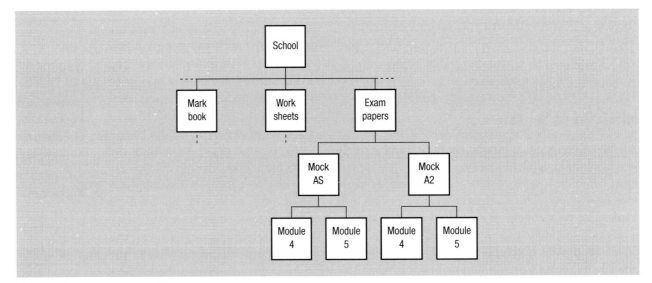

Figure 42.1 **Hierarchical file structure**

This particular file is stored on drive C which is normally the hard disk in a home computer. The root folder is called `Windows`. This contains a subfolder called `Desktop` which in turn contains a folder called `School` In this folder is the file which is called `2002GCSE`. The `.xls` on the end of the filename is called the 'file extension' and it is used to inform the operating system that the data in this file is stored in a format that Microsoft Excel can read.

The file system will also need to record what sort of access rights the user has to this file. For example, if another user is already using this file, then the file will be set to 'read only'.

All these details explain how an operating system can keep track of files on a home computer. Now try to imagine how complex the structure must be on the network in a school or college.

Summary Questions

3 Explain how it is possible for two files with the same name to be stored in a file structure.

4 Explain the difference between resource and file management.

Study Question

1. Most modern computers are sold with a version of Microsoft's Windows, but there are other operating systems available. Research other operating systems and compare them with Windows.

Examination Questions

1. For each of the following suggest a suitable type of operating system. Give one reason for your choice.
    (a)   A computer system consisting of several PCs capable of sharing each other's files.   [2]
    (b)   A computer system dedicated to controlling the engine management system in a modern car.   [2]
    (c)   A computer system dedicated to processing, at the end of each day, a building society's transactions stored on magnetic disc.   [2]

2. (a) In the context of file management what is meant by archiving? [2]

The directory structure shown in the figure below contains a root directory (\) and four subdirectories, named Documentation, Project, Source and BackUp. The root directory and its subdirectories are mounted on logical drive C: The subdirectory names Documentation and Project will be stored in the directory structure.

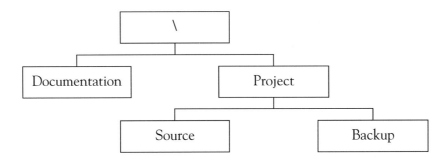

(b) In which part of the directory structure will these names be stored? [1]

Two files each with the filename Main.exe are stored in the system with the directory structure shown in the figure. The subdirectory Project contains one entry for Main.Exe and the BackUp directory contains another.

(c) What is the pathname for the subdirectory Project's entry for Main.exe? [1]

(d) What is the pathname for the subdirectory BackUp's entry for Main.exe? [1]

(e) In addition to file management, name one other type of resource managed by an operating system. [1]

AQA June 2002 Module 2

3. Computer controlled central heating and the computer controlled engine management system in a modern car would both be run using a real time operating system.

Explain two major differences in the requirements of these two examples of real time systems. [4]

CHAPTER:43
Advanced operating systems

In Chapter 42 we looked at how operating systems could be classified by the time they took to process a task. The other way that operating systems are classified is the way in which they can deal with the users and their tasks or jobs.

Single purpose (dedicated) operating systems

Early computers were designed to deal with just one task at a time, and there is still a big need for computers that are dedicated to just one task. Computers that use this type of OS are said to be time- or mission-critical. This includes situations such as the engine management system of a car or the guidance system in a missile. If you want a computer to concentrate all its efforts on just one task you are most likely to use a dedicated operating system. This is also known as an 'embedded' operating system. It is designed to do just one job, indeed it cannot be used for anything else.

Multiprogramming and multitasking

Multiprogramming is the process that allows a number of programs to appear to be running simultaneously on one computer.

There is only one CPU in a multiprogramming computer and so only one program can actually be 'live' at any one moment in time. In order to allow more than one program to appear to run simultaneously the operating system has to allocate access to the CPU and other resources such as peripherals and memory. One of the main tasks that a multiprogramming operating system has to do is to make sure that all these allocations make the best possible use of the available resources.

Multitasking can be seen as one user using one computer to carry out more than one task at a time. The operating system in even the simplest modern PC supports multitasking. It is possible to have many tasks or applications loaded and available on a home PC, but you would normally only be actively using one application at any one time.

There are exceptions to this. For example, you might use a home PC to download a file from a web site, print out a document and carry on working on a spreadsheet all at the same time. In these circumstances it is the job of the operating system to make sure that all three tasks are serviced as efficiently as possible.

Multitasking and multiprogramming are therefore very similar but multitasking involves one user running many applications on one computer whilst multiprogramming will involve a number of users sharing the processing power of one computer.

Summary Questions

1   Give an example of a device that uses an embedded operating system, and explain why this is the most suitable type of OS for this task.

2   Distinguish between a multitasking and a multiprogramming operating system. Is it possible for the operating system to be both at the same time?

Scheduling and time slicing

Usually the most heavily used resource in a computer is the CPU. The process of allocating access to the CPU and other resources is called 'scheduling'. The simplest way that an operating system can schedule access to the CPU is to allocate each task a 'time slice'. This means that each task is given an equal amount of CPU time. This process of passing access to the CPU from one task to the next is also known as 'round-robin' scheduling.

Time slicing is a crude system because a particular task might not need all or even any of its allotted time slice with the CPU. For example, a word processor might be waiting for the slowest part of any computer system, the user, to press a key. Waiting for this to happen is a waste of CPU time and so a more sophisticated 'scheduler' might pass the time slice on to the next task before the word processor's time slice has expired.

Other scheduling systems include 'shortest job first' and 'priority scheduling'. Shortest job first involves the scheduler either being told or estimating how long a particular task will take and putting those jobs that will take the least time at the front of the queue.

Priority scheduling involves the user allocating a priority to each job. The operating system then identifies all the jobs with the highest level and deals with them first, leaving lower priority jobs until later. It is possible that if a high priority task arrives whilst a low priority task is being executed that the lower priority task is temporarily stopped whilst the high priority task is dealt with.

Some sophisticated operating systems allow the user to control the way the operating system copes with the tasks or jobs it is given. This is done through a 'job control language'. For example, the user might want to alter the priority of the tasks or tell the computer which resources a job will need.

Multi-user

Multi-user operating systems are normally associated with network operating systems. A multi-user operating system allows more than one user to access a computer at one

Photograph 43.1 **A multi-user computer network**

time. This will mean that each user will have to have access to at least a keyboard and monitor. Each user appears to have unique access to the computer though this view can become increasingly hard to maintain as more and more users access the computer at the same time.

An example of a multi-user operating system can be seen in a supermarket where each of the tills seems to have unique access to the database that holds details of the goods. At the same time that the till operators are accessing the database to find the cost and description of goods the manager could be accessing the same data to carry out an analysis of sales. The concept of allowing more than one user to access a central database this way is known as 'multi-access'.

Parallel processing

One of the main bottlenecks in any computer is the CPU. All the instructions have to be processed by it and the more users and tasks you ask the CPU to cope with the harder it is for the CPU to keep up. One way to relieve the pressure is to fit more than one CPU. This process is called parallel processing. There is still one primary CPU that oversees the work, but it is able to pass parts of the work to one or more 'slave' CPUs. In some situations such as weather forecasting where there are large numbers of calculations to carry out there may be several CPUs acting together and so sharing the workload.

Centralised and distributed processing

As the use of networks has grown the pressure on the file servers has increased. This is especially true in situations where all the processing is carried out by the file server itself. This is called 'centralised processing'. File processing is an example of centralised processing.

One way round this problem is to use 'distributed processing'. This method makes different computers on a network 'responsible' for different aspects of a task. One computer would handle all the processing for the sales department of a company whilst another might deal with orders and a third customer support. Because the computers are part of a network they are still able to pass data between departments.

Client–server network operating systems

Networks in schools and colleges use a 'client–server' operating system. The 'clients' are the workstations used by the users. When a user asks for an application or a file to be loaded on to their workstation, the request is sent to the 'server' that acts as a central resource. This means that the user should be able to access the applications and files from any workstation on the network. It is the job of the operating system to manage these central resources. It controls which users have access to which applications and files and which computers can be used for this work.

Most school and college networks also support network printing. When a user asks for a job to be printed the server sends the request to a print server. The main server often performs this task.

When the print request is being processed the document that is going to be printed is spooled – this is the process of sending it to the print server where it is temporarily stored until the printer can deal with it. The print job also contains other information such as the quality or resolution needed for the job, and details about which printer the user wants to use to print the job. The user might also be able to set the priority of the print job. It is the job of the print server to interpret these details.

Summary Questions

5 Compare centralised and distributed processing and explain the benefits of each system.

6 What is a job control language?

7 What is a print server, and how does a print server use spooling to cope with the demands placed upon it?

Examination Questions

1. For each of the following situations, state which of the terms multiprogramming, multiuser and multitasking bests describes the type of operating system involved.
   (a) A user on a stand-alone PC is working on a report which involves switching between a word-processed document and a spreadsheet, while occasionally looking at the Internet for information. [1]
   (b) A computer system is running in batch mode overnight with a queue of jobs to be done. While one job is waiting for input or output, another job is using the processor. [1]
   (c) A number of terminals communicate with a central computer which allocates processing power to each terminal in turn. [1]

AQA January 2003 Module 4

2. A job control language is used to control how jobs are run in a batch processing system.
   (a) List two pieces of information which might be specified in the job control language script for a particular job. [2]

   Some job control languages allow statements which specify to the operating system the amount of input and output expected relative to the amount of processor time required.
   (b) How would a batch multiprogramming operating system use this information? [3]

   AQA January 2002 Module 4

3. A process is a program whose execution has started but not yet finished. Give three reasons why a process might not execute continuously in a multi-programming operating system. [3]

   AEB Summer 2001 Paper 3

4. (a) What is an embedded system? [2]

   Give an example of an embedded system that you might expect to find:
   (b) in the home; [1]
   (c) not in the home. [1]

   AEB Summer 2000 Paper 2

5. A school network includes a number of printers. To manage outputs to the printers the network operating system uses spooling.
   (a) Give two reasons why spooling is used in this situation. [2]

   The spooling routine stores data about the files waiting to be printed.
   (b) Suggest three items of data which need to be recorded for each output file. [3]
   (c) Suggest a suitable data structure for this data. [2]

   AEB Summer 1999 Paper 2

6. In a batch multiprogramming environment, the following three programs are ready and waiting to be run.

   - **a payroll program;**
   - **a complicated scientific calculation;**
   - **the printing of a long queue of reports.**

   (a) Give one reason why the queue of reports would be allocated the highest priority. [2]
   (b) Give one reason why the scientific calculation would be allocated the lowest priority. [2]

   AEB Summer 1998 Paper 2

CHAPTER:44
Advanced user interface design

As we have already seen the operating system of a computer acts as an interface between the user and the computer itself, but there are times when the user needs to be able to communicate with the computer. There are a number of ways in which a user might communicate with the operating system or an application package.

Command line interface

A command line interface (CLI) involves typing in commands for the operating system via a keyboard. Probably the most well known example is Microsoft DOS (MS-DOS). This screen shows MS-DOS in use.

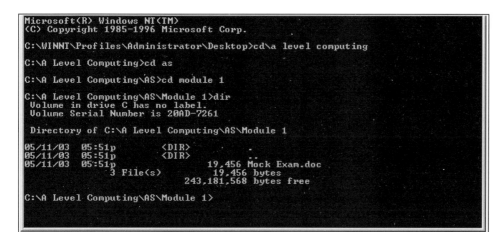

Figure 44.1 **Command line interface**

A CLI is probably the least user-friendly user interface. This is because the user must know a large range of text-based commands and understand the syntax that goes with them. For example, in DOS the command 'dir' would list all the directories and files in the current folder and 'del' would be used in conjunction with a file name to delete files.

A CLI allows the user the most direct control of the operating system. This is because there are many more commands available to the user than can be displayed at any one time on the screen. The user does not have to follow a sequence of menus or windows to get to the option they want – they can save time by entering the commands directly.

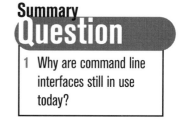

Summary Question

1 Why are command line interfaces still in use today?

Menu-driven interface

A menu-driven interface provides the user with a list of options. The user then uses either a sequence of key presses or a mouse to select the option they wanted. This in turn might lead to another menu where the user would select a further option and so on.

The problem with this is that the commands are text based and as a result their purpose might not be immediately obvious. The other problem is that the menus take up a lot of screen space and users might find themselves working their way through a large number of menus to reach the process they are looking for.

Despite these problems menu-driven systems are still common. Most mobile phones seem able to carry out a bewildering range of processes and most of these are reached by working through menus. Some televisions and video recorders use on screen lists of commands and an automatic teller machine (ATM) at a bank uses buttons to allow users to select items which in turn carry out a number of functions such as asking for cash or a printing a mini-statement.

The benefit of using a menu-driven interface is that you can control what the user does next very precisely – ideal in situations where an untrained user has to make decisions in a set order.

Almost all commonly-used applications include drop-down menus as part of their user interface.

Graphical user interface (GUI)

The advent of GUIs in the 1980s revolutionised personal computers. They allowed users to interact with their computers without having to understand a large number of technical words or work their way through seemingly endless menus.

The concept of a GUI is that the user uses a device, such as a mouse, to move a pointer and press a button over an icon. The mouse can also be used to control frames or windows on

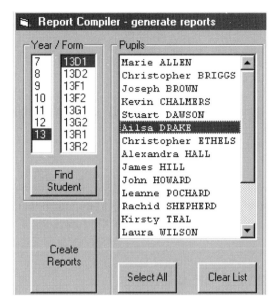

Figure 44.2 **Graphical user interface**

the screen. The GUI system is sometimes referred to as a WIMP environment – Windows, Icons, Menu (or Mouse) and Pointer.

This innovative system allows more or less anyone to interact with a computer – the user no longer needs a high level of specialist knowledge to be able to interact with their computer. A good GUI should be intuitive, with the icons and screen layout designed to make using the computer as easy as possible. Other facilities that make a GUI very popular are the ability to customise the screen layout and the built-in help system.

Natural language interface

One of the latest developments in the way that users can interact with their computer is using a natural language interface. These are operated either via voice or keyboard commands.

The difference between natural language and command line interfaces is that natural language allows the user to phrase their commands in a language such as English. The operating system then has to try and interpret what the user has requested. The main problem is this interpretation. The English language is full of ambiguities and potential pitfalls. For example, the command 'back up' could mean back-up a file or move back up through a file structure.

Despite years of research, true natural language interfaces are rare.

Summary Questions

2 Explain why mobile phones use a menu-driven system to control their operation.

3 What features of a GUI make it particularly useful for a non-expert to use?

4 Using a good GUI is said to be intuitive. What features of a GUI support this claim? Do you agree with this claim?

5 Give three examples where a natural language interface might be used instead of a GUI.

Examination Questions

1. (a) What type of operating system interface is shown below? [1]
   (b) What program receives the instructions entered via this interface and analyses them? [1]
   (c) Give two advantages of this type of interface over alternative types of operating system interface. [2]
   (d) Give one disadvantage of this type of interface over alternative types of operating system interface. [1]

```
P:\TL01>cd May 2001


P:\TL01>cd May 2001

Volume in drive P has no label.

Volume Serial Number is E04F-F00A


Directory of : May 2001


.          <DIR>            28/05/01  11.37a

..         <DIR>            28/05/01  11.37a

Seniors    <DIR>            30/05/01  04.16p

Juniors    <DIR>            30/05/01  04.15a

Summer               92,160 31/05/01  10.37a

         5 File(s)  92,160 bytes
```

AQA January 2003 Module 4

CHAPTER:45
Advanced operating system concepts

File management

The operating system controls how files are stored on storage media. It does this by using an index called a FAT or File Allocation Table. The FAT splits the storage capacity of the storage media up into blocks. These blocks are also known as 'clusters' or allocation units. The size of a cluster is dependent on the size of the hard disk, the larger the disk capacity the larger the cluster size – a 10 Gb hard disk drive is likely to use a cluster size of 8 Kb.

A cluster is the smallest block of data that can be assigned to a file. Using the example above this means that even if a particular file is only 20 bytes long, it will still be allocated 8 Kb, so most of the cluster will be wasted. This also means that the hard disk on your home computer has almost certainly got lots of capacity that you cannot use. This is because every file you have saved on your computer will fit into one or more 8 Kb blocks. A word-processed file that is 45 Kb long will take up six 8 Kb blocks, but the last one will have 3 Kb that cannot be used.

The operating system also has to cope with the fact that that same 45 Kb file will not necessarily be stored in six consecutive blocks – they are just as likely to be spread right across the storage media. This is because as you expand or reduce the size of a file the number of blocks needed is continually increasing and decreasing. The more work you do with the files, the worse the situation becomes. A file split between six widely spread parts of the hard disk will be slower to load and save than one held in six consecutive blocks. It is for this reason that an operating system often supports a utility called a drefragmentation (defrag) program. This program attempts to reorganise files into sequential blocks and it also puts all the unused blocks together so there is more chance that future files will be allocated sequential blocks.

Because the details of where a file is stored are themselves stored in the FAT, deleting a file is actually very easy – the OS just removes all details of the file from the FAT. Deleting files this way leaves the file itself intact – all you are doing is removing the references to it in the FAT. This means that files can easily be recovered. Many computer users have, at one time or another, been thankful that deleting files merely places them in a recycle bin from which they can be subsequently recovered. In fact the only way to delete the contents of a file is to overwrite it with another file. This goes some way to explain why some companies will not pass on their used computer equipment to second users. Some companies will even go as far as removing and physically destroying the hard disk to make sure that any data that it might still hold cannot be extracted.

Summary
Questions

1 The files in a FAT are held in a hierarchical file structure. What do the terms FAT and hierarchical file structure mean?

2 What are the benefits of defragmenting a hard disk?

The FAT contains details of where the files are physically stored on the disk surface in terms of tracks and sectors (see Chapter 49), but the view that the user sees is governed by the directory structure. This is called a logical to physical relationship.

When a user asks for a file or an application to be loaded it is the job of the file management routines to locate the file, check to see if the file is already in use and make sure the file has not been corrupted.

File buffers

One of the problems with accessing data or program files from a secondary storage device such as a hard disk is that the device will be operating at a much slower speed than the CPU. Every time an item of data is downloaded from the device there is a time delay. One way round this problem is to download more than just the data item the program has requested from the storage device. Instead a whole block of data is loaded into a section of the RAM called a buffer. It is likely that the next item of data that the program requests will be in this same block and because this data is already in RAM the access time will be much faster.

For example, if you are searching through a database for all the references to a particular customer then the computer will probably need to load in all the records one after the other so they can each be checked in turn. Note that the records are not checked on the secondary storage media they are kept on, they have to be loaded into main memory and then checked from there.

Memory management

In the same way that the operating system of a computer controls the way files are stored on a secondary storage system, such as a hard disk, the operating system also controls how the primary memory or RAM is used.

The operating system stores details of all the unallocated locations in a section of memory known as the 'heap'. When an application needs some memory, this is allocated from the heap, and once an application has finished with a memory location or perhaps an application is closed, the now unneeded memory locations are returned to the heap.

When a user asks for a file to be loaded, it is the job of the memory management routines to check to see if enough memory is available and then allocate the appropriate memory and load the file in to those locations.

The operating system controls the use of main memory by creating a memory map, which shows which blocks of memory have been allocated to each task. This way an operating system can control more than one task in the RAM at any one time. The amount of memory needed by each task is dependent on the size of the program itself, the variables that will be needed and any files that might be generated by the task but it is up to the operating system to decide how much space can be allocated.

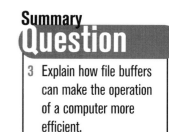

Summary Question

3 Explain how file buffers can make the operation of a computer more efficient.

When the operating system processes a request to load an application or file from the hard disk it is the job of the memory management system to decide whereabouts in the RAM the file will be stored. As you add to a file it is highly likely that the work will need more than one block of RAM. In this case a type of linked list is used to show where each subsequent block is stored.

App 1	File 1	unused

In this stylised example of a memory map, the application, 'App 1', was loaded first and work started on 'File 1'.

App 1	File 1	App 2	File 1	unused

After a while the application 'App 2' is loaded, then work carried on 'File 1'. Because 'App 2' is now in the memory, 'File 1' is now spread across two sections of RAM.

App 1	File 1	App 2	File 1	File 2	File 1	unused

A little work is done using 'App 2' which generates 'File 2', and then work recommences on 'File 1' which is now spread across three sections of RAM and so on.

App1	unused	App2	unused	File 2	unused

'File 1' is now saved and then deleted from RAM, the memory map now looks something like this.

App1	App2	File 2	unused

The operating system might now decide to rationalise this and move the applications and existing files so that all the unused space is put together.

Even with this simple example you can see that managing the memory can be a complex task for the operating system to control.

Virtual memory and paging

In some cases the application or file you are trying to work with will be too big to fit in the available RAM. In this case a process called 'virtual memory' can be used. This involves using secondary storage such as a hard disk to store code or files that would normally be held in RAM. The operating system then treats that part of the hard disk as if it is part of the RAM, hence the name virtual memory.

An alternative method is to hold a 'kernel' or central block of the code in RAM. Other sections of code known as 'pages' are loaded from the secondary storage as and when they are needed. Using this method allows very large applications to run in a small section of RAM. This in turn frees up memory for other applications to use.

A word processor will hold instructions about how to cope with the text itself in the kernel but if the user selects a less commonly used task, such as spell checking or mail merging the appropriate page of the program will be loaded into RAM from the hard disk. This down-loading often causes a noticeable delay in the operation of the application.

Code sharing, re-entrant code and threading

A computer program is described as being re-entrant if it is designed so that one single copy of the program can be shared by more than one user or process. It is possible for more than one copy of the same program to be executed on a computer but this is a waste of resources. It is more efficient to have just one copy of a program being executed but allow different users to be at different points in the one version of the program.

If two or more users or tasks are code sharing in this way, then the CPU will be able to use the same instruction without having to recall it from memory which will make the processing even quicker as the process does not have to be called from RAM. This process of running more than one task through the same software is called multi-threading.

Input/output management

Each input/output device in a computer has its own hardware control unit which can transmit to or receive data from the CPU. Each control unit is able to send a signal called an 'interrupt' to the CPU to indicate that it needs access to the resources on the computer. Each peripheral that is attached to a computer needs a device driver. This program allows the operating system to interact with a peripheral such as a hard disk, a mouse or a printer.

Dynamic link library (DLL)

There are some processes that are common to a large number of applications; for example, most programs use the same routines to save files. Instead of having a block of identical code in each of the applications the code is kept in a dynamic link library (DLL). Access to these DLLs is controlled by the operating system. Accessing code that is stored elsewhere in this way also means that the application programs themselves will not be so large.

Summary Questions

4 Compare virtual memory and paging as a way to execute programs that would not normally fit into the RAM in a computer.

5 Explain how code-sharing and threading allow more than one user to use an application at any one time.

6 Explain what a DLL is and how they are used by the operating system.

Study Question

1. A floppy disk has a stated maximum capacity of 1.44 Mb, but you will not be able to store a file of this size on a floppy. Why not?

Examination Questions

1. (a) How can an operating system allow two files with the same name to be stored on the same floppy disk? [2]
   (b) A computer has a multitasking operating system with a command line user interface.
      (i) What is a multitasking operating system? [1]
      (ii) What is a command line interface? [1]

2. In the context of memory management, explain the following terms:
   (a) virtual memory; [3]
   (b) paging. [3]

   AQA June 2003 Module 4

3. (a) A process is a program whose execution has started but not yet finished.
      Give two reasons why a process might not execute continuously in a multiprogramming environment. [2]
   (b) Distinguish between processes and threads in a multiprogramming environment. [2]

   AQA June 2003 Module 4

CHAPTER:46
Input and output devices

The purpose of this chapter is to identify the range of input and output devices that are available and to identify the most appropriate devices for the user and the application. An explanation of how these devices work is not needed for AS Level. A2 students must understand the principles of operation of these devices and these are covered in Chapter 47.

There is constant flow of new devices coming on to the market all the time. This includes 'peripherals' – devices which are attachments to the main system. As A Level students, you should be aware of the latest trends in input, output and storage technology. Appendix 2 contains information on useful publications and web sites.

Input devices

An input device is any piece of hardware that takes data from the 'outside world' and puts it into the computer.

KEYBOARD

This is the most common device for inputting text into PCs. Most systems use the standard QWERTY keyboard. The extent to which a keyboard is used varies depending on the application. For example, most 'office' applications, such as word processing and databases rely heavily on keyboard entry. This can present problems in that keyboard entry is prone to error. Consequently, validation and verification techniques are used extensively to ensure the integrity of the data.

KEYPAD

This is a variation on the keyboard but used for specific devices such as PDAs, microwave ovens, calculators, alarm systems, and ATMs.

CONCEPT KEYBOARD

Used in specific situations where a standard keyboard is impractical, the 'keys' are touch sensitive areas on a plastic surface. These are typically used in addition to a till in pubs and fast-food restaurants. Rather than having a standard till the concept keyboard is a flat rectangular device which will have icons that represent different products. By pressing the icon, the price of that product is input. They are physically robust and tend to be used in places where a QWERTY keyboard would get damaged.

MOUSE

There are many variations on the mouse. The standard mouse plugs into a serial port and has two buttons. Recently, a third button has been added to provide access to menus and a scrolling wheel allows the user to move up and down a screen page more quickly. There are also infra-red mice that do not need cables and others that reflect a light beam to register movement rather than using a ball. Laptop computers tend to use built-in mouse balls which are basically small tracker balls, or mouse pads so that the user does not have to carry a mouse with them. The mouse is used extensively when operating a graphical user interface (GUI) and is the main input device for navigating the Internet.

SCANNERS

A standard document scanner or flat-bed scanner allows printed text and images to be converted into digital form. A very common use is the inputting of family photographs. However, scanners come in a variety of forms. Hand-held scanners are portable and only have a small scanning area which is passed across the document. Local council employees use these to scan financial documents when they visit pensioners in their homes and need documentary proof of earnings for pensions claims. Scanners of different types are also used to scan bar codes and biometric data and are the underlying technology used in OMR, OCR and MICR technologies described below.

BAR CODE SCANNER

Bar codes are primarily for inputting product details at the point of sale. Typical uses include food, electrical products and books. The patterns of black lines and white spaces represent information about the product. Bar codes on food products are passed over a scanner built in to the checkout. Products that are physically bigger than food items, such as those sold in DIY stores, are more difficult to scan so hand-held scanners tend to be used. There are different classifications of bar codes, the most common being the European Article Number (EAN) which is standard for food products sold in the UK.

BIOMETRIC SCANNER

Biometrics are individual physical characteristics that uniquely identify each individual. A biometric scanner will scan the parts of the body, for example, the eye retina or the fingerprint, and by linking to a database, can identify the individual being scanned.

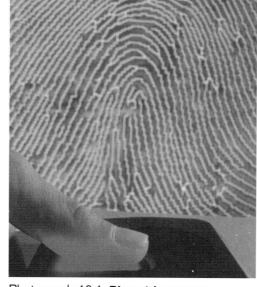

Photograph 46.1 **Biometric scanner**

Biometrics are used where proof of identity is required. For example, they could be used in place of passwords to give users access to computer systems. Alternatively, they could be used to enhance the security of passports or even replace them.

OPTICAL MARK READER (OMR)

Commonly used to collect data from tests and questionnaires, an OMR recognises and inputs marks made on a page. For example, with school tests, students are asked to place their answers onto a marks sheet by drawing small pencil lines into pre-printed boxes. The OMR will scan in the boxes and record where marks have been placed. They are also used to scan national lottery tickets and are used by meter readers to input electricity and gas meter readings.

OPTICAL CHARACTER RECOGNITION (OCR)

Standard scanners with OCR software scan written or printed text and then convert the document into a word-processed document that can then be edited. This is useful if you want to digitise a document that you do not have in electronic form.

LIGHT PEN

Used in conjunction with character recognition software, a light pen or stylus is shaped like a pen and used to 'write' or mark on the screen. The trace of what has been written or drawn is then converted using the software. It is used on personal digital assistants (PDAs) to input text. A PDA has become the accepted term for hand-held computers which used to be known as 'palm-tops'.

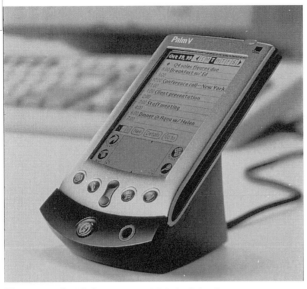

Photograph 46.2 **Personal Digital Assistant**

Doctors in hospital use PDAs and light pens to write patient notes at source rather than having to type them in at a later stage.

MAGNETIC INK CHARACTER RECOGNITION (MICR)

This is similar to OCR and OMR but is used specifically to read characters printed using magnetic ink. The most common application is on bank cheques where various bank details are printed at the bottom of each cheque and then read by a MICR reader.

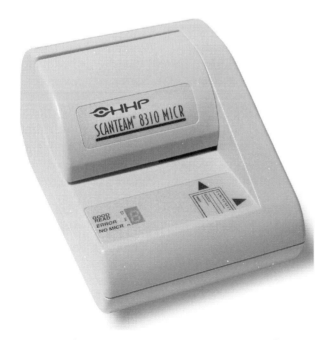

Photograph 46.3 **Combined MICR and magnetic stripe card reader**

MICROPHONE (VOICE RECOGNITION)

The spoken word can be digitised using sampling techniques (as described in Chapter 19) and then converted into text. A number of large software companies have experimented with 'voice recognition' software which will convert the spoken word into text in a word-processed document. This has not been as successful as was predicted as it has proved difficult to write software that reliably recognises and converts continuous speech. There is also a problem with background noise in busy environments such as an office or classroom. Voice recognition is used by some disabled users who cannot use a mouse or keyboard. It is also used in some automated telephone systems where the human voice activates certain options rather than pressing a key on the telephone.

TOUCH SCREEN

A screen is usually considered to be an output device but it can be used for input and output. Touch screens have proved to be popular devices for applications where the user interface needs to be very simple. A common use is in tourist information centres, museums and estate agents where users are given information and asked to press an on-screen button that links them to various choices. It is a useful way of presenting a limited amount of information and the user is only able to make limited inputs by pressing one of the buttons from the choices presented. Another benefit is that they are physically robust and less likely than a keyboard to get damaged or stolen. Some cash terminals use touch screens.

MAGNETIC STRIPE READER

Magnetic stripes are found on the back of plastic cards such as credit cards. Data, such as a bank customer's account number, is stored in the stripe and read when the card is swiped through a 'reader'. For example, an ATM and a till at a supermarket will both incorporate a card reader. There are some concerns over how safe these cards are as the data can easily be read from the stripe with fairly basic home-made equipment. Many application that used to use magnetic stripes are being replaced by 'smart cards'.

SMART CARD READER

These look the same as the magnetic stripe cards but instead of a stripe, they contain an embedded microchip that stores the data. These are more expensive to produce due to the cost of the chip. However, they are more secure as specialist equipment is needed to read them. They can also store much more data than a magnetic stripe and, consequently, can be used for a much larger range of applications. The banks in particular have been keen to introduce smart cards in this country.

One possible application for smart cards is for every individual in the country to carry a card that contains all their personal data. This could include medical details, driving licence, employment details, benefits and tax information. The benefit to the individual is that one card contains all the data that they need so they would only need to carry the one card. However, civil liberties groups are very concerned that this could lead to a national identity card. In some countries, smart cards are already being used in this way. For example, France has health smart cards and many states in the USA use them for driving licences.

SENSOR

Computer-controlled environments receive most of their data via inputs from sensors. For example, an automatic door will open when the infra-red sensor detects an object; a smoke alarm is activated when it senses a change in the air particles. A number of physical factors can be input using sensors including: temperature, light, movement, pressure, acidity, moisture, strain, voltage, wind speed and radiation.

Output devices

An output device is any piece of hardware that gets data from the computer to the 'outside world'.

SCREEN

Also known as the 'monitor' or 'visual display unit' (VDU), the screen is the most common output device for a standard PC, laptop and PDA. Even mobile phones are now using small colour liquid crystal display (LCD) screens. The size of the screen is measured diagonally across the viewable area and 17" is becoming the standard for PC monitors. Some graphics and CAD/CAM packages require larger screens to allow images to be viewed in more detail.

PRINTER

INKJET PRINTERS

These produce good quality printouts. They are relatively quiet in operation and cheap to buy. At the time of writing, colour inkjets range in price from £30 to £350. However, inkjet cartridges are relatively expensive and the speed of printing is slow compared to laser printers. A standard inkjet printer would typically produce four pages per minute but will slow down when producing detailed graphics with large amounts of fill colour. Inkjets are currently the most commonly used printer in the home and are also used in offices and schools.

LASER PRINTERS

These have been reducing in price over recent years and colour versions are available. The cheapest black and white laser is around £100 with colour lasers going up to around £700. They are more expensive than inkjets but print more quickly, typically around 20 pages per minute. They are virtually silent in operation, produce very high quality printouts and the running costs are lower than inkjets. Laser printers used to be found only in larger organisations and businesses who had a requirement to print large volumes of high quality output, for example, businesses that needed to send letters to thousands of customers. However, as the price has reduced, laser printers are now affordable for home users.

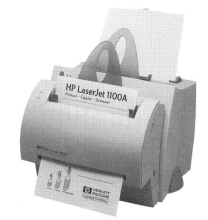

Photograph 46.4 **Laser printer**

DOT-MATRIX PRINTERS

These are still used though it is uncommon to find one in an office or school these days as they are slow, noisy and produce poor quality output compared to inkjet and laser printers. They are 'impact' printers which means that they physically strike the paper.

Summary Question

1 Define the following terms ensuring that the difference between them is made clear:
(a) OCR;
(b) OMR;
(c) MICR.

They are still used where a 'carbon copy' of the print-out is required. For example, when a business prints an invoice for goods that they have sold, they give one copy to the customer and keep one for their own records. For this use, rather than printing it out twice, a dot-matrix printer can use a special paper that has a top copy and a carbon copy behind it. When the pins strike the ribbon, the ink is transferred onto the top copy and the impact creates the carbon copy.

PLOTTERS

These are used to produce specialised printouts such as technical drawings and maps. Most laser and inkjet printers will only produce printouts on A4 or less. Some printers go up to A3 but for anything bigger than that, a plotter is used.

SPEAKER

With an increase in multimedia content on the Internet and on CD-ROM, speakers have become standard devices on work and home systems. The operating system also uses the speakers to provide an audible signal to indicate that certain tasks have or have not been com-

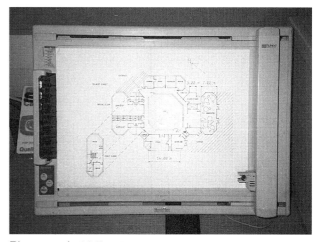

Photograph 46.5   **Plotter**

pleted. For example, Windows will play a tune when it loads and shuts down. Speakers are used in the same way in a number of embedded systems such as microwave ovens and burglar alarm systems.

ACTUATOR

An actuator is any device such as a motor, solenoid switch or pneumatic device that is used as an output by a computer-controlled system. For example, a motor is used to open an automatic door; a solenoid switch is used to switch a central heating system on.

Summary Questions

2 Why might a plotter be used rather than a printer?

3 Identify the most appropriate input and output devices in the following scenarios:
(a) a till used in a pub/restaurant;
(b) an ATM;
(c) flight simulation software.

Study Questions

1. A national fast-food restaurant is in the process of replacing their computer systems at all their outlets. Identify three input and three output devices that they could use, explaining why you think each is appropriate to the scenario.

2. Identify three possible applications that would benefit from voice recognition.

3. Identify two possible problems with the use of OCR software.

4. Provide a detailed comparison of inkjet and laser printers in terms of speed, quality, initial cost and ongoing costs.

5. Suggest three possible practical applications for biometric scanning.

Examination Questions

1. For each of the following appli]ations suggest one suitable input device, excluding keyboard and mouse.

    (a) Desk-top publishing;   [1]

    (b) Sale of goods at a supermarket checkout desk.   [1]

    AQA June 2002 Module 2

CHAPTER:47
Advanced input and output devices

In Chapter 46 we introduced the various input and output devices that are available and discussed the appropriate use of each device. The purpose of this chapter is to identify the concepts behind how the main devices work.

Scanner

Scanner technology is used in a number of different ways. It can be used to scan images and documents; for OCR, OMR and MICR; for bar codes; and for biometrics, such as fingerprint scanning. The principle of scanning is the same regardless of the application:

- **Light is passed over the object. In the case of a flat-bed scanner, a motor is used to move the light source over the whole document.**

- **Light reflected from the object is passed via mirrors and lenses to a 'photosensitive array' which converts light into electrical pulses.**

- **The data is then passed from the photosensitive array to the CPU and into memory where it can be manipulated by scanning software.**

The photosensitive array contains thousands of sensors each of which handles a different portion of the image. An A4 flat-bed scanner will typically use 2500 sensors to provide a black and white image with a resolution of 300 by 300 dots per inch. (Resolution is covered in greater detail in the section on printers).

To scan colour images, the object may be scanned three times: through a red, a green and a blue (RGB) filter. Using light, all colours are created from these three primary colours. Modern scanners will scan for RGB in one pass by splitting out the red, green and blue in the image.

CRT monitor

CRT stands for 'cathode ray tube' and is the same technology used in televisions. In the back of the monitor an electron beam is scanned onto the screen using a technique called 'raster scanning'. This means that the beam scans from left to right in horizontal lines starting in the top left-hand corner and finishing in the bottom right. The beam then starts again in the top left-hand corner.

The screen is made up of thousands of phosphor dots which will hold a charge for a very small amount of time. Each dot is referred to as a pixel which is a 'picture element'. As the beam passes over each dot, it glows. The electron beams scans

Summary
Question

1 Describe how a scanner works.

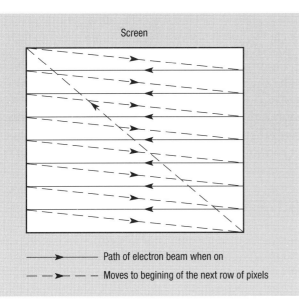

Screen

Path of electron beam when on
— — ▸ — — Moves to begining of the next row of pixels

Figure 47.1 **Raster scan**

the screen at a speed which is sufficient to create a picture from the glow created by the dots. Therefore, the image you see on screen is not a solid image at all, but a combination of thousands of different coloured dots. The number of dots or pixels on the screen determines how clear the image is. For example, increasing the number of pixels leads to a sharper image, whereas reducing the number of pixels creates a more jagged image.

The number of pixels determines the 'resolution' of the screen. Pixels are organised in a grid across the surface of the screen. The resolution is stated as the number of pixels on the horizontal axis by the number of pixels on the vertical axis. A standard screen size of 1024×768 means that there are 1024 pixels along the x-axis and 768 down the y-axis.

Another factor to consider is the physical size of the screen. Screen sizes are quoted in inches and are measured diagonally across the screen. Assuming that the resolution doesn't change as the size of the screen increases, the sharpness of the image will degrade. This is because the same number of pixels are spread across a larger area.

In order to create colour images, three electron beams are used. Each phosphor dot is in fact made up of three further dots, for red, green and blue. The three electron beams control the three colours, mixing them as required to create the desired colour.

Graphical images are stored and manipulated in memory and it is the job of the graphics card to control the display. It is common to assign one byte of memory to each of the three primary colours, red, green and blue. This means that the graphics card is a 24-bit card giving 2^{24} different combinations which represents 16 777 216 different colours.

Liquid crystal (LCD) monitor

Liquid crystal displays are starting to replace CRT monitors as they are thinner and require less power. Originally, they were only found on laptops but the falling manufacturing costs mean that they are now used for desktop computers. An LCD monitor consists of thousands of liquid crystals. A constant light source is provided behind the crystals which is passed through an RGB filter which in combination provide all the necessary colours. Varying degrees of electrical charge are then applied to each crystal which will alter the state of the crystal allowing differing amounts of light to pass through.

Laser printer

A laser printer works in the same way as a photocopier to produce high black and white and/or colour images. It works in the following way:

- **A rotating drum inside the printer is coated in a chemical which hold an electrical charge.**

- **The laser beam is reflected onto the drum and where the light hits the drum the charge is discharged. The laser switches on and off creating the image to be printed.**

- **As the drum rotates it picks up toner which is attracted to the charged part of the drum.**

- **Paper is passed over the drum and by charging the paper, the toner is transferred from the drum to the paper.**

- **The paper is heat treated to 'fuse' the toner onto the paper.**

**Summary
Questions**

2 How many different colours can be created using a 16-bit graphics card?

3 Describe how a CRT monitor differs from an LCD monitor.

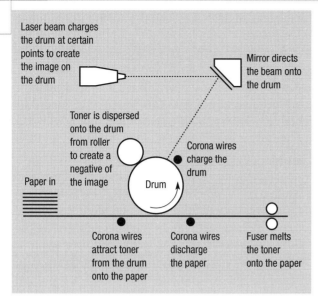

Figure 47.2 **Laser printer**

To achieve colour printing, four different coloured toners are used, and the paper is passed around the drum four times to pick up each colour. Printed colours mix in a different way to light. Using light, creating all possible colours needs three primary colours: red, green and blue (RGB). When printing, four colours are needed: cyan, magenta, yellow and black (CMYK).

Inkjet printer

An inkjet printer, also known as a bubble jet, uses ink cartridges and a printing head. The ink cartridge contains either black, cyan, magenta or yellow ink depending on whether it is a black only, or colour printer. Ink is dispensed onto the page through a tiny print-head which controls the flow and mix of ink

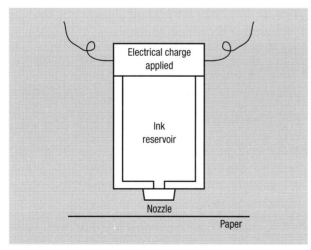

Figure 47.3 **Inkjet printer**

being applied to the page. The flow of ink is controlled either by electrical charge or by applying heat.

The print-head assembly is located on a bar which runs the width of the printer. A motor is used to move the print-head along the bar while another motor moves the paper round the roller. The print-head therefore is running on the x-axis as the paper is running on the y-axis. The print out is coordinated so that the entire page can be printed.

Dot-matrix printer

A dot-matrix printer has a print-head which is made up of a number of pins arranged in a column. The original models had only nine pins, but newer models have 24. The pins strike a ribbon which is soaked with ink and the physical impact of the pins transfers the ink from the ribbon onto the paper.

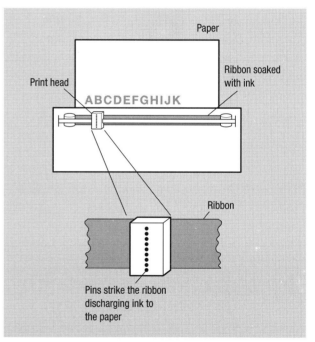

Figure 47.4 **Dot-matrix printer**

Printer resolution

The printer resolution is a measure of the clarity of the printed output. It is measured in dots per inch (dpi). A dpi of 300 means that the printer prints 300 dots per inch. Therefore, in one square inch on the paper there will be 90 000 dots. As the dpi increases, the sharpness of the printout improves. However, the amount of memory required to print the image also increases as resolution gets higher.

Typical printing requirements do not need more than 600 dpi to produce good quality output. The exception to this might be photograph quality print-outs which could be 1200 dpi or 2400 dpi. Some printers use 'dithering' techniques which can produce high quality images from lower resolution printers. Dithering involves printing different combinations of dots so close to each other that they appear to the human eye to mix together to create the desired colour or shade.

Summary Questions

4 What is the purpose of an RGB filter in a monitor or scanner?

5 Millions of colours are created by mixing primary colours together. What are the primary colours used:
(a) for printing;
(b) for visual display on a monitor?

Study Questions

1. Explain how biometric scanning could be used in conjunction with a database as a method of allowing secure access to a building.

2. Toll bridges and roads are becoming a common feature in the UK. Explain how OCR can be used in conjunction with digital cameras and a database to identify vehicles using a toll bridge or road.

3. Biometric scanning can be used on a number of human features. Identify all human features that can be scanned explaining the technical details of how the scanning process takes place.

Examination Questions

1.   'Firemen will be able to respond faster to emergency calls thanks to a system that relays data from the control room computer to the fire engine.' Data that could be transmitted included maps or directions to give the best route to the fire and information about hazardous chemicals that might be stored at the site of the fire. Suggest and justify appropriate devices that could be used effectively in a fire engine cab of this system for input and output. [4]

AEB Summer 1999 Paper 2

2. Video RAM (VRAM) is separate memory on the graphics card, into which the processor writes screen data which is then read to the screen for display. A computer has a colour monitor and 1 Mb of VRAM, and its screen display has been set to a resolution of 1024×1024.

   (a) Exactly how many bytes are 1 Mb? [1]

   (b) What is a pixel? [1]

   (c) (i) What does a resolution of 1024×1024 mean? [1]

   (ii) How many bytes would be available to represent each pixel in the above computer system? [1]

   (iii) How many colours can this computer system display? [1]

   AQA January 2002 Module 1

CHAPTER: Storage devices 48

The purpose of this chapter is to identify the range of storage devices that are available and to identify the most appropriate devices for the user and the application. An explanation of how these devices work is not needed for AS level. A2 students must understand the principles of operation of these devices and this is covered in Chapter 49.

There is constant flow of new devices coming on to the market all the time. This includes 'peripherals' which are devices that are attachments to the main system. As A Level students, you should be aware of the latest trends in storage technology. There is a resources list in Appendix 2 which contains information on useful publications and web sites.

Storage devices are referred to as either primary or secondary storage. Secondary (backing storage) provides permanent storage of data. Primary storage is another term for RAM which is volatile. Storage devices vary in terms of speed of access, storage capacity and cost. It is important that appropriate storage devices are selected based on the purpose for which they are being used.

Floppy disk

A standard floppy disk can store up to 1.44 Mb of data which by modern standards is very small. It is suitable for transferring small files between computers or for creating back-ups. Files that contain images of any sort, such as graphics or photographs, are likely to be bigger than 1.44 Mb so floppy disks are only really used for text- or number-based documents such as word processing and spreadsheet files. It is likely that floppy disks will become redundant in the next few years.

Hard disk

A typical hard disk at the time of writing is 60 Gb. The storage capacity of hard disks has increased enormously in recent years as it has become cheaper to manufacture them. Contained within the computer, they store all the applications and data and provide reliable and relatively fast access to your data. Although it is possible to buy removable hard disks, most hard disks are not portable.

CD-ROM

It is important to distinguish between CD-ROM and other types of CD. A CD-ROM is 'read-only', which means that you cannot write to it. Software is usually supplied on CD-ROM which can store between 650 Mb and 850 Mb of data. It is particularly useful for software, as modern applications often require several hundred megabytes of storage space. The CD-ROM also acts as a back-up allowing the user to reinstall the software if it is lost or corrupted on the hard disk. Access is relatively slow compared to a hard disk which is one of the reasons why software takes a while to install.

The storage capacity of CD-ROMs is sufficient to be able to store large volumes of multimedia data. It is common, therefore, to find reference material supplied on CD-ROM. For example, encyclopedias, atlases and maps, aerial photographs, the census, and the electoral roll are all stored on CD-ROM.

Re-writeable CD

Summary
Questions

1   Identify the most appropriate storage device in the following scenarios. Justify your choice:
(a) creating a back-up of a school network each night;
(b) transferring a document from home to school;
(c) creating a back-up of all the work on a stand-alone computer;
(d) storing a feature length movie;
(e) storing a number of audio files.

This type of CD can have data written to it as well as reading data from it. It is common to refer to 'burning' a CD, which means that data is copied on to it. There are different types of writeable CDs. The main difference between writeable CDs is the number of times that they can be written to. CD-R is a 'recordable' CD which is known as a WORM – write once, read many. This means that data can be only be written to the CD once. CD-RW is 'rewriteable' which means that it can be written to over and over again. Virtually every computer manufactured after 2000 is supplied with a rewriteable CD drive which means that CDs are now being used in the same way that floppy disks used to be.

Digital Versatile Disk (DVD)

DVD works in exactly the same way as a CD. They have become the standard format for films which is why the 'V' is sometimes referred to as 'video'. Although the underlying technology is the same, a separate DVD drive is needed to read from and write to DVDs as the format of the data is different from CD. A standard DVD can store up to 17 Gb of data.

Smart media

There has been a growth in the use of 'smart' media. You will find smart storage devices in your mobile phone in the form of a SIM card. They are also used in digital cameras to store photographs which can then be transferred to your hard disk using a smart card reader. Manufacturers are now producing smart storage in a number of formats including a 'memory stick' which plugs directly into a USB port. Most of these devices use techniques such as erasable programmable read-only memory (EPROM), or electrically erasable programmable read-only memory (EEPROM), which use either ultraviolet light or electricity to write data to memory chips. Some versions of EEPROM are also known as 'flash memory'. Standard storage size for this kind of media at the time of writing is anything from 8 Mb to 1 Gb.

Magnetic tape

Access to data on tape is very slow compared to other storage methods, but tape has the largest storage capacity of any of the portable storage devices. A typical tape could store 120 Gb of data which would be enough to back-up the contents of a typical school or college network. In fact, this is the most common use of magnetic tape as a technician can leave a back-up running overnight.

Medium	Typical storage capacity	Typical uses
Floppy disk	1.44 Mb	Transfer and back-up of small files
Hard disk	10 to 60 Gb	Permanent storage of all software and data
CD-ROM	650 to 850 Mb	Software, games and reference material
CD-R and CD-RW	650 to 800 Mb	Transfer and back-up of all types of data files
DVD	4.7 to 17 Gb	Films and audio
DVD-R	4.7 Gb	Recording films and audio
Magnetic tape	120 Gb	Backups of entire networks; archiving large volumes of data
Flash media	128 Mb to 1 Gb	Transfer and back-up of larger files. Portable.

Study Questions

1. Some computer manufactures are no longer including floppy drives with their new systems. Give two reasons why you think they are taking this course of action.

2. Identify two different types of magnetic storage media and two types of smart storage media.

3. Suggest one suitable use for each of the following storage devices:

(a) floppy disk;

(b) CD-ROM;

(c) CD-R;

(d) Magnetic tape.

4. Zip drives remain popular amongst some users. A typical zip disk can store 100 Mb of data. Why might users prefer this to a writeable CD?

5. Smart media are becoming increasingly popular. Research the devices currently available comparing them in terms of cost, capacity, speed of access and compatibility.

Examination Questions

1. Suggest the most appropriate storage medium for distributing the electronic form of a mail order catalogue through the post. The catalogue occupies 500 Mb of storage space. [1]

AQA January 2002 Module 2

2. Name the most suitable storage medium for each of the following:
   (a) backing-up a 30 Kb file; [1]
   (b) backing-up 2 Gb of data; [1]
   (c) distributing a software package requiring 500 Mb of storage space. [1]

AQA January 2001 Module 2

CHAPTER:49
Advanced storage devices

In Chapter 48 we introduced the various storage devices that are available and discussed the appropriate use for each device. The purpose of this chapter is to identify the concepts behind how the main devices work.

Floppy disk

Inside the outer casing of a floppy disk is a thin brown magnetic material which stores data. The disk spins at around 360 rpm while read/write 'heads' scan the top and bottom surface of the disk and read or write the data. The surface of the disk is organised into concentric tracks and each track is split into sectors each of which can be individually addressed by the operating system.

Each sector has the same capacity and a large file will be stored over a number of sectors. The operating system groups sectors together into 'clusters' to make storage easier to manage. There will be many occasions when a whole cluster is not needed. For example, a file may require five whole clusters and only part of a sixth. In this case, the whole cluster is allocated to the file even though it is not needed. This means that the disk is likely to have redundant space on it.

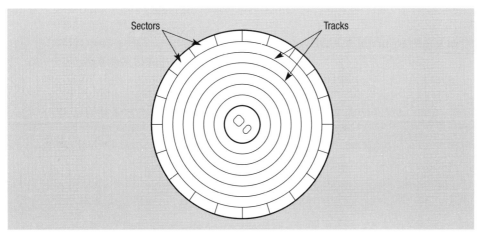

Figure 49.1 **Tracks and sectors on a floppy disk**

Hard disk

Hard disks work in the same way as floppies though they are constructed of hard metallic material and are hermetically sealed inside the computer. This is to protect them from being corrupted by dust or other debris. Many hard disks are in fact made up of a number of disks arranged in a stack.

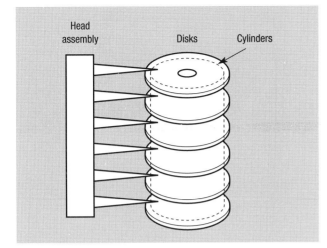

Figure 49.2 **Typical hard disk**

Photograph 49.1 **Hard disk**

Hard disks spin at speeds between 3600 and 12 500 rpm as a series of heads read from and write to the disks. The heads do not actually touch the surface of the disk but float slightly above it by virtue of the speed at which the disk spins. The surface of the disk is split into tracks and sectors in the same way as a floppy disk. However, because the head assembly can read any one of several disks, a cylinder reference is also used to identify which of the disks in the stack is being addressed.

CD/DVD ROM

CD and DVD both use the same technology, which is the use of lasers, to read and write data. A CD is made up of one single spiral track that starts in the middle and works its way to the edge of the CD. The laser will read the data that is contained within this

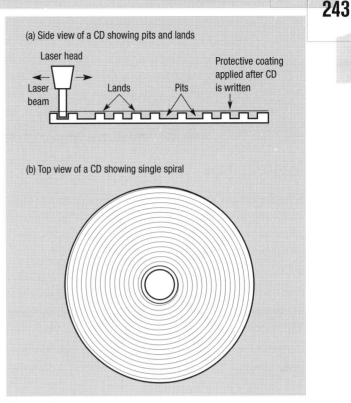

Figure 49.3 **CD**

track. The data is represented using a series of 'pits' and 'land'.

When a CD is written, the laser 'burns' pits into the surface of the CD at a set depth. Therefore, the single track is made up of a series of pits where the laser has burnt and a series of lands where the laser has not burnt. A protective layer is then put over the surface to prevent any corruption of the data. The pattern of pits and lands are used to represent data. When the CD is read, the pits and lands are read by the laser which then interprets each as different electrical signals. In turn the electrical signals can be converted into binary codes.

CD-R and CD-RW

In order to write data to a CD a different type of CD is required. There are two main types:

- **CD-R which is recordable. This means that data can be written to a CD once.**

- **CD-RW which is rewriteable. This means that the CD can be written to over and over again.**

Summary Question

1 Explain the difference between CD-ROM, CD-R and CD-RW.

Both types work in a similar way in that rather than burning pits onto the CD, they alter the state of a dye that is coated onto the surface. The dye reflects a certain amount of light. A 'write' laser alters the density of the dye and a 'read' laser interprets the different densities to create binary patterns which in turn can represent sound or images.

Magnetic tape

Magnetic tape works in the same way as video tape. The tape itself is a brown magnetic material which passes over a head that will read and write data onto the tape.

The surface of the tape is divided into blocks, and files are allocated as many blocks as are needed. The blocks are a fixed size, so there will be occasions when parts of the blocks remain unused.

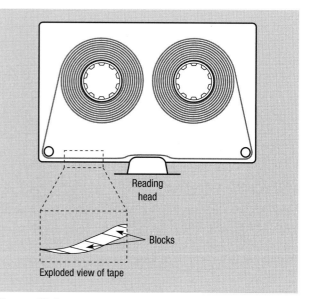

Figure 49.4 **Magnetic tape**

Summary
Question

2 Explain why data stored on a floppy disk is less secure than data stored on a CD.

Magnetic tape provides good value for money in terms of the amount of storage that is available. However, it can only provide serial access, which means that if users need a file that is stored at the end of the tape, they will have to read through up to 120 Gb of data before they can get at it.

means that if you need a particular file, you can access it directly. Magnetic tape is serial which means that files can only be accessed one after the other.

A useful analogy would be comparing video to DVD. With video, if you want to move to a certain scene, you must fast forward or rewind until you find the part you want. DVD is indexed which means you can choose a scene and move directly to it.

Random and serial access

Floppy disks, hard disks, CDs and DVDs all allow random access to the data stored on them. This

Study Questions

1. What are the key differences between the way a CD works and the way a DVD works?

2. How does a mini-CD work?

3. Some people believe that DVD will replace CD and floppy disks completely. Why might this be the case?

4. How much data can be stored on a standard 'smart' media storage device. How does this compare with other media?

CHAPTER:50
The system life cycle

The systems life cycle is the cycle of events that is used to solve computer/ICT-based problems. Definitions of the stages of the life cycle vary and there is no consensus about precisely how many stages there are. A system is more than just the programs that will be needed – it might include the file structures, hardware, operating system and people that will be working with it.

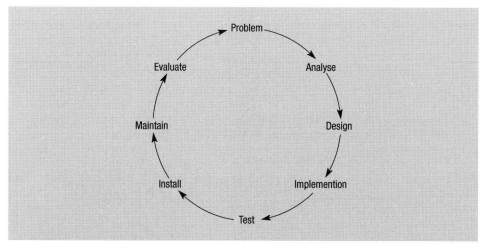

Figure 50.1 **The system life cycle**

Prompts for a new system

There are many reasons for creating a new computer system. Many of these are based on the ever-increasing demands that are made on existing systems and the ever-changing advances in computer technology.

- Some existing systems simply cannot cope with the increased volume of data they are being asked to handle. For example, the way in which a bank maintains its data has changed beyond all recognition in the last 20 years, and banks have spent many millions of pounds updating their systems.

- New technology has meant that existing systems soon become outdated. At one time it took a lot of time and effort to book a holiday. Now it can all be done in real time with the flights you want booked in a matter of minutes.

- The current system may be inflexible. The number of people flying is increasing every year and this has placed pressure on the airport immigration authorities. Computer-readable passports allow immigration far greater control and instant access to details of the person in front of them.

- New technology has created new opportunities. You have only to look at the way the use of the Internet has exploded to realise how many new opportunities such as e-commerce and e-banking there are. Other developments such as computer control and GPS have created other totally new fields. For example, guidance systems in vehicles that can plan routes and advise the driver on details such as where to turn and the estimated time of arrival.

- The current system might be inefficient.

- Commercial reasons. Many new systems are created in order to generate demand from customers. There isn't necessarily a need for a new system but companies introduce them because customers will buy them.

- New operating systems – businesses create new systems to take full advantage of new operating systems. For example, new programs have been written specifically for the Linux OS.

- Increased processing power. The new Intel chip allows wireless networking so new software is written to take advantage of this.

Defining the problem

Having identified that there is a problem with an existing system or perhaps seen a new area that needs developing, it is very important to keep an open mind and concentrate on getting to grips with what the problem involves rather than looking for possible solutions.

This involves identifying the scope of a problem and being realistic about how much of the problem a new system can solve. Any constraining factors may be identified here.

If you are creating a solution for someone else it is important that you agree the specification and scope of the work before you start. In general the more you can involve the end users, the less likely you are to do something they do not want.

METHODS OF GATHERING INFORMATION

If the problem that you are going to tackle is based on an existing system then it may well be worth while investigating how it currently works though there are times when a completely fresh approach to a problem might lead to a better solution. Asking for opinions about a possible new system is a good idea too. There are several ways in which you can gather data about an existing system.

- Interview people that are involved with the current system. This will probably include the systems administrator, the people actually using the system and their customers or clients. Although this can be a time-consuming process, talking to the people that are actually using the existing system will give valuable first-hand knowledge and you can follow up on any comments that they might make. A drawback is that the person you talk to may give you a very personal view of the system.

- Unless it is carefully structured the data collected from an interview can be hard to make use of. Asking someone to fill in a carefully designed questionnaire or carrying out a survey will allow you to carry out a more accurate analysis of the responses, but these tend to restrict the data you gather to definite, closed answers. Questionnaires allow you to gather a lot of data relatively quickly.

Summary Question

1 You have been asked to gather data about an existing system from the employees that use it. You can either interview them or ask them to complete a questionnaire, or possibly even both. Compare the benefits and drawbacks of these two methods.

- Although it can be very time consuming, observation of current practices will help to identify problem areas. It is objective rather than subjective and you may spot something that everyone else has missed.

- Examination of the current system including the files, paperwork and processes used will help to identify the data requirements of the new system. It will also help with the creation of the human–computer interface (HCI) of the new system. This process will also help you to see the overall scope of the problem.

FEASIBILITY STUDY

A feasibility study is a preliminary report to the person that asked for the new system in the first place. It will identify possible solutions and suggest the best way forward.

The report will indicate how practical a solution is in terms of time and other resources, such as the availability of suitable software and hardware and the abilities of the end user to cope with the proposed method of solution.

Possible solutions might include doing nothing, having bespoke software written for you, writing the software yourself or buying an existing package 'off the shelf' and tailoring it to your needs.

MODULAR AND TOP-DOWN

Before work can start on the actual creation of the solution the availability of appropriate hardware and software is assessed. The choice of hardware will be driven by the users' needs and by the way in which data will be manipulated and stored. Work will begin on the file structures and algorithms that are going to be used.

Most big projects are far too big to be considered as one complete problem. The best solution is often to break them down into smaller modules. Each module will be self-contained, and the programmer

will test it on its own. This approach will allow more than one person to work on the solution. Often the view a user has of the system will need to be defined so that all the modules will have the same 'feel'.

The process of looking at a big problem and breaking it down into smaller problems and then breaking each of the smaller problems down, and so on until each problem is manageable is known as the 'top-down' approach. The benefits of this approach are similar to the modular system mentioned above, though there is the potential problem of getting too engrossed in small details such as the fine-tuning of the human–computer interface. It makes more sense to solve the overall problem first before you get too involved in screen layouts.

DATA FLOW DIAGRAM (DFD)

There are a number of ways of representing a problem and its possible solution. A data flow diagram is concerned purely with how data is moved round a system and as such it only needs four symbols.

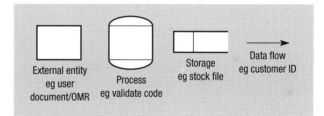

Figure 50.2 **DFD symbols**

The next diagram shows how a DFD might be used. It shows what happens after the electricity meter at a house has been read.

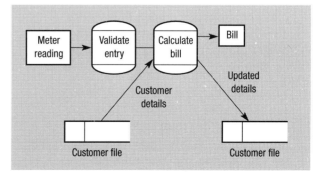

Figure 50.3 **DFD for an electricity meter**

Summary Question

2 What are the benefits of using a top-down approach to solve a problem?

Implementation

Having been through the analysis and design phases of the project it is finally time to implement it. This is the process of creating the fully working system using the appropriate tools identified in the feasibility study. The process of implementing a system is based on the design, and the programmer(s) will need to be fully aware of the requirements set out in the design.

THE HUMAN–COMPUTER INTERFACE (HCI)

The human–computer interface is the term given to any form of communication between a computer and its user. For the majority of us this might seem limited to the computer screen with its familiar graphical user interface (GUI), but it can also include the layout of buttons on a mobile phone or house alarm system and the way information is presented on a VCR or the flight controls of a new aircraft.

Summary
Question

3 What is prototyping?

There are a number of aspects that need to be considered when designing an effective HCI. These include:

- **Ease of use – there is no point creating sophisticated software if the functions are hidden behind a series of screens and button presses. A good HCI will feel almost intuitive.**

- **Target audience – what suits a child might not necessarily suit an adult so it is important that the programmer is aware of who the end user is gong to be.**

- **Technology – there is little point in creating a screen layout that works comfortably on a 17" monitor if the target audience mostly use laptops or PDAs.**

- **Ergonomics – the interface should be 'comfortable' to use. This is important if the user is likely to be sitting with the interface for a long period of time, for example, an airline pilot or a tele-sales operative.**

Prototypes

Creating a solution to a problem can be very costly both in terms of finance and time. There is little point in presenting the end user with a completed project if they are going to ask you to alter various details. In this case it would be a good idea to produce a prototype.

A prototype has all the major functions that are required in a system, but the human–computer interface is likely to be fairly primitive and minor functions that will be present in the completed project may be incomplete. Navigation buttons might not do anything and validation routines are likely to be incomplete but the program does what it is supposed to do. A prototype will only have a limited data set to work with.

At this stage the end user is asked to comment on the product so far, and they will check to make sure all the major functions work as expected.

Testing

It is important that the system is tested to make sure it performs as expected. There are a number of test strategies that can be used.

Test data is data that generates a known result, and test data will need to be devised that tests every aspect of the solution from the expected responses to the extremes that humans can subject a computer program to. As individual units or modules are completed they are tested to ensure they carry out the functions they contain. As the project proceeds modules can be fitted together and at this stage integration testing takes place. This process makes sure that the modules work together. Other aspects of testing will be discussed in the next chapter.

Maintenance

Once the solution has been created and installed it is important that the system is maintained. There are three types of maintenance:

- **Perfective – Although you will expect the solution to function correctly it is highly unlikely that everything will be exactly as the end user wants – there may be a need to** change a range check on a variable, or add a navigation button to move to a different part of the program.

- **Adaptive** – All situations change. There may be a need to add an additional attribute to an entity, or allow the system to input data from a new device.

- **Corrective** – No matter how thoroughly you test your solution there will always be somebody somewhere that will press the buttons or keys in a sequence that your program cannot cope with. Corrective maintenance fixes these unforseen problems.

Evaluation

The final stage of the systems life cycle is the evaluation. The solution that has been created was designed to match the specification that was agreed with the user. An evaluation compares the actual outcome with this specification. It should also con-

tain suggestions for future improvements. It is these improvements and refinements that start off the whole cycle all over again.

Summary Questions

4 Explain why the systems life cycle is a cycle.

5 An evaluation has to be based on some sort of criteria. At what stage of the systems life cycle are the criteria created?

6 After a new system has been installed it is important that it is maintained. Explain the difference between installation and maintenance.

Study Questions

1. Describe five features of a good HCI (human–computer interface).

2. Describe the benefits and drawbacks of using off-the-shelf software, having bespoke software created or writing it 'in house'.

3. Draw a data flow diagram to show what happens when you take money out of your bank account via an ATM. Remember it only shows the flow of data.

Examination Questions

1. Explain why a technical manual might be provided with a new software system. [1]

2. Give three reasons why a software system will require maintenance after it has been implemented. [2]

3. The development of computer-based systems is commonly broken down into a number of stages collectively called the systems life cycle. Briefly describe the following stages of this cycle:
   (a) feasibility study;
   (b) systems analysis;
   (c) systems design;
   (d) implementation;
   (e) evaluation. [5]

   AEB Summer 2000 Paper 2

4. The maintenance of a computer program can take much more time and effort than its initial development.
   (a) State three reasons why a program might require maintenance. [3]
   (b) Apart from documentation, state three techniques of good programming that aid maintainability. [3]

   AEB Summer 1998 Paper 3

5. Software developers use prototyping for different reasons in different situations.
   (a) What is prototyping? [1]
   (b) Briefly explain two reasons for using prototyping. [2]

   AEB Summer 1998 Paper 2

6. A library loans system identifies each book in its stock by a unique BookID. The BookID is encoded in a bar code and attached to the book. When a borrower returns a book it is scanned and any fine that is due is calculated by extracting from the library database the date that the book was due back. Copy and complete the given data flow diagram that describes this part of the library system. [5]

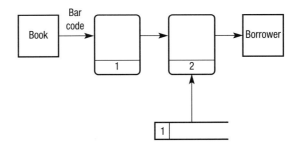

AQA June 2002 Module 5

7. A company is replacing its existing paper-based data processing system with a more modern computer based system. After consultation, two alternative methods for converting from the old to the new system are proposed.

    (a) What is meant by:

        (i) Phased conversion?   [1]

        (ii) Parallel conversion?   [1]

    (b) State two tasks that may have to be carried out when converting from the old to the new system.   [2]

CHAPTER:51
Advanced systems development

Data dictionary

It is important that the programmer decides at an early stage what data will be used and how it will be stored. Careful planning at this stage will reduce the number of problems that will be encountered later in the project.

Details of the data to be stored, including the data type, length, title and any validation checks, will be stored in a data dictionary. This can be seen as a database about the database – it hold background details but not the data itself. This diagram shows part of the definition of a table in Microsoft Access. This forms part of the data dictionary that defines the whole solution.

Field Name	Data Type	Description
CustomerID	AutoNumber	
Surname	Text	max length 30
Forname	Text	max length 20
Date of Birth	Date/Time	dd/mm/yy
Height (cm)	Number	between 150 and 210

Figure 51.1 **Data dictionary definition of a table**

Variable tables

It is important to decide what variables a program will need and what purpose they will serve. Some programming languages will only let the programmer use variables that have been declared. Declaring variables at the start of the program allows the programmer much tighter control of their program. The programmer will need to decide about certain characteristics of the variable – type, length, name and whether the variable is local or global. This example shows how three global variables might be set up in Visual Basic.

```
Public Age As Integer
Public Name As String
Public WearsGlasses As Boolean
```

Summary
Question

1 Explain why it is important for a programmer to define the variables they intend to use before they start writing the code itself.

In Chapter 50 we met the concept of using blocks or modules to make a project more manageable. Allocating names to these procedures and defining local variables used within them is also best carried out at this stage.

Volumetrics

The volume of data that a system will be asked to handle both now and in the future will have a bearing on how the programmer decides to store and handle the data. They will need to consider the throughput of data – how many transactions the system will need to cope with in a given time span – and also how much data the system will need to store at any one time. This will affect the storage media that is used, and it will also be a consideration when back-up strategies are being decided.

The programmer will also need to consider how many users will be allowed to access the files and programs at one time.

It is important to realise that the databases that most students see in their time at school or college are generally small. Even a pupil database in a school with 1200 pupils is very small compared to the high street banks that have literally millions of customers each with hundreds of fields of data stored about them. The computers used by the DVLA store details of well over 20 million cars which means the planning needed for this project is very different to planning how the secretary of a swimming club will store their data.

Testing strategies

The importance of testing was discussed in the previous chapter. The aim of this section is to look at the various testing strategies that can be employed during the development of a project. There are two phases to testing. The first involves tests that are carried out during the development of a project and the second testing that is carried out once the solution has been created.

A lot of these processes make use of test data. Test data is data that will generate a known response.

DEVELOPMENT TESTING

- **Black box testing involves entering test data into a routine or** procedure and checking the resulting output against the expected outcome.

- **White box testing involves testing every aspect of a routine or procedure. Whilst black box testing is concerned with testing the data handling, white box testing considers all the other processes that are involved – for example, how, the program reacts if it fails to find a suitable printer; what happens if buttons are pressed in the wrong sequence; and so on.**

- **Unit testing is making sure each unit carries out the function it has been designed for. It will incorporate both black box and white box testing.**

- **Once all units have been tested, they are put together to form bigger sections. Integration testing is the process of making sure that the different modules that have been tested as individual units will work together.**

SYSTEM TESTING

System testing involves testing the system as a complete unit rather than as individual modules and making sure that it satisfies the specification agreed with the user.

Alpha testing is carried out on the finished system. This involves creating test data 'in-house'. This test data will try to cover all the possible eventualities, so it will allow the system to be tested under 'normal' conditions. The benefits of this process are that any problems that are found can be rectified before true 'live' data is used by the end user. Another benefit of using a known set of test data is that if necessary the system can be stopped and restarted.

Some program developers will release an early or 'beta' version of their new program to their potential users. At this stage the software is bound to

Summary Questions

2 What is meant by the term 'volumetrics'?

3 Explain the difference between white box and black box testing.

have 'bugs' in it and the users are expected to send details of the problems they have encountered back to the programmers for them to resolve. This process is known as beta testing.

The benefits of this system are that passing your software to a number of people that have not been involved with the development will mean the testers will all use the system in slightly different ways and so highlight faults that might not have been found by normal means.

Although the developers will test the system they have developed as thoroughly as possible it is the end-users that need to be satisfied that the solution does what they wanted it to. Acceptance testing is carried out by the intended user. They enter their own 'live' data and make sure the system matches the specification that was agreed with the program writers.

Some problems may only come to light some time after the system has been implemented by the user. These might include issues involving the volume of data the system is asked to cope with. Problems such as these will be resolved as part of the systems maintenance.

Implementation – Conversion methods

Many new computer systems are, in fact, new versions of old, existing systems. This means that when the new system is finally ready for use it has to take over from the old system in some way.

There is a lot of work involved in introducing any new system whether it is computer based or not. Data has to be converted to work on the new system, hardware might also have to be updated and staff may have to be trained how to use the new system. There are a number of strategies for dealing with this:

- **Pilot implementation involves running a full-sized version of the new system, but with only a limited amount of data. For example, a mail-order company may only put new customers on the new system,** and transfer existing customers as and when they place an order. This would mean running both the old and the new systems alongside each other as existing customers are migrated across.

- **Direct implementation needs very careful planning. The concept is that you stop using the old system on one day and start up with the new system the next. If you are converting to a new computer system, then you may have no choice, but there is a definite element of risk with this method. If anything should go wrong with the new system then it would be almost impossible to go back to the old one. There would also be a need for considerable staff training before the change over and ongoing support after the event. There might also be problems with data that is held on the old system but is not on the new. It might be possible to start up with just enough to make the system viable and gradually add more features as time goes on.**

- **Parallel implementation involves running the old and the new systems alongside each other. This is a strong fail-safe method – if something goes wrong with the new system you can always revert to the old, but it is obviously very costly to run both systems at the same time, especially if staff are trying to get to grips with the new system. It also means that all the data has to be processed twice – once on the old then again on the new.**

- **Phased implementation involves introducing one section of the new solution at a time then checking it is working as expected before introducing another section. This sounds like a good idea, but often this is just not practical –**

circumstances will often mean that you cannot follow an ordered plan.

Support

Once the new system has been handed over to the users there are bound to be some initial problems, and as the users get used to the new system and begin to explore the functions of the system other problems will come to light as well. There are a number of ways in which the users can get help.

- **Training** – Some software companies will carry out training sessions. This human contact allows the users to ask questions that might be unanswerable by any other means, but training can be very expensive whether it is carried out on-site or at the software company's premises.

- **User manual** – Most modern systems still come complete with a user manual. This should explain what the system requirements are, how to get started and how to use the various functions. There might also be some sort of troubleshooting section. The good thing about a printed manual is that it is truly portable and users often find it easier to flick through pages in a book than on a web site. The low cost of CDs means that many companies supply a help system on CD so that they can use multimedia.

- **Technical manual** – this will give details that will allow a programmer to adapt a package to their own needs. As the name suggests, it will include technical details such as variable names and details of the file structures that have been used.

- **Internet** – An increasing number of companies are putting their help resources on a web page. The benefits of this are that every time a new problem occurs, a solution can be added to the web pages. That way customers can access the very latest solutions.

- **Help desk** – A help desk allows a user to talk to a real person and so they can explain their problem in their own words. Some help line systems allow the helper to access the new system remotely so they can either resolve the problem or show the other person how to solve the problem.

- **Interactive/built in** – Most modem software has built-in, interactive, context or problem-sensitive help routines. The program can recognise whereabouts in the program the problem has occurred, what has gone wrong and report back to the user with suitable solutions.

Study Question

1. A company has developed an electronic system for registering pupils in a school. Draw up a table comparing the pros and cons of the various methods of delivering support for this program.

Examination Questions

1. Name two manuals supplied with a large software system. [2]

2. Several testing strategies are used during the software development stages of a new system. Integration testing is one example. Name one other that can be used. [1]

3. A company is developing a new version of its data storage system. For the following testing methods, briefly describe at which stage of the development of a new software system each occurs.
   (a) black box testing; [1]
   (b) integration testing; [1]
   (c) acceptance testing. [1]

4. Some software developers make their core software available free of charge whilst others charge their customers. Give three reasons why developers might not charge users. [3]

   AEB Summer 2001 Paper 3

5. A large secondary school is updating its computer network. The new network is going to be installed in four classrooms in a new purpose-built building, and the old computers will be passed on to a charity. The new network will include recent developments in both hardware and software.
   (a) Once the hardware and software have been chosen, briefly describe three tasks which need to be carried out when implementing the new system. [3]
   (b) What changeover method is appropriate in this situation? Explain how your method would be applied and justify your choice. [3]

   AEB Summer 2001 Paper 2

CHAPTER:52
Machine architecture

The central processing unit (CPU) is what most people would call the computer itself – all the decisions are made here and all the instructions that come from any program that the computer is executing, including the operating system, must be processed by the CPU.

The CPU consists of a number of units which all have to act together to make the computer function correctly. The principle components and the part they have to play in the running of the computer are set out below.

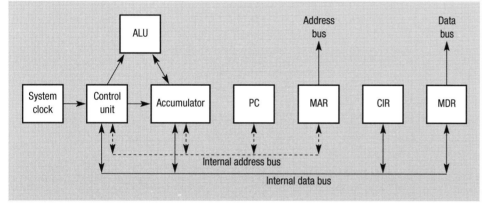

Figure 52.1 **Machine architecture – the CPU**

The control unit

The control unit is the part of the CPU that supervises the machine code cycle – the fetch, decode and execute. The control unit also makes sure that all the data that is being processed is routed correctly – it is put in the correct register or section of memory. The 'fetch-decode-execute' cycle was introduced in Chapter 4 and it is described in more depth in the next chapter.

The arithmetic logic unit (ALU)

The ALU carries out two types of operation – arithmetic and logic.

The ALU can be used to carry out the normal mathematical functions such as add, subtract, multiply and divide, and some other less familiar processes such as 'shifting'. This process is explained in Chapter 56.

The ALU is also used to compare two values and decide if one is less than, greater than or the same as another. Some comparisons will result in either 'true' or 'false' being recorded.

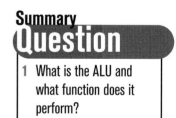

Summary
Question

1 What is the ALU and what function does it perform?

The ALU is sent an 'operation code' (op-code) and the operands (the data to be processed). The ALU then uses logical operations such as OR, AND and NOT to carry out the appropriate process. In some computers a separate arithmetic unit (AU) is used to cope with floating-point operations.

The clock

All computers have an internal clock. The clock generates a signal that is used to synchronise the operation of the CPU and the movement of data around the other components of the computer. Generally speaking each phase in the 'fetch-decode-execute' cycle takes one pulse of the clock to be executed though some complex instructions will take more.

Some users state the clock speed as a measure of the performance of their computer but there are other factors, such as bus width, which also need to be taken into consideration, not least of which is just how efficiently the CPU can make use of the clock pulse. There is no point fitting a faster clock to a computer if you do not change the components that are going to make use of that pulse as well. A better way to increase the performance of a computer would be to increase the 'bus width' – the number of bits that can be transferred in one go along the various system buses.

The speed of a clock is measured in either megahertz (MHz – millions of cycles per second) or gigahertz (GHz – 1000 million cycles per second). In 1990 a clock speed of between 4 and 5 MHz was the norm. In 2000, 1 GHz clock speeds were common. The speed of the system clock has been doubling roughly every 18 months.

Registers

The control unit needs somewhere to store details of the operations being dealt with by the 'fetch-decode-execute' cycle and the ALU needs somewhere to put the results of any operations it carries out. There are a number of storage locations within the CPU that

are used to store this sort of data. They are called registers and although they have a very limited storage capacity they play a vital role in the operation of the computer.

A register must be large enough to hold an instruction – for example, in a 32-bit instruction computer, a register must be 32 bits in length. Some of these registers are 'general purpose' but a number are used for a specific purpose.

- **The status register keeps track of the status of various parts of the computer – for example, if an overflow error has occurred during an arithmetic operation.**

- **The interrupt register is a type of status register. It stores details of any signals that have been received by the CPU from other components attached to the CPU, for example, the I/O controller for the printer. We will be looking at the role of interrupts in Chapter 54.**

There are four registers that are used by the CPU as part of the 'fetch-decode-execute' cycle:

- **The current instruction register (CIR) stores the instruction that is currently being executed by the CPU.**

- **The program counter (PC) stores the memory location of the next instruction that will be needed by the CPU.**

- **The memory data register (MDR) holds the data that has just been read from or is about to be written to main memory.**

- **The memory address register (MAR) stores the memory location where data in the MDR is about to be written to or read from. We will be taking a closer look at what addressing is all about in Chapter 55.**

Perhaps the most important register of all is the accumulator.

The accumulator plays a key role in the operation of a program. It is the only truly 'live' memory location in the whole computer. All the other registers and

Summary Questions

2 Explain what the clock in a computer does.

3 The CPU has access to many registers. What is a register?

4 The control unit uses four registers to control the execution of a program. They are the CIR, PC, MAR and MDR. Explain what each of these is and the part it has to play in the execution of a program.

RAM are used to hold data – they can have data taken from them or new items of data can overwrite what is already there. The accumulator is the only memory location that can have its contents modified rather than overwritten. If the CPU writes to any other register, its contents will be overwritten – what was already in the register will be lost. All calculations must, at some stage, pass through the accumulator. More details about how the accumulator is used can be found in Chapter 56.

Examination Questions

1.   (a)   What is a register in a computing context?   [1]

      (b)   Give one reason for using general purpose registers rather than main memory.   [1]

      (c)   Some registers are used in the processor for a specific reason. Name three such registers and explain the purpose of each use.   [3]

AQA June 2002 Module 4

2.   (a)   Explain how each of the following can lead to faster execution of instructions:

         (i)   modifying the width of the data bus;   [1]

         (ii)   altering the clock rate.   [1]

CHAPTER:**53**
The 'fetch-decode-execute' cycle

In order for a program to be executed the machine code instructions that make it up have to be processed. This processing is carried out by the CPU and is known as the 'fetch-decode-execute' cycle. The 'fetch-decode-execute' cycle is carried out once for each machine code instruction.

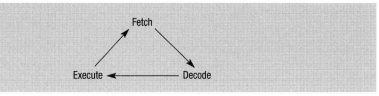

Figure 53.1 **The 'fetch-decode-execute' cycle**

How the cycle works

Before you read through the next section you need to make sure you know what the program counter (PC), the current instruction register (CIR), the memory address register (MAR) and the memory data register (MDR) do. An explanation of these four registers can be found in the previous chapter.

Fetch

The PC holds the address of the next instruction. The CPU sends this address along the address bus to the main memory. The contents of the memory location at that address are copied to the CIR and the PC is incremented. The CPU will not always know whether it is loading data or part of the code from the program so all details of addresses are initially loaded into the MAR and the data initially goes to the MDR.

Some instructions need to load a number of bytes or words, so they may need to be fetched as successive parts of a single instruction.

Decode

The CPU then takes the instruction from the CIR and decides what to do with it. It does this by referring to the 'instruction set'. These instruction sets are either classed as a RISC (reduced instruction set) or a CISC (complex instruction set).

An instruction set is a library of all the things the CPU can be asked to do. Each instruction in the instruction set is accompanied by details of what the CPU should do when it receives that particular instruction. This might be to send the contents of the MDR to the ALU or to load the accumulator with the contents of the MDR, and so on.

Execute

Once the instruction that has just been taken from the memory has been decoded, the CPU now carries out the instruction.

It then goes back to the top of the cycle and fetches the next instruction. A simple instruction will require only a single clock cycle whereas a complex instruction may need three or four. The results of any calculations are written either to a register or a memory location.

A worked example

The following program adds two numbers together. The code has been written in pseudo-assembly code to make it easier to follow, but this would have to be converted into machine code for the CPU to be able to use it.

200	MVI	Acc 4	loads the value 4 into the accumulator
203	STD	129	stores the contents of the accumulator at address 129
205	MVI	Acc 7	loads the value 7 into the accumulator
208	ADD	129	adds the contents of location 129 to the accumulator
210	STD	130	stores the contents of the accumulator at address 130

In order to start executing the program the program counter (PC) is loaded with the address of the first command – in this case 200.

200 MVI Acc 4

Fetch   CPU takes the value 200 from the PC.

The command 'MVI' (move immediate) is loaded via the MDR into the CIR.

The operands 'Acc' and '4' are fetched and placed in the MAR.

PC is incremented to 203.

Decode   CPU takes the content of the CIR and looks up what to do in the instruction set.

Execute   CPU now 'knows' it has two operands – the address to load data to and the data itself, and places the value '4' in the accumulator.

The command MVI has now been completed so the CPU goes to the PC for the location of the next instruction (203).

203 STD 129

Fetch   CPU goes to location 203 and reads the command 'STD' (store direct) and places this in the CIR.

CPU fetches '129' and places it in the MAR.

PC is updated to 205.

Decode   CPU takes the content of the CIR and looks up what to do in the instruction set.

Execute   CPU takes the value contained in the accumulator and places a copy at the memory location stored in the MAR – in this case 129.

205 MVI Acc 4

This line of code is almost identical to the first. Once it has been carried out the PC contains 208 and the accumulator 7.

208 ADD 129

Fetch   CPU goes to the PC for the location of the next instruction (208).

CPU goes to location 208 and reads the command 'ADD' (add direct) and places this in the CIR.

CPU fetches '129' and places it in the MAR.

PC is changed to 210.

Decode   CPU takes the content of the CIR and looks up what to do in the instruction set.

Execute   CPU now 'knows' it needs to add the contents of memory location 129 to the accumulator.

CPU reads the value 4 from memory location 129.

Sends value 4 and content of accumulator (7) to the ALU and tells it to add them together.

Result from the ALU is placed in the accumulator.

The command ADD has now been completed so the CPU goes to the PC for the location of the next instruction (210).

210 STD 130

Fetch   CPU goes to location 210 and reads the command 'STD' (store direct) and places this in the CIR.

CPU fetches '130' and places it in the MAR.

Decode CPU takes the content of the CIR and looks up what to do in the instruction set.

Execute CPU takes the value contained in the accumulator and places a copy at the memory location stored in the MAR – in this case 130.

As you can see this is a very complex process, and all this program does is add two numbers together.

CHAPTER: Interrupts 54

The CPU in a computer is always working irrespective of whether there is an application active or not. This is because the operating system, which is itself a large collection of programs, is always active. This means that the 'fetch-decode-execute' cycle is always in use. If an error occurs or the user wants the computer to start doing something else then we need some way to grab the CPU's attention. The way to do this is to send an interrupt. An interrupt is a signal sent to the CPU by a program or an external source such as a hard disk, printer or keyboard.

There are a number of different sources of an interrupt. These are some typical examples:

- a printer sends a request for more data to be sent to it;
- the user presses a key or clicks a mouse button;
- an error occurs during the execution of a program, for example, if the program tries to divide by zero or tries to access a file that does not exist;
- an item of hardware develops a fault;
- the user sends a signal to the computer asking for a program to be terminated;
- the power supply detects that the power is about to go off;
- the operating system wants to pass control to another user in a multitasking environment.

How the interrupt works

What happens is that an additional step is added to the 'fetch-decode-execute' cycle. This extra step fits between the completion of one execution and the start of the next. After each 'execution' the CPU checks to see if an interrupt has been sent by looking at the contents of the interrupt register.

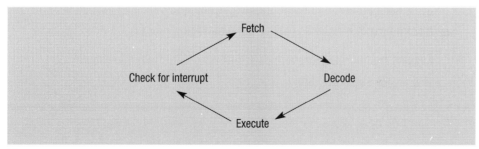

Figure 54.1 **The 'fetch-decode-execute' cycle with interrupts**

If an interrupt has occurred the CPU will stop whatever it is doing in order to service the interrupt. Most interrupts are only temporary so the CPU needs to be able to put aside the current task before it can start on the interrupt. It does this by placing the contents of the registers, such as the PC, CIR and accumulator, on to the system stack. Once the interrupt has been processed the CPU will retrieve the values from the stack, put them back in the appropriate registers and carry on.

Priorities

Sometimes the program that has interrupted the running of the CPU is itself stopped by another interrupt. In this case the CPU will either place details of its current task on the stack or it will assess the priority of the interrupts and decide which one needs to be serviced first.

Assigning different interrupts different priority levels means that the really important signals, such as a signal indicating that the power supply is about to crash, get dealt with first.

This table shows some of the processes that can generate an interrupt, and the priority level that is attached to that interrupt. Level 1 is the highest priority, 5 the lowest.

Interrupts with the same priority level are dealt with on a first-come first-served basis.

Vectored interrupt mechanism

Once the values of the registers have been dumped to the stack, the CPU is then free to handle the interrupt. This can be done using a technique called a 'vectored interrupt mechanism'.

Each interrupt has an associated section of code that tells the CPU how to deal with that particular interrupt. When the CPU receives an interrupt it needs to 'know' how to find that code. Every type of interrupt has an associated memory address known as a vector. This vector points to the starting address of the code associated with each interrupt.

So when an interrupt occurs, the CPU identifies what kind of interrupt it is, then finds its associated interrupt vector. It then uses this to jump to the address specified by the vector.

Summary Questions

1   Why are the contents of the registers put on the stack before an interrupt is processed?

2   Why is it important that different types of interrupts have different priorities?

3   Explain how the 'vectored interrupt mechanism' works.

Level	Type	Possible causes
1	Hardware failure	Power failure – this could have catastrophic consequences if it is not dealt with immediately so it is allocated the top priority.
2	Reset interrupt	Some computers have a reset 'button' or routine that literally resets the computer to a start-up position.
3	Program error	The current application is about to crash so the OS will attempt to recover the situation. Possible errors could be variables called but not defined, division by zero, overflow, misuse of command word, etc.
4	Timer	Some computers run in a multitasking or multiprogramming environment. A timer interrupt is used as part of the time slicing process.
5	Input/Output	Request from printer for more data, incoming data from a keyboard to a mouse key press, etc.

Study Question

1. Some of the major causes of interrupts are listed in the chapter. Find out about other causes of interrupts and try to decide what priority level you would give each.

Examination Questions

1. (a) Define an interrupt.   [1]
    (b) Describe how an interrupt from a printer is handled   [3]

2. (a) Describe the vectored interrupt mechanism.   [3]
    (b) How does this mechanism make the use of interrupts more flexible?   [1]

AQA June 2003 Module 4

CHAPTER: **55**
Addressing modes

In order to access anything that is held in memory you need to know its address. The address is a number that tells the computer where in memory to go to find a specific item of data.

You might visualise the memory of a computer as a vast set of pigeon-holes, each with its own name or address. There are several ways in which you can access these addresses, either to put data in or to take it out. These methods are called addressing modes. Incidentally you cannot 'take' data from an address – you can only copy what is already at that address.

Each address mode will need its own assembly language mnemonic to carry out the same basic process. It is important to realise that each assembly language has its own codes. You can read more about assembly language in Chapter 56.

Immediate addressing

Calling an 'immediate' address an address is rather misleading because the number that is going to be loaded into the accumulator doesn't actually need fetching at all. A command such as **ldaa #12H** would place the hexadecimal number 12 (18 in base 10) directly into the accumulator. In this particular example the **#** symbol tells the CPU that it is to load a number (not an address) and the H on the end of the number tells the computer that this is a hexadecimal number. You might use an immediate address if you wanted to start a count from a set point or if you wanted to store a constant.

Direct addressing

Using a direct address mode tells the CPU which address contains the data you want to access. So **ldaa 100** would load the accumulator with the contents of memory address 100.

A problem with using a direct address is that the number of memory locations that can be directly addressed is limited by the size of the address bus. If the bus is eight bits wide, then only 256 (2^8) addresses can be accessed directly and they would have to be locations 0 to 255. Even with 16 bits you can still only address 65 536 memory locations directly.

Another potential problem is that the number of bits allocated to a direct address is sometimes less than the address bus width of the computer.

Summary
Question

1 Explain why direct addressing can only access a small area of the computer's main memory.

Indirect addressing

Like direct addressing, indirect addressing points to a particular memory location. Unlike direct addressing the memory location that is pointed to does not contain the data you want, but another memory address. The CPU then uses this new address to locate the data it needs.

So **ldai 132** would point the CPU to memory location 132. The CPU would then read the number stored at location 132 and use the number it found there to identify the address of the data item. The benefits of this are that the same location can be used to point the CPU to other locations within the main memory.

You could use this mode to read the data from a sequence of adjacent addresses. The address of the first location could be stored in 132, then after this has been read, the value in 132 is incremented so that the next time 132 is accessed the CPU looks at the next memory address on.

Displacement addressing

Direct and indirect addressing have an inherent problem in that they can only address a limited range of addresses. One way round this problem is to supply the computer with an address and an offset or displacement.

This system works by looking in an address or a register for a starting point then adding on the offset.

The mnemonic **ldx** is generally used for displacement addressing. **ldx** has two operands. There are two very similar ways of carrying this out.

INDEXED ADDRESSING

Index addressing uses two operands. The first points to an index register. The contents of this register are then added to the second operand to generate an address. The command **ldx R1 32** indicates that the starting point is stored in the 'index register' **R1** and that **32** must be added to the contents of the register to generate the address of the data that is needed.

This system is used when only small numbers need to be added to the register. Indexed addressing would be used to address the elements of an array. The index address points to the start of the array, and the second operand is used to locate a particular element within that array structure. The index value tends to be small and changes frequently.

BASE REGISTER ADDRESSING

Base register addressing uses nearly the same method as indexed addressing. The only difference is that the register used to store the 'root' is called the 'base register'. The value stored in the base register rarely changes during the execution of a program. This method is used to access the variables used in a program.

Summary Questions

2 Explain the difference between direct and indirect addressing.

3 Explain the difference between indexed and base register addressing.

Examination Questions

1. **(a)** Describe each of the following addressing modes:
   (i) immediate addressing; [1]
   (ii) direct addressing; [1]
   (iii) indexed addressing. [1]

   (b) Storage locations 120 onwards hold the values as shown below.

120	1
121	2
122	3
123	4
124	5
125	6

   The following instructions are part of a program. If the accumulator and register X both initially hold the value zero, what value would each hold after each instruction in the program is executed? [4]

   (i) `LDX#5`   ;load immediate 5 into register X
   (ii) `LDA#120`   ;load immediate 120 into Accumulator
   (iii) `ADD 120`   ;add direct 120 into Accumulator
   (iv) `ADD X (120)` ;add indexed 120 into Accumulator

   AQA January 2003 Module 4

2. Storage locations 99 and 145 contain the values 145 and 256, respectively.
   (a) What value would the accumulator hold after each of the following instructions has been executed? (The instructions are to be executed one after the other.)
   (i) LDA #99   load immediate 99;
   (ii) ADD 99   add direct 99;
   (iii) ADD (99)   add indirect 99. [3]

   (b) If register X holds the value 10, in which storage location would the final answer be stored after the following instruction has been executed.
   STA 99(X)   store relative 99 [1]

   AQA January 2002 Module 4

3. Distinguish between indexed addressing and base register addressing in machine code, and give one example of the use of each. [2]

4. Explain base register addressing and its role in a multiprogramming operating system. [5]

   AEB Summer 1999 Paper 3

CHAPTER:56
Assembly language instructions

The fundamentals of assembly languages were discussed in Chapter 5. The aim of this chapter is to take a deeper look at the code itself. The assembly code used in this chapter is not based on any specific assembly language.

A typical assembly language statement consists of four parts. Here is a typical example.

```
Reset MOV    Acc    45        'store acc in 45'
```

Label

The label is the left most item – in this case 'reset'. The label can serve two purposes. It can be used to help identify sections within the program, and it can also act as a pointer to show where a jump command might move to.

Operation code

The operation code, or op-code as it is more commonly called, is shown as a mnemonic consisting of two, three or four characters. The mnemonic usually uses letters that help to explain what the command does. For example, ADD, MOV and JIZ translate into 'add', 'move' and 'jump if zero'. There are more details about operation codes later in this chapter.

Operands

The number of operands following an operation code and the way they are interpreted depends on the sort of code it is. For example the command MOV must be followed by two operands – the first identifies the memory address or register that is to be accessed and the second the data that is to be put there.

In the MOV example, the second operand is an immediate address.

Comments

The comment part of the statement is optional. Assembly language programs can be hard to follow. The one-to-one relationship between assembly language and machine code means that assembly language programs tend to be very long, so being able to add comments makes them easier to understand.

Our example has a label called reset, the mnemonic is a move command, and this particular 'move' entails putting the value 45 into the accumulator.

Summary Questions

1 What is an operation code?

2 Some, but not all, operation codes are followed by one or more operands.
   (a) What is an operand?
   (b) Why does the number of operands vary from one operation code to the next?

3 A programmer can add both labels and comments to an assembly language instruction. Explain the purpose of these two features.

Types of operation codes

The operation codes of an assembly language can be placed in one of four groups: data transfer, arithmetic operations, logical operations, and branch operations.

DATA TRANSFER

These include commands (such as the one detailed in the example above) that move data between the registers and main memory. Typical instructions include Move, Store and Load.

ARITHMETIC OPERATIONS

Apart from the four normal arithmetic functions – add, subtract, multiply and divide – this section also includes the increment (increase by one), decrement (reduce by one), negate (reverse the sign) and shift instructions. The status register is used to record certain features of a calculation. These include if the calculation has generated an overflow error or if the result is zero or negative.

Shift instructions are used to move the bits within a register. Shifts can move bits either left or right.

LOGICAL SHIFT

A logical shift can be used to extract the content of just one bit. This is achieved by repeated shifting until the bit you want is put in the carry bit.

If this bit pattern

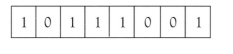

is operated on with a shift right then it becomes

4 Give an example to illustrate each of the following types of operation code:
(a) data transfer;
(b) arithmetic operation;
(c) logical operation;
(d) branch operation.

5 For each of the following instructions state whether it is a data transfer, arithmetic operation, logical operation or branch operation.
(a) compare two values;
(b) load data from a register;
(c) multiply the content of the accumulator by a given number;
(d) check to see if a variable has become zero;
(e) save data to memory.

The least significant bit (the right-hand most) is placed in a carry bit; in this case it is a 1, and a 0 is placed in the most significant bit (left-hand most).

ARITHMETIC SHIFT

An arithmetic shift can be used to multiply or divide a number. Shifting all the bits one place left has the effect of multiplying by two, shifting one place right will divide by two.

This works in the same way as the logical shift, but the sign bit (the most significant bit) remains unaffected. In the example the original sequence, when arithmetically shifted right

1	0	1	1	1	0	0	1

becomes

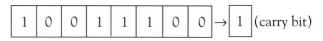

as all the bits shift right one place (except for the sign bit).

LOGICAL OPERATIONS

This includes the logical functions AND, OR and NOT. These can be used to compare values. They can also be used to mask out or ignore the contents of some of the bits in a byte.

For example, if you want to check to see if the two least significant bits in a byte are set to 1 you could check the value of the byte ANDed with 3. If this returns a value of 3, then both bits are set to 1. This works because the value of 3 in an 8-bit binary byte is 00000011 and ANDing would force the six most significant bits to be ignored.

BRANCH OPERATIONS

Without the ability to 'jump' all assembly programs and by extension all high-level languages, would have to be linear. There are a number of ways you can create a branch or jump.

A JMP command carries out an unconditional jump round a section of code. This means that there are no conditions attached so the jump will take place regardless of any prevailing conditions.

Conditional jumps take the form of 'Jump if Zero', 'Jump if Negative', and so on. The value stored in the accumulator will determine if the jump is executed or not. This is where the labels come in. This line of assembly language will force the program to jump to the line with the label 'reset' attached to it.

```
JIZ reset
```

All the complex structures that are taken for granted in high-level languages such as arrays and iterative routines can be constructed from these basic operation codes. Using a high-level language hides a lot of the complex nature of the assembly language.

Sample assembly language code

There are a number of problems associated with writing an assembly language program. They tend to be long and not very user friendly and because they are CPU-specific, assembly code that works on one computer might not necessarily transfer to another.

The following block of code causes a very short delay whilst the accumulator 'counts' from 0 to 100. Note how the program uses both immediate and direct addressing (details of which can be found in Chapter 55).

This code will have to be translated into machine code by an assembler before it can be executed.

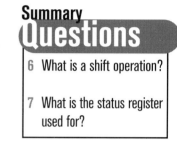

Summary Questions

6 What is a shift operation?

7 What is the status register used for?

Label	op-code	operand(s)		Comment
Start	MVI	R1	0	put the value 0 in register R1 – immediate address
Loop	LDD	Acc	R1	load the accumulator with the contents of R1 – direct address
	ADI	Acc	1	add 1 to the contents of the accumulator – immediate address
	MVD	R1	Acc	copy the contents of the accumulator to R1 – direct address
	SUI	Acc	100	subtract 100 from the accumulator – immediate address
	JIN	loop		jump if negative – If the accumulator is negative then jump to the line labelled 'loop'. Note how this operand is a label on an earlier statement.

Examination Question

1. Write a sequence of assembly language instructions, with annotation, which
    correspond to the following high-level language code: [5]

```
x ← 0;
Repeat
  Do x ← x + 1;
Until x=10
```

CHAPTER:57
Documenting a major project

Selecting a project

The information given in this chapter relates specifically to the documentation required for AQA A2 coursework. All of the main exam boards require students to undertake a major piece of coursework. For AQA, this module accounts for 20 per cent of the total A level mark. This coursework involves working through the stages of the systems life cycle (described in Chapter 50) in the production of a solution to a chosen problem. The student is expected to identify a realistic problem with a real end user and the system created must allow interaction with the user and involve the storage, manipulation and output of data. Most projects are completed in a programming language or in a database package.

The exam board does not accept any programs or solutions on disk. Therefore, the documentation that is produced must be sufficient to prove that the system created works fully and meets the user's requirements. You should also note that marks are awarded for 'quality of communication' which includes good use of English as well as good presentation.

Choosing a problem

Considerable thought should be given to the choice of project. Many students choose problems that are either too easy or too hard and as a consequence, they do not give themselves the opportunity to score highly in this area. AQA students must have a real end user and this is sometimes the hardest part of the project. Try to find a user who you can speak to throughout the project rather than just at the beginning and end.

- **Start with your close family and see if there is anything they do on which you could base a project. For example, you could choose something based on their work.**

- **Many students base projects on their own work experience placements particularly if they still have contacts at the organisation.**

- **Another source of projects is your own hobbies and interests. You may be able to create systems for clubs or societies that you are involved in.**

You should also base your choice on the tools and skills that you know are available in your centre, and on your level of expertise with different software. For example, it is easier to produce your coursework using a database package such as Microsoft Access or Lotus Approach and you will probably find that there is more help available on these packages than with a programming language. Solutions that use programming languages such as Visual Basic, C++ or Java may prove more difficult to produce but often lead to much better solutions.

The following is a sample of project ideas that have been used successfully in recent years:

- Stock control and ordering system for a pub.
- Stock control and invoicing system for a computer shop.
- Booking system for a holiday company.
- Booking system for a dentists' surgery.
- System for recording GP prescriptions.
- System for recording exercise programs in a gym.
- System for tracking investment performance for a shares syndicate.
- Team selection systems for sports teams, for example, football, cricket.
- Membership management systems for sports clubs, for example, golf, tennis.
- System for generating school reports.
- Student timetabling system.
- Fantasy league systems, for example, football, basketball.

It is worth noting that the best projects are often the most realistic. It is much better if there is a real problem rather than a pretend one. Don't be scared to do something original even if it is very specific in what it will do. Examiners see hundreds of library systems and video shop databases every year so they know what to expect and will spot errors easily.

Analysis

This is possibly the hardest part of the project as it involves identifying and interviewing a real user. If your user has a genuine problem that needs solving then this section is much easier as they will provide much of the information you need. Your analysis should include:

- General background information on the organisation or person you are creating the system for.
- A description of the problem.
- An interview or questionnaire involving the user.
- Source documents from the current system.
- Observation of the existing system.
- A list of the user's requirements and any limitations.
- A list of general and specific objectives that are realistic, achievable and measurable.
- A feasibility study with full justification of the chosen solution.
- Data flow diagrams (DFDs) for the existing and proposed system using recognised methods.
- Entity relationship models if a relational database is being made.

Design

AQA do not require full designs of every button, form, report, etc. It is often sufficient to supply a sample of your designs to prove that you have the skills – check with your exam board.

This section should include:

- The overall system design, perhaps in the form of a top-down design diagram or a system flow chart. Database solutions should include a description of the database structure and the entity relationship model.
- A description of the main modules that will make up the system.
- A table that describes every item of data that will be stored in terms of its name, field type and length and any special formatting including use of validation techniques.

- An explanation of the storage medium that will be used and the file organisation and processing involved.

- Explanation of the main calculations that will be used. It may be appropriate to use pseudo-code.

- A sample of rough designs of inputs and outputs including forms and reports. You should not use screen grabs of the finished system.

- A sample of data that will be input.

- An explanation of the data validation techniques to be used.

- A sample of output either on-screen or printed.

- An explanation of measures for system and data security and integrity.

- A test strategy to include valid, invalid and extreme data as well as a whole system tests.

- Evidence that the user has been consulted and their opinions acted upon. It is preferable to show stages of development and any changes made as a result of user feedback.

Technical solution

You must include enough evidence to prove that you have fully implemented the design. This will vary depending on whether you have used a programming language or a database project. It is sufficient to use the same evidence here as that supplied in the maintenance section and it must include:

For a program:

- Annotated code from the program.

- Annotated macro listings.

- A list of variables including variable type and purpose and whether they are local or global.

- Samples of annotated screens showing forms, buttons and reports.

- Output – either screen grabs or hard copy.

For a database package:

- Annotated print-outs of tables, forms, relationships, queries and reports.

- A list of macros which could include any customisation of VBA code (don't claim credit for package-generated code).

- Annotated QBE screen grabs to explain queries (don't claim credit for package-generated SQL).

- Ensure that you have customised your solution as much as possible and provide evidence of this customisation (don't rely on the wizards).

System testing

You should refer back to the test plan produced in the design section. There must be evidence that the tests have been carried out. Use screen grabs or actual print-outs as evidence.

This section should include:

- An overview of the test strategy including an explanation of the valid, invalid and extreme test data used. There should also be some 'whole system' tests that prove that the original objectives of the system have been met.

- Evidence that tests have been carried out including annotated hard copies.

- Cross-referencing of the evidence to the original test plan.

- All possible outcomes should be tested.

Systems maintenance

Your project only requires you to work through the systems life cycle once. In reality, there may be a version 2 and 3 and so on. Therefore, you must provide enough documentation to allow someone else to take control of your project in order to maintain and extend it. You are not expected to explain how to use the language or package itself. However, you must:

- **Summarise the features of the package you have used.**

- **Provide one or two samples of the algorithm design using pseudo-code.**

- **Provide a commented code listing.**

- **Where a package was used – print out the forms, queries, tables, relationships and reports in design view and annotate them.**

- **Where a program was used – print out the procedures and variables and the forms and macros.**

User manual

This must be a stand-alone document and only needs to be four or five pages long. It is not necessary to produce a full user guide covering every part of the system. Instead, you should produce a detailed sample for one part of your solution. It is designed for a user who has not used the system before and must be written in a style that is appropriate to their level of ability.

The manual should include:

- **A brief introduction to your software.**

- **Screen grabs of the main components with explanations of how to use the system.**

- **Clear instructions of how to use the system.**

- **Samples of error messages and error recovery routines.**

Appraisal

It is important to be honest about whether the project has been a success or not:

- **Copy the original objectives that you wrote in the analysis section. Go through each and explain**

whether you met the objective. If you met the objective, explain how and if you did not meet the objective, explain why not.

- **Give your user a chance to use the system and ask them for general and specific comments. Don't invent the user feedback – it will be obvious.**

- **Address the user feedback explaining how you may incorporate any changes they have requested.**

- **Based on these comments and your own opinions, identify any ways in which the system could be improved or enhanced.**

General advice on projects

The A2 coursework is a major undertaking if you want to get a good mark. Students who do well with coursework tend to get the best A level grades overall. It's a comforting feeling when you go into the exam to know that you already have a good mark in your coursework. The reverse is also true – a poor coursework mark leaves you with a lot to make up in the exam room.

Students who do well in coursework:

- **Plan the project well.**

- **Stick to deadlines.**

- **Ask their teachers lots of sensible questions.**

- **Have a copy of the AQA specification.**

- **Use the AQA project log.**

- **Have a real user.**

- **Consult with the user throughout the project.**

- **Have an interest in the problem they have chosen to solve.**

- **Work on the project outside lesson time.**

APPENDIX: 1
Communications and networking look-up table

Section 4 splits into five main topics: communication methods, local area networks, wide area networks, the Internet and the World Wide Web. Many of the concepts covered fall under more than one topic heading. For example, 'broadband' is covered under communication methods but is also a feature of the Internet. Each concept is covered under the most appropriate topic heading and this table is provided to help you identify which other topic headings each concept relates to.

Chapter reference	Concepts covered	Main topics				
		Communication methods	Local area networks	Wide area networks	Internet	World Wide Web
20 Communication methods	Serial and parallel transmission	✓				
	Baud rate, bit rate and bandwidth	✓	✓	✓	✓	
	Synchronous and asynchronous data transmission	✓	✓	✓		
	Start and stop bits	✓				
	Handshaking and protocols	✓	✓	✓	✓	
	Odd and even parity	✓				
21 Networks	Introduction to networks		✓	✓		
	Wide area network (WAN)			✓		
	Local area network (LAN)		✓			
	Network topologies		✓			
	Network adapter		✓			
	Modem	✓		✓	✓	

Appendix: 1 **Communications and networks look-up table**

Chapter reference	Concepts covered	Communication methods	Local area networks	Wide area networks	Internet	World Wide Web
22 Advanced networks	Baseband and broadband	✓	✓	✓	✓	
	Circuit switching	✓		✓	✓	
	Packet switching	✓	✓	✓	✓	
	Datagram virtual circuit	✓		✓	✓	
	Asynchronous transfer mode (ATM)	✓		✓		
	Protocols	✓	✓	✓	✓	
	Layers of TCP/IP	✓		✓	✓	
	Sockets	✓	✓	✓	✓	
23 Advanced local area networks	Cable types	✓	✓	✓	✓	
	Hubs	✓	✓			
	Segments	✓	✓			
	Bridges	✓	✓			
	Ethernet	✓	✓			
	Client–server networks		✓	✓	✓	
	Peer-to-peer networks		✓	✓	✓	
24 Advanced wide area networks	Electronic data interchange (EDI)			✓		
	Value added networks (VAN)			✓		
	Cable modem	✓		✓	✓	
	ISDN	✓		✓	✓	
	Asymmetric digital subscriber line (ADSL)	✓		✓	✓	
	CODEC			✓	✓	✓
	Video conferencing			✓	✓	
	Inter-networking	✓			✓	

Chapter reference	Concepts covered	Main topics Communication methods	Local area networks	Wide area networks	Internet	World Wide Web
25 The Internet	Internet service providers (ISP)				✓	✓
	On-line service providers				✓	✓
	Uniform resource locator (URL)				✓	✓
	Domain name				✓	✓
	IP address				✓	✓
	Intranet		✓		✓	
26 Advanced internet	The World Wide Web (WWW)				✓	✓
	Web browsers				✓	✓
	Internet registries and registrars				✓	
	Hypertext transfer protocol (HTTP)				✓	
	File transfer protocol (FTP)				✓	
	Telnet				✓	
	Usenet				✓	
27 Advanced web sites	Web page construction and HTML					✓
	Organisation of web pages on a web site	Java and applets				✓
	Active server pages (ASP)					✓
28 Advanced uses of the World Wide Web	E-mail				✓	✓
	Internet relay chat (IRC)					✓
	On-line shopping and banking					✓
29 Advanced issues on the Internet	Firewall		✓	✓	✓	
	Encryption		✓	✓	✓	
	Digital certificates					✓
	Moral, ethical, social, and cultural issues		✓	✓	✓	✓

APPENDIX 2:
Resources

The resources listed will be useful to teachers and students. Web resources given may have changed since publication.

Books

British Computer Society. *Glossary of Computing Terms* (Tenth Edition 2002), Addison Wesley.

Ray Bradley. *Understanding Computer Science for Advanced Level* (Fourth Edition 1999), Stanley Thornes.

Journals

Computing	Computing industry journal
Computing Weekly	Computing industry journal
On-line	Weekly supplement in The Guardian (Thursday)
Wired	Weekly supplement in The Telegraph (Tuesday)

Web sites

www.AQA.org.uk	AQA exam board web site which includes the full specification for computing AS and A2 and Chief Examiners' Reports and Mark Schemes from previous exams.
www.bbc.co.uk	Follow the technology links for the latest technological news.
www.bcs.org.uk	British Computer Society website includes their code of conduct and various links.
www.cw360.com	Computer Weekly's website. Very good for up-to-date case study material with a searchable archive.
www.dataprotection.gov.uk	Information on the Data Protection Act and Freedom of Information Act and other data protection issues.
www.homeoffice.gov.uk	Information on Acts of Parliament including the RIP Act.
www.Howstuffworks.com	Good section on computers. Particularly good on input, output and storage devices.
www.ost.gov.uk	Office of Science and Technology. Useful for identifying current trends in the use of new technologies and their impact on society and the economy.
www.pito.org.uk	Details of use of computing and ICT within the Police Force.
www.unicode.org	Official web site of the Unicode consortium.
www.w3.org/MarkUP/Guide/	Getting started guide to HTML.
www.webopedia.com	On-line encyclopaedia of computing terms.
www.whatis.com	Searchable site for definitions and links. Particularly good on networking and communications terms.
www.wombat.doc.ic.ac.uk/foldoc	On-line dictionary of computing terms supported by Imperial College, London.

APPENDIX 3:
AQA GCE Computing Specification 2004

AS Module 1 – Computer Systems, Programming and Network Concepts

10.1 Fundamentals of
     Computer Systems

Hardware and Software	Candidates should understand the relationship between hardware and software and be able to define both.
Classification of Software	Candidates should be aware of how software is classified. They should be able to explain what is meant by system software and application software.
System Software	Operating system software Utility programs Library programs Compilers, assemblers, interpreters
Application Software	Candidates should be able to describe the different types of application software. General purpose applications software Special purpose applications software Bespoke software
The generation of Bit Patterns in a Computer	Explain the different interpretations that may be associated with a pattern of bits. Bits, bytes Concept of a word Program and data
Internal Components of a Computer	Outline the basic internal components of a computer system. (Although questions about specific machines will not be asked it might he useful to base this section on the machines used at the centre.) Processor, main memory, address bus, data bus, control bus, I/O port, secondary storage, their purpose and how they relate.
Functional Characteristics of a Processor	Describe the stored program concept whereby machine code instructions stored in main memory are fetched and executed serially by a processor that performs arithmetic and logical operations.

10.2 Fundamentals of Programming	
Generations of Programming Language	
First generation – Machine code	Describe machine code language and assembly language. Some discussion of the development of programming languages and the limitations of both machine code and assembly language programming would be useful
Second generation – Assembly language	
Third generation – imperative high-level language	Explain the term 'imperative high-level language' and its relationship to first and second generation languages.
Types of Program Translator	
Assembler Compiler Interpreter	Define each type of language translator and illustrate situations where each would be appropriate or inappropriate
Features of Imperative High-Level Languages	
Data types Built-in/User defined	Illustrate these features for a particular imperative, third generation language.
Programming statements Type definitions Variable declarations Constant definitions	Describe the use of these statement types.
Procedure/Function declarations Assignment Iteration Selection Procedure and function calling	Explain the advantages of procedure/functions.
Constants and variables Procedure and function parameters.	Explain the advantages of named variables and constants. Describe the use of parameters to pass data within programs.
Fundamentals of Structured Programming	Candidates should be familiar with the structured approach to program construction and should be able to construct and use structure charts when designing programs, use meaningful identifier names, procedures/functions with interfaces, use procedures that execute a single task, and avoid the use of GoTo statements. Candidates should be able to explain the advantages of the structured approach.
Abstract Data Types Binary tree Stack Linear queue	Candidates should be able to recognise and use these in very simple ways. They will not be expected to have knowledge of how to implement these in a programming language. Uses of these should include a binary search tree and using a stack to reverse the elements of a linear queue.

Data Structures

One and two dimensional arrays	Candidates should be familiar with each of these and their uses.
Simple Algorithms	Candidates should understand the term algorithm and be able to hand trace simple algorithms.

10.3 Fundamentals of Information and Data Representation

Relationship between Data and Information

Data	Explain the term data.
Sources of data	Consider sources of data, both direct and indirect.
Meaning of the term Information	Consider data as an encoded form of information and information as any form of communication that provides understandable and useful knowledge to the recipient.

Number Representation Systems

Binary number system	Describe there presentation of unsigned decimal integers in binary. Perform conversion from decimal to binary and vice versa.

Pure binary representation of decimal integers

Binary-coded decimal (BCD) representation	Describe the representation of unsigned decimal integers in binary-coded decimal. Perform conversions from decimal to BCD and vice versa. Explain advantages of BCD.

Information Coding Schemes

ASCII EBCDIC Unicode	Describe standard coding systems for coding information expressed in character form and other text-based forms. Differentiate between the character code representation of a decimal integer and its pure binary representation.

Representing Images, Sound and other Information

Bit-mapped graphics Vector graphics	Describe how bit patterns may represent other forms of information including graphics and sound.

Sampled Sound

Sound Synthesis

Analogue and digital signals	Differentiate between analogue and digital signals.
Analogue to digital converter (ADC)	Describe the principles of operation of an analogue to digital converter.

10.4 Communication and
Networking

Communication Methods

Serial data communication Parallel data communication	Define both serial and parallel methods and illustrate where they are appropriate. Consider the effect of distance on the transmission of data.
Baud rate, bit rate and bandwidth	Define these terms. Differentiate between baud rate and bit rate. Consider the relationship between bit rate and bandwidth.
Asynchronous data transmission	Define
Start and stop bits	Describe the purpose of start and stop bits in asynchronous data transmission.
Odd and even parity	Explain the use of parity checks.
Handshaking in parallel data transmission and meaning of the term protocol	Explain what is meant by a protocol in this context.
Modem	Describe the purpose and the method of operation of a modem.

Networking

Network	Define these networking terms.
Local area network (LAN) Bus, Ring and Star topologies Wide area network (WAN) The Internet Intranet Network adapter Leased line networking Dial-up networking	Candidates should be familiar with LAN topologies but will not be required to know details of their operation. Candidates should be aware of the advantages and disadvantages of each LAN topology. Candidates should be able to compare local area networking with stand-alone operation.
Uniform Resource Locator (URL)	Describe the term URL in the context of Internetworking.
Domain names and IP addresses	Explain the terms domain name and IP address. Describe how domain names are organised.

AS Module 2 – Principles of Hardware, Software and Applications

11.1 Applications and Effects

A study of one Major Information Processing Application of Computing	Consider the purpose of the application. Discuss the application as an information system in the context chosen. Examine specific user interface needs. Examine the communication requirements of the application. Discuss the extent to which the given system satisfies both the organisation's and users' needs. Discuss the economic, social, legal and ethical consequences of the application.

General Purpose Packages

Database, spreadsheet, word processing,	Candidates should have experience in using a database and a spreadsheet package as part of their skills' development. In addition,
Desktop publishing, presentation package, e-mail	they should be aware of how the listed packages facilitate the execution of particular tasks. Candidates should be able to assess the suitability of a given package for a particular task as well as its limitations.
Social, Economic and Ethical Consequences of Current Uses of Computing	Discuss the social and economic implications for an individual in relation to employment, government, education and leisure. Discuss issues relating to privacy in the context of electronic mail and data. Consider the impact of encryption technology on the privacy of the individual, organisation and the state.
Legal Implications of the Use of Computers	Discuss issues of ownership of information and programs, and protection of data. Consider current legal controls on computerised data and programs and the implications of current legislation.

11.2 Files and Databases

File Types

Text and non-text (binary files) file	Define a file. Describe the meaning of the terms, text and non-text files.
A file as a collection of records	
Records and fields (data items), primary and secondary key field	Illustrate how key fields are used to locate and index heterogeneous records.
Fixed and variable length records	Describe the use of fixed and variable length records. Consider the advantages and disadvantages of each.
File structure	Define what is meant by the structure of a file.
File size	Calculate the size in bytes of a given file.
File Organisation	
Serial	Describe the organisation of these files.
Sequential	Explain hashing.
Direct access	
File Processing	Explain the principle of master and transaction files and methods used to retrieve, insert, edit and delete data.
Security and Integrity of Data in a Data Processing Environment	
The meaning of the terms Security Integrity	Define these terms.
File Security Methods	
Backing up strategies Encryption	Describe hardware and software protection of online files against unauthorised access and system failure.

Data Processing Integrity Methods	Explain how corrupted data can be detected and prevented using techniques such as batch totals, control totals, hash totals, check digits, virus checking, parity checking, check sums.

Database Concepts

Data sharing Data consistency Primary key Alternate key/ Secondary key Indexing Secondary index	Consider a database as an integrated collection of non-redundant, related data accessible from more than one application and stored in different record types together with a mechanism for linking related records. Consider how data inconsistency may arise in an application based on a separate file approach and how this is avoided in a database approach. Consider why indexing is used and how databases support multiple indexes.
Validation	Describe typical built-in validation controls.
Relational Databases	Explain the concept of a relational database. Define the term attribute.

Querying a Database

Querying by Example (QBE)	Illustrate the use of QBE to extract data from several tables of a relational database.

11.3 Operating Systems

Role of an Operating System

Provision of a virtual machine	Candidates should understand that the role of the operating system is to hide the complexities of the hardware from the user.
Resource management	In addition, it manages the hardware resources in order to provide for an orderly and controlled allocation of the processors, memories and I/O devices among the various processes competing for them.

Operating System Classification

Batch Interactive Real time Network	Define each type of operating system and explain their operational characteristics.

File Management

File Filename Directory Directory structure Logical drives	Define the terms File, Filename and Directory. Describe the use of directories. Explain the relationship between the root directory and subdirectories and the use of pathnames.
Access rights Backing-up Archiving	Explain the term access rights in the context of file management. Distinguish file backing-up from archiving.

11.4 Hardware Devices

Input and Output Devices	Consider how the application and needs of the user affect the choice of input and output devices. Candidates should be able to make appropriate selections based upon knowledge of the usage of contemporary devices. Principles of operation will **not** be required.

| Secondary Storage Devices | Explain the need for secondary storage within a computer system and discuss the difference between archived data and directly accessible data. Compare the capacity and speed of access of various media including magnetic disk and tape, optical media and CD-ROM storage. Give examples of how each might be used. |

AS Module 3 – Practical Systems Development

12.1 Systems Development

The Classical Systems Life-cycle

| Problem definition / problem investigation / feasibility study, analysis, design, construction / implementation and maintenance | Describe the stages of development and maintenance of a hardware/software system including evaluating the operational, technical and financial feasibility of developing a new system. The importance of testing the specification, design and implementation. The importance of evaluating the effectiveness of the implemented solution in meeting the users' needs. |
| Evaluation | |

Analysis

| Methods of gathering information
Data flow Diagrams | Describe methods of deriving the user and information requirements of a system and its environment. Evaluate the feasibility of a computer-based solution to a problem, specify and document the data flow and the processing requirements for a system to level one and identify possible needs for the development and maintenance of the system. |
| Entity-Relationship Diagrams | Produce a data model from the given data requirement for a simple scenario involving two or three entities. |

Design

Modular and top-down design Pseudo-code Simple algorithm design	Specify and document a design that meets the requirements of the problem in terms of human–computer interface (usability and appropriateness), hardware and software, using methods such as structure charts, hierarchy charts, pseudo-code, relations.
Prototyping	Define prototyping.
Human–Computer Intertace	Examine and document specific user interface needs.
Testing Strategies	Dry run testing. Unit testing. Integration testing. Identify suitable test data. Test solution.
Construction/Implementation	Make use of appropriate software tools and techniques to construct a solution to a real problem.
Maintenance	Understand the need for and nature of maintenance. Understand how technical documentation aids the process of maintenance.
Evaluation	Evaluate methods and solutions on the basis of effectiveness, usability, and maintainability.

A2 Module 4 – Processing and Programming Techniques

13.1 Machine Level Structure, Operation and Assembly Language Programming

Structure and Role of the Processor

Arithmetic Logic Unit, Accumulator and Control Unit, Clock	Explain the role and operation of a processor and its major components. Explain the effect of clock speed, word length and bus width on performance.
General purpose and dedicated registers.	
Machine code and processor instruction set. The Fetch-Execute cycle and the role of registers within it.	Explain how the FE cycle is used to execute machine code programs including the stages in the process with details of registers used.

Processing Concepts

Interrupts in the context of the FE cycle.	Define an interrupt, showing how it might be used within the computer system and its effects. Describe the vectored interrupt mechanism.
Addressing modes including direct, indirect, immediate, indexed and base register addressing.	Describe the various modes of addressing memory and justify their use. Examples from actual machines might be useful.
Assembly language instructions and their relationship to machine code, memory addressing and use of the registers.	Describe the nature and format of assembly language statements. Illustrate their use for elementary machine operations.

13.2 Programming Concepts

High-Level Languages

The characteristics and classification of high level languages	Examine the characteristics and use of a number of high-level languages, (including both declarative and imperative) for developing applications.
Choice of programming languages to develop particular applications	Discuss criteria for selecting programming languages for particular tasks.
Programming Paradigms	Candidates should have practical experience of at least one programming paradigm and should have knowledge of and reasons for the range of paradigms referenced in section 13.2. Candidates should be aware of the application areas for which particular paradigms are best suited.
Imperative and declarative languages	Distinguish between programming language types and generations.

Structured programming
techniques

Procedural–oriented
programming

Object-oriented
programming

Candidates should be familiar with the concept of an object, an object class, encapsulation, inheritance, polymorphism and containment, and event-driven programming.

Logic programming

Candidates should be familiar with the concept of logic programming for declaring logical relationships.

Data Structures

Lists
Trees
Queues – linear and circular
Stacks
Pointers

Candidates should be familiar with the concept of a list, a tree, a queue, a stack, a pointer and be familiar with the methods (data structures) for representing these when a programming language does not support these as built-in types.

Linked lists.

Distinguish between static and dynamic structures and compare their uses.
Use of free memory, heap and pointers.

Standard Algorithms

Linear search
Binary search
Bubble sort
Tree traversal algorithms
Stack, queue and list operations
Creating and maintaining linked lists.

Describe, using algorithms or programming examples, the methods used by programmers when manipulating structured data. Discuss methods used in relation to efficiency criteria. Candidates should be aware of the link between choice of algorithms and volume of data to be processed. Describe the creation and maintenance of data within lists, trees, stacks, queues and linked lists.

Recursive Techniques

Illustrate the use of recursive techniques in both procedural and logic programming languages.

13.3 Data Representation in Computers

The concept of number bases denary, binary and hexadecimal

Describe the conversion of a denary number to binary form and vice versa. Describe the conversion of a denary number to hexadecimal form and vice versa. Describe the use of hex as shorthand for binary.

Number Representation

Integer and real numbers

Draw a distinction between integers and reals in a computer context. Describe how an unsigned real number is represented in fixed-point form in binary.

Representation of negative numbers by Two's Complement

Describe the use of Two's Complement to perform subtraction. Convert denary number into Two's Complement and vice versa.

Floating point number

Describe the format of floating point numbers including the concept of mantissa and exponent and the need for normalisation.

13.4 Operating Systems

Operating System
Classification

Batch Interactive Real time	Describe the role of job Control Languages and systems that combine batch and interactive modes.
Multilprogramming, multi-user, multitasking systems	Describe the principles of muldiprogramming.
Client–server systems, distributed file systems and network operating systems	Outline the principles of chentyserver operation. Explain the terms distributed file and network operating systems.

Operating System Concepts

User interface	Classify methods of user interface including command-line, graphical and job-control.
Memory Management	Outline how operating systems manage memory including the concepts of virtual memory and paging, code sharing (re-entrant code), dynamically linked libraries or DLLs.
File Management	Outline how operating systems manage file space. Explain the concept of an addressable block and the use of the file buffer.
I/0 Management	Outline the concepts of handlers and drivers and the use of interrupts.
Process/Task/Management	Explain the concept of a process, process states, threads and the need to schedule processes in a multiprogramming operating system.

A2 Module 5 – Advanced Systems Development

14.1 Applications and Effects

The applications of computing in a variety of contexts	These could include science, education, manufacturing industry, commercial data processing, publishing, leisure, design, communication, embedded systems, information systems, the Internet, artificial intelligence and expert systems. Candidates should: consider the purpose of the application; discuss the application as an information system in the context chosen; examine specific user-interface needs; examine the communication requirements of the application; discuss the extent to which the given system satisfies both organisation's and user's needs; discuss the economic, social, legal and ethical consequences of the application.

Generic Packages

Database, spreadsheet, word-processing, desktop publishing, presentation packages, expert system shells	As part of their skills development candidates should have sufficient experience of using a database to understand how a database management system controls access to the data via user views. In addition, they should be aware of how the listed packages facilitate the execution of particular tasks. Candidates should be able to assess suitability of a given package for a particular task as well as its limitations. Candidates should also appreciate how these packages might be integrated or share common data and be customised by the use of macros.
Social, Economic and Legal Consequences of Computerisation	Discuss issues of software failure such as in safety critical systems, errors in commercial transactions and error, caused by poorly specified systems. Discuss the possible effect, from a social, economic and legal point of view.

14.2 Databases

Database Concepts

Three level architecture of a DBMS External or user schema	Describe the structure of a Database Management System (DBMS). Distinguish between the use of a database and the use of a Database Management System (DBMS).
Conceptual or logical schema Internal or storage schema	Consider how a DBMS improves security and eliminates unproductive maintenance.
Program/data independence	
Concurrent access to data	Discuss how a DBMS overcomes problems that arise with multi-user access.
ODBC (Open Database Connectivity)	Explain the term and consider situations where it is used.
Data Definition Language (DDL)	Explain the terms DDL and DML. Candidates should be familiar with the use of a DDL to define a database.
Data Manipulation Language (DML)	
Database Design and the Relational Model	
Entity-relationship modelling Normalisation techniques	Illustrate the principles of database design using these techniques in the production of normalised tables that control redundant data, studied up to BCNF
Querying a Database	
Structured Query Language (SQL)	Illustrate the use of a Structured Query Language using the constructs Select, From, Where, GroupBy and OrderBy to extract data from several tables of a relational database.
Database Server	Define and explain the operation of a database server.
Object-oriented Databases	Define and explain the need for object-oriented databases. Candidates need to understand that databases may need to store complex data types and their associated methods of access.

14.3 Systems Development

Analysing a System

Fact finding techniques	Interview, observation, survey, examination of paperwork.
Reporting techniques	Data flow diagrams, Entity Attribute Relationship Modelling (EAR)
Data dictionary	Explain a data dictionary.
Volumetrics	Data volumes
	Characteristics of users
Designing a System	System flowcharts, prototyping, user interface design.
Testing Strategies for the development of a System	Top down, Bottom up; Black-box testing, white box testing, Unit testing, Integration testing.
System Implementation	
Conversion	Consider the problems that may arise when converting from the old to the new system.
Parallel, direct, pilot, phased	Describe the four main methods of converting from the old to the new.
System testing Acceptance testing	Define the different types of testing that may be applied to the developed system.
Alpha and beta testing	
Training	Consider the training needs for the new system.
Installation manual, user manual, operations manual, training manual documentation.	
Evaluation	Consider the purpose and timing of the evaluation.
Maintaining a System	Explain the need for maintenance.
	Consider the factors that affect the maintainability of a solution and evaluate a solution for maintainability in terms of the ease with which a program/solution can be corrected if an error is encountered, adapted if its environment changes, or enhanced if a customer changes requirements.

14.4 Hardware Devices

Input and output methods	Examine the role of computer devices in relation to both the nature and volume of the data being input and the characteristics of the user. Consider how the application influences the input method. Discuss the choice of output method in relation to applications and user needs, including the issue of whether printed reports, visual display, sound or other outputs are most appropriate. Consider how computers may assist in situations where the user may be unable to utilise conventional methods of input and output. Discuss situations where output may control machinery. Candidates should be able to select appropriate hardware by making an informed choice, rather than by learning a list of devices. Comprehension questions, based on contemporary devices and the principles of their operation and use, would be most suitable for this area of the syllabus.

14.5 Networking

Methods

Baseband and broadband modes of network operation	Define each method and illustrate where each is appropriate.
Synchronous data transmission Time-division multiplexing	
Circuit switching Packet-switching Datagram Virtual circuit	Describe and contrast the operation of these three network types – circuit-switched, packet-switched, ATM.
Asynchronous Transmission Mode (ATM)	
Standard Protocols TCP/IP protocol stack	Explain the concept and need for standard protocols both across a network and linking computers. Describe the layers of the TCP/IP protocol stack.
Sockets	Candidates should be aware that sockets can connect an application to a network protocol, such as TCP/IP.
Local Area Networks	
Types of cable	Twisted pair, baseband coaxial cable, broadband coaxial cable, optical fibre.
Topology	Define the term topology.
Bus	Describe in general terms the operation of these networks.
Ring	Compare the advantages and disadvantages of each.
Star	
Switched Ethernet and Hubs	
Segment	Define the term and explain why local area networks based on a bus topology are segmented.
Bridge	Define the term and explain why it is used.
Peer-to-peer networking	Explain what peer-to-peer networking is and compare with server-based networking.
Wide Area Networks	Contrast wide area and local area networks.
Electronic Data Interchange (EDI)	Describe EDI.
Value-Added Network (VAN) providers	Contrast private and public networks.
On-line service providers Internet Service Providers (ISP)	What is meant by an on-line service? Explain why such services are provided.

Internet

Connecting to a wide area network	Compare the various methods that may be used and consider where it would be appropriate to use each method.
Leased line ISDN	
cable modem dial-up line and modem Asymmetric Digital Subscriber Line (ADSL)	
CODEC	Short for Coder/decoder, a device that encodes or decodes a signal e.g. to convert binary signals transmitted on a digital network to analogue signal on an analogue network.
Inter-networking	Explain the meaning of the term inter-networking.
Routers / Gateways	Define these terms and consider where and why they are used. In particular consider how routing is achieved across the Internet and how local area networks are connected to the Internet.

The Internet and its Uses

World Wide Web (WWW) Internet registries and Internet registrars	Candidates should be familiar with the structure of the Internet and the facilities that it provides to users.
Client/server model of Internet	
HTTP protocol Hyperlinks	Candidates should be familiar with elementary syntax and use of by hypertext mark-up language.
Web site Web page construction	Candidates should have some experience of creating Web pages and be familiar with how Web pages can be organised on a Web site.
The organisation of Web pages on a Web site	
FTP	Candidates should be familiar with the use of FTP to transfer files such as Web pages from a local machine to a Web server.
Telnet	Candidates should be familiar with how Telnet can be used to manage a remote Web site or to access a remote machine including retrieving e-mail.
Role of URLs in retrieval of Web documents	
Internet search engines	Candidates should have some experience of using a search engine and understand its purpose.
Web browser Java and applets	Candidates should be aware of how applications may be executed on a Web site and how Java applets allow programs to be executed through browsers.
Active Server Pages (ASP)	Candidates should be aware that ASPs can combine HTML, scripts and components to create dynamic web pages. They will not be expected to be able to produce such a page.

E-mail Usenet Internet Relay Chat (IRC) Videoconferencing On-line shopping and banking	Candidates should be familiar with the use of these facilities, their advantages and disadvantages.
Moral, Ethical, Social and Cultural Issues	Candidates should be made aware of its use and misuse by individuals, or groups. The World Wide Web as a force of empowerment.
Security and the Internet	
Firewalls Encryption Digital certificates	Describe and explain the need for these in the context of the Internet and understand the issues that surround these.

A2 Module 6 – The Practical Project

15.1 Systems Development

Analysis

Data Flow Diagrams Entity Relationship data modelling E-R diagrams Object-analysis diagrams	Specify and document die data flow and the processing requirements for a system to the appropriate level and identify possible needs for the development and maintenance of the system. Establish the data requirements and produce a full conceptual data model from these, document any constraints and assumptions. Produce a preliminary data dictionary. Document any requirements for specific mathematical algorithms e.g. calculating interest payments.

Design

System Flowcharts Algorithm design Object-oriented design Hierarchy charts Structure charts Pseudo-code Relations	Consider and evaluate alternative ways of developing a solution to a problem on the basis of effectiveness, cost and ease of development and maintainability. Specify and document a design that meets the requirements of a real problem in terms of hardware and software, using methods such as system flowcharts, structure charts, hierarchy charts, pseudo-code, relations.
Prototyping	Consider the impact of prototyping on the design and development process.

Human–Computer Interface (HCI)	Good HCI design:
	    Considers
	
	        The User – type of use and context – e.g. business or home – User needs/ Usabilitw
	
	        Input/output devices – choice of and appropriateness of Dialogues to be relevant, simple and clear
	        Colour – use of and colour combinations
	        Icon usage and presentation – 3D effects and depth perception

Provides
    Feedback
    Exits – clearly marked
    On-line help
    Shortcuts
    Helpful error messages

Prevents errors occurring
Minimises the amount the user has to remember

Testing Strategies	Top down, bottom up; Black-box testing. White-box testing. Identify suitable test strategies and select and document suitable test data.
	Unit testing, Integration testing, System testing, Acceptance testing. Test solution and document the results of testing.
Construction / Implementation	Make use of appropriate software tools and techniques to construct a solution to a problem.
Maintenance	Develop and document a solution for maintainability. For maintainability a solution should be evaluated in terms of the easy with which it can be corrected if an error is encountered, adapted if its environment changes, or enhanced if customer changes requirements.
Evaluation	Evaluate methods and solutions on the basis of effectiveness, usability and maintainability.

Glossary

Acceptance testing	Testing carried out by the end user to ensure the system meets the specification set.
Access rights	Permissions set on a system/file that limit which users can use them and what they can do with them.
Accumulator	Special register at the heart of the CPU that handles all data that is to be used by the CPU.
Active server page (ASP)	A web page that can be updated online without reference to other software.
Address	A place either in main memory or possibly a register where data is either written to or copied from.
Address bus	A set of conductors (wires or pcb tracks) that connect the processor to memory. They carry details of the memory location that needs to be accessed.
Algorithm	A sequence of instructions designed to carry out a specific task.
Alpha testing	Testing a whole system 'in house' using test data. Attempts to test all possible situations.
Analogue	Data transmitted as a continuous variable signal.
Analogue to digital conversion	The process of converting analogue data into digital data.
Analogue to digital converter (ADC)	A piece of hardware that carries out the conversion from analogue to digital.
AND	Logical operation that returns a value of 'true' only if all inputs are true.
Append	Add to the end of – usually with reference to adding data to a file.
Applets	A small self-executing application.
Application software	Programs that are designed to carry out user tasks – what the computer is actually used for, for example, word processing, spreadsheets.
Arithmetic logic unit (ALU)	The part of the CPU that carries out calculations and compares values.
Array	A variable that has two or more elements with each element being addressed by an index. Often visualised as a table.
Artificial intelligence (AI)	Any computer system or program that attempts to mimic human intelligence.
ASCII code	An internationally recognised 7-bit code used to represent all of the keyboard characters.

Assembler	A program that converts assembly language into machine code.
Assembly language	Low level computer language based on mnemonics.
Assignment	Giving a variable or a constant a value when programming.
Asymmetric digital subscriber line (ADSL)	A technique for transmitting data to and from the Internet where an adapter is used to transmit digital signals at high speeds. More bandwidth is allocated to downloading than uploading.
Asynchronous data transmission	Sending data from one device to another where a start and stop bit are sent with each character.
Asynchronous transfer mode (ATM)	A method of communication that uses packet switching to transmit data of different types at very high rates.
Attribute	A field in a relational database (in databases).
Backbone	A high speed cable used to connect the main nodes of a network.
Backdoor	System set up by programmers that will allow them to access a password-protected system even if the master password has been changed.
Back-up copies	Copy of data kept remotely from the master files.
Bandwidth	The range of frequencies available for transmitting data.
Base register addressing	Very similar to indexed addressing. Address mode where the address that needs to be accessed is calculated by adding together the content of a register indicated by the first operand to the value of the second operand. Used to access the values held in variables in different programs in a multitasking environment.
Baseband	Data transmitted over a single carrier wave.
Basic input/output system (BIOS)	A series of instructions stored in ROM that contain the basic set-up instructions for a computer.
Batch	A type of operating system where jobs or tasks are processed one after the other.
Batch total	Integrity check that indicates how many records there are in a file.
Baud rate	A measure of the speed of transmission of serial data.
Bespoke software	Software written for a specific user to carry out a specific task.
Beta testing	Copy of a system sent to potential users to see if they can find any faults with it.
Binary coded decimal (BCD)	A method of representing denary numbers in binary form using blocks of four bits.
Binary digit	A zero or one.

Binary search	Search routine that checks the middle value in a sequential list, rejects the half that does not contain the search item, then repeats this process until the required record is found.
Binary tree	Dynamic data structure that can be visualised as a series of nodes with branches to the left and right that can lead to other nodes.
Biometric scanner	A device used to scan personal physical characteristics such as the retina or fingerprint.
Bit	A binary digit – a zero or one.
Bit rate	The number of bits that can be transmitted within a given time frame – usually measured in bits per second.
Bit-mapped graphics	A method of representing a graphic where the image is constructed from a series of dots (pixels).
Black box testing	Using test data then checking the results against what was expected/predicted.
Boolean	A variable that can be either true or false.
Bridge	A piece of hardware that connects two segments of a network together even where the topologies of the two parts are different.
British Computer Society (BCS)	A national organisation that represents the interests of everyone involved in the computer industry.
Broadband	Data transmitted over a number of carrier waves of different frequencies allowing larger amounts of data to be transmitted in the same time frame compared to baseband.
Bubble sort	Simple sort routine that works by comparing a sequence of adjacent pairs of data and swaps if needed. Also known as ripple sort.
Buffer	Section of memory set aside as a temporary store. Allows two devices that operate at different speeds (such as the keyboard and the CPU) to communicate.
Bus network	Workstations are connected to each other and to one or more file servers via one central cable shared by all workstations.
Buses	The collection of microscopic wires that connect the internal components of the computer.
Byte	A collection of bits – usually eight.
Cable modem	A device used to connect high speed coaxial or fibre optic cables to computers to allow Internet access.
Call	Line of a program that looks for, then starts up a procedure or function.

Carrier sense multiple access with collision detection (CSMA/CD)	A protocol used on Ethernet networks to prevent two items of data colliding when being transmitted though the cable.
CAT standard	The specification of twisted pair cable typically used in LANs.
Central processing unit (CPU)	The unit within the computer that carries out the 'fetch-decode-execute' cycle of instructions.
Centralised processing	Concept of using one central file server to carry out all the processing needed on the files it stores.
Certification authority	An organisation that authenticates digital certificates used on the Internet.
Check digit	Digit or character added to a field in order to check the integrity of the data.
Checksum	An integrity check that works by adding all the values of the characters in a block of data.
Child node	One point of a binary tree that stores data. There will be a 'branch' leading back up the tree.
Chip	A microprocessor or integrated circuit which is silicon implanted with millions of microscopic circuits.
Circuit switching	The process of establishing a fixed connection between two computers communicating over a network, for the duration of the communication.
Circular queue	A queue such that once the last place in the queue has been taken up, the next item of data goes in the first position in the queue.
Class	List of processes and facts that define a group of related data items in an object-oriented language.
Client–server network	A network of computers where one computer provides the data and resources (server) to the others (clients).
Clock	Device that generates a signal used to synchronise the components of a computer.
Clock speed	Measure of the number of synchronising pulses the systems clock generates each second.
Cluster	Smallest unit of storage space used in a secondary storage device.
CMYK	Cyan, Magenta, Yellow, Black – the four colours used to create all other colours when printing.
Coaxial	A type of heavily insulated cable used in networks.
CODEC	Coder/Decoder – a device that converts analogue data to digital and vice versa, and also compresses and decompresses data.
Comma separated variable (CSV)	A file format used for transferring data between applications packages. Fields are separated by commas.

Command line interface (CLI)	Operating system that is controlled by a sequence of commands typed in on a keyboard.
Compiler	Program that translates an entire high-level language program into machine code before it is executed.
Composite key	Two or more attributes combined to create a primary key in a relational database.
Compression software	A program that reduces the size of a file.
Computer	A programmable machine that processes data in digital form.
Computer Misuse Act 1990	Sets out rules relating to unauthorised access and damage to computer systems and data.
Computer program	A list of instructions that control the operation of a computer.
Constant	A value that does not change throughout the execution of a program.
Control bus	A set of conductors (wires, pcb tracks) that connect the components of the computer. They carry instructions between the various components of the computer and control the memory and data buses.
Control total	Integrity check that totals some value such as sales of a product. Sent as a separate data item that can be checked when the data is received. Unlike a hash total, a control total can be used for more than just checking the integrity of the data.
Control unit	Part of the CPU that manages the execution of instructions.
Counter	A variable used to count how many times a particular condition has been met.
Current instruction register (CIR)	Register that stores the instruction that the CPU is currently decoding/executing.
Data bus	A set of conductors (wires or pcb tracks) that connect the internal components of the computer – used to read and write data.
Data definition language (DDL)	Language used by a database manager to control the way that data is stored in a database via a data dictionary.
Data dictionary	File maintained by the DBMS that stores details of the logical data structure being used by a database.
Data flow diagram (DFD)	Graphical representation of a system that only deals with the how the data is used.
Data lock	Process of limiting access in some way to avoid two or more users trying to update the same item data.
Data manipulation language (DML)	Language that allows a user to access, sort and search the data in a database. SQL is an example of a DML.

Data/program independence	Where the data stored in a database is separate from the program used to access it.
Data Protection Act 1984/1998	Sets out rules relating to how personal data can be stored.
Database management system (DBMS)	A program that acts as an interface between a database and the programs that need to access it.
Database schema	The three ways of seeing a database – external, conceptual and logical.
Database server	A server that stores a database that is accessed remotely by the users. The database is kept centrally rather than copies being sent out to the users.
Datagram virtual circuit	The route that a packet will take when being transmitted around a network.
Datagram	Another term for a packet.
Declaration	Defining the name of a variable or constant that you intend to use in a program.
Declarative language	Programming language based on a set of data and rules that link the data together.
Defragmentation	Utility program that manipulates the physical organisation of a disk to maximise the space available and improve access times to files.
Denary	Number base 10.
Dial-up	A method for connecting to the Internet whereby the user dials in for access each time it is needed and the cost is based on the amount of time spent on-line.
Dictionary attack	Device used by hackers to try and break through a password. A program works through a dictionary, trying each word in turn on the password system.
Digital certificate	Authorisation that a web site is genuine.
Digital signals	Data transmitted as a sequence of zeros and ones.
Dimension	Same as 'declaration' – tells the computer the name of a variable or constant that you intend to use.
Direct access file	File structure based on fixed length fields/records that allows a program to access any given field directly.
Direct addressing	Address mode where the operand contains the address that it is to be accessed.
Distributed control	Different points of a WAN have responsibility for different tasks.
Distributed processing	Using a number of networked file servers, each of which controls its own distinct files and programs.
Dithering	A method of printing that can create high quality images without a high resolution.

Domain name	The part of the URL that identifies the web site to be accessed, for example, www.bbc.co.uk.
Double entry verification	A technique whereby data is entered into a computer system twice, and the two entries compared.
Dry run	To run through a program, or part of it, on paper.
Dumb terminal	A device or devices connected to a mainframe that have no processing power of their own – usually a screen and keyboard.
Dynamic data structure	Data structure that can hold varying amounts of data – it is the amount of data that can change rather than the data itself that makes a data structure dynamic.
Dynamic link library (DLL)	Library of commonly used programs or routines that are shared by a number of application packages.
e-commerce	Any commercial activity carried out on the Internet.
Electronic data interchange (EDI)	A technique for transmitting documents over networks where the format of the document is standard, for example, company invoices.
Electronic funds transfer at point of sale (EFTPOS)	The transmission of data from bank cards allowing automatic payment for goods when scanned at a checkout.
Electronic point of sale (EPOS)	The transmission of sales data from the checkout using the product bar code to a central database using a WAN.
Embedded systems	A computer system built in to another device.
Encapsulation	Concept of keeping data and its related processes together when using an object-oriented language.
Encryption	The process of turning data into a meaningless form using code so that if it is intercepted, it cannot be understood.
Encryption key	Short section of coded text used to encrypt data.
Entity	A table in a relational database (in databases).
Entity relationship (ER) modelling	Defining the nature of relationships between tables in a relational database: one-to-one, one-to many or many-to-many.
ER diagram	Entity relationship diagram – a method to show the nature of the relationship between entities.
ER modelling	Abbreviation of entity relationship modelling.
Ethernet	A method of constructing a LAN based on a bus network.
European article number (EAN)	A unique code encoded as a bar code and used on products.
Evaluation	Process of assessing a project to see if it has met the specification that was originally set.

Even parity	See parity bit. The parity bit is set either to zero or one to ensure that the total number of ones in the code is even.
Expert system	Software that contains a knowledge base provided by subject experts. The system can then be queried to help solve problems, for example, medical diagnoses.
Extended binary coded decimal interchange code (EBCDIC)	A method of representing data commonly associated with data stored on magnetic tape.
External components	The physical components of a computer that are not contained within the casing, for example, printer, screen.
Feasibility study	Examination of the alternative solutions to a problem, and the viability of each.
Fetch/decode/execute cycle	Cycle used by the CPU when it is executing a program.
Field	One item of data about a person or thing stored in a file.
FIFO	First in first out – the first item of data added to a FIFO structure will be the first to be taken out.
File	A collection of related data.
File allocation table (FAT)	Lookup table that stores details of files on a storage device. Kept on a secondary storage device that links the logical layout the user sees to the physical layout that the device uses.
File buffers	Section of RAM put aside to store blocks of data that are read in from a secondary storage device.
File management	The part of the operating system dedicated to managing any secondary storage devices that are linked to it.
File transfer protocol (FTP)	The set of rules that dictate the way in which files are downloaded from the Internet.
Filename	The name a user gives to a file when it is saved.
Firewall	Hardware and software used to prevent external hacking into a network.
Fixed field length	Field where a pre-determined amount of memory is put aside for a data item.
Fixed point number	A method of representing real numbers in binary form where the binary point remains in a fixed position during processing.
Flag	A variable used to indicate whether or not a condition has been met when programming.
Flat file (database)	Storing the contents of a database in a single file.
Floating point number	A method of representing real numbers in binary form where the binary point can move in either direction during processing.

Flowchart	Diagrammatic way of representing the processes that make up a system or program.
Foreign key	The attribute (field) that is placed in a table in a relational database in order to create a join with another table.
Format check	A validation check that ensures data is entered in a set format, for example, DD/MM/YY. Often referred to as a 'mask'.
Freedom of Information Act 2000	Sets out rules relating to access to personal data.
Frequency division multiplexing (FDM)	A technique that allows several separate transmissions to take place down the same cable at the same time. Each transmission uses a different frequency.
Function	Routine that returns a value based on data it is given when running a program.
Gateway	An access point to the Internet provided by an ISP.
General purpose software	Applications that can be used in a number of different ways, for example, word processor, spreadsheet.
Generations of files	Process of keeping old versions of a file so that data can be recovered if necessary.
Generic software	Another term for general purpose software.
Global variable	A variable that can be used throughout an entire program.
Grandfather/father/son	Name given to the generations of files used in an updating process.
Graphical user interface (GUI)	User interface that uses a WIMP (Windows, Icons, Mouse, Pointer) environment to control the software.
Hacker	Anyone who gains or attempts to gain unauthorised access to computer systems and data.
Handshaking	An exchange of signals between two devices before they can transmit and receive data.
Hardware	The physical components of a computer.
Hash total	Integrity check created by adding a set of values together. Unlike a control total, a hash total has no use beyond that of checking the integrity of the data.
Hashing algorithm	Processing the value of the primary key of a record to produce an address that can be used to access the appropriate record details.
Hexadecimal	Number base 16.
Hierarchical file structure	Concept of folders or directories which can contain files and/or other folders and so on. Sometimes shown as a tree diagram.
High-level language	Portable, programmer-friendly computer language.

Home page	The first page of a web site.
Hub	A device that sits between the workstations and the file server in a network. Also used to boost signals from the file server to the workstations.
Human–computer interface (HCI)	The part of the program that a user actually sees – the screen displays, buttons and graphics that the user uses to interact with a program.
Hypertext mark up language (HTML)	Text-based code that is used to define the contents and layout of a web page.
Hypertext transfer protocol (HTTP)	The set of rules that dictate the transmission of viewable content on the Internet.
I/O management	The part of the operating system dedicated to communicating with external device such as hard disk drives and monitors.
Immediate access store (IAS)	Another term for main memory or random access memory.
Immediate addressing	Addressing mode where the operand is the data that is to be used.
Imperative language	Same as procedural language – language based on a set of 'must do' commands.
Implementation	Process of converting a specification and design into a working computer system.
Indexed addressing	Very similar to base register addressing. Address mode where the address that needs to be accessed is calculated by adding the content of a register indicated by the first operand to the value of the second operand. Used to identify the values held in an array.
Indexing (databases)	The process of assigning numbers to all the records in a relational database so that their relative position in the file is known.
Indirect addressing	Addressing mode where the operand contains an address and the contents of that address in turn point to another address that contains the data that is needed.
Information	Data that has structure and therefore is of practical use to a user.
Inheritance	Process whereby one object 'inherits' all the data and processes from another in an object-oriented language.
Input device	Any piece of hardware used to get data into a computer from the outside world.
Input/output (I/O) controller	A piece of hardware that is the interface between the I/O devices and the processor.
Input/output (I/O) port	A physical connector made up of a series of pins on the computer that enables external devices to be connected.

Insert	Put a record in the correct place in a sequential or direct access file.
Instruction set	List of instruction codes and details of what the CPU needs to do if it receives each of those codes.
Integer	Whole number (positive or negative).
Integrated digital services network (ISDN)	A technique for transmitting data to and from the Internet, where an adapter is used to send the data in digital form so that no conversion is required.
Integrated package	Application software that includes elements of a number of general purpose packages, for example, a combined word processing, database and spreadsheet package.
Integration testing	Testing to see if the routines that make up a computer system can work together.
Integrity checking	Process of ensuring data has not been corrupted before it is used.
Interactive	An operating system that allows the user to have a dialogue with the computer.
Internal components	The physical components of a computer that are contained inside the casing for example, hard disk, processor.
Internet	A global network of networks, computers and other devices. Relates to the physical components and not the content.
Internet protocol (IP) address	The unique number that identifies any device attached to the Internet. Also relates directly to a domain name.
Internet registrar	An organisation that controls the use of domain names and IP addresses.
Internet relay chat (IRC)	Real-time typed conversations that take place with any number of users within chat rooms.
Internet service provider (ISP)	A company that provides users with a gateway/access to the Internet.
Inter-networking	The process of communication between networks
Interpreter	Program that translates and executes one part of a high-level language into machine code at a time.
Interrupt	Signal sent by a device or program to the CPU requesting its attention.
Interrupt register	Stores details of any incoming interrupts.
Intranet	An internal internet used within one institution such as a school.
ISDN adapter	A device that transmits data in digital form down an ISDN line.

Iteration	Program structure designed to repeat a process a number of times.
Jackson structure chart	Diagrammatic way of representing a system as a sequence of subsystems, and each of those subsystems as a number of systems and so on.
Job control language (JCL)	Language used to control the jobs or tasks in a multiprogramming operating system.
Key field	A field that contains data that uniquely identifies a record.
Leaf node	A point in a binary tree that has no other points leading from it.
Leased line	A method for connecting to the Internet whereby the user pays a fixed rate for the line, and they can use it as often as they need with no additional costs.
Least significant bit (LSB)	The right-most bit in a binary number.
Library program	An add-on program available to multiple users of the same system designed to carry out routine tasks associated with the main program.
LIFO	Describes how data is added to a data structure – last in first out.
Linear search	Search based on looking at each item in a dataset one after the other.
Linked list	A set of data where each item includes a pointer that shows which is the next item in the list to visit.
List	A one-dimensional array – literally a collection of data that can be viewed as a list.
Local area network (LAN)	A connection of computers over a small geographical area, usually one building or site.
Local variable	A variable that only exists inside a specific module or function.
Logic programming	Programming based on a set of data and rules that link the data together.
Look-up check	A validation check that ensures that data entered must appear in a predefined list.
Loop	Same as 'iteration' – program structure designed to repeat a process.
Low-level language	Collective name for machine code and assembly language.
Machine code	Sequence of zeros and ones that the CPU of a computer uses to represent data and instructions.
Machine-oriented language	Programming language designed to work with a particular CPU.

Macro	A commonly used routine or sequence of instructions that can be stored and then run using a single command.
Magnetic ink character recognition (MICR)	A method of scanning and identifying characters printed on a document, usually bank cheques.
Mail merge	The process of creating a standard letter using a word processor and then combining it with data stored in a database.
Main memory	Another term for immediate access store.
Mainframe	A computer with a large amount of processing power and storage capacity that connects to hundreds of terminals.
Maintenance	Processes needed to keep a computer system running.
Memory	Microchips used to store data.
Memory address	How memory is organised – a means of identifying the location where data can be sent to or retrieved from. Main memory is broken down into a series of memory addresses.
Memory address register (MAR)	Register that stores the location of the address that data is either to be written to or copied from by the CPU.
Memory data register (MDR)	Register that holds data that is to be either written to or copied from the CPU.
Memory management	The part of the operating system dedicated to managing the RAM of a computer.
Memory map	A diagrammatical way of showing how blocks of memory addresses have been allocated to different programs.
Menu-driven interface	Operating system that is controlled by the user selecting from a list or menu of options.
Merging	Process of creating a new generation file by combining parent and transaction files.
Metropolitan area network (MAN)	A connection of computers over an area between 1 km and 10 km.
Microcomputer	The original term for a personal computer.
Microprocessor	Also known as the central processing unit (CPU) it is a 'chip' that carries out all the processing of data and instructions.
Microwaves	Carrier wave used for mobile phones and satellite communications.
Minicomputer	A smaller version of a mainframe usually serving around 50 terminals.
Mnemonics	A system of abbreviated commands, such as LDA, used in assembly language.
Modelling	Re-creating real life scenarios on a computer.

Modem	A device that converts analogue data to digital and vice versa for transmission using telephone lines.
Modulus-11	Check digit system used on certain bar codes, such as the ISBN on a book, to ensure the code has been read correctly.
Most significant bit (MSB)	The left-most bit in a binary number.
Multi-access	An operating system that allows more than one user to access the same data at the same time.
Multiprogramming	An operating system that can allow more than one program to be executed at any one time.
Multitasking	Similar to multiprogramming but usually used to describe a home computer that can be running a number of tasks simultaneously.
Multi-user	Operating system that allows more than one user to access their files at any one time. Users seem to have unique access to the computer.
Musical instrument digital interface (MIDI)	A piece of hardware that allows musical data to be passed between a musical instrument and a computer system. The original data may be in digital or analogue form.
Natural language interface	Operating system that allows a user to either speak or type commands using normal, text-based phrases.
Nest	Concept of putting one iterative or selection process inside another when programming.
Network adapter	A piece of hardware that is fitted into a computer enabling it to connect to a network.
Network interface card (NIC)	Another term for a network adapter.
Network operating system	A suite of software that manages and controls the hardware and applications software which contains features specific to running a network.
Network printer	A printer that is shared by two or more computers across a network.
Network topology	The conceptual layout that identifies how the computers in a network will be connected together.
Nibble	Part of a byte – usually four bits.
Node (binary tree)	Each separate point in a binary tree.
Node (network)	Each point of a network, for example, each individual workstation.
Normal form (database)	A relational database that has been normalised.
Normal form (numbers)	A floating point number that has been normalised.
Normalisation (database)	The process of ensuring that a relational database has been set up as efficiently as possible.

Normalisation (of numbers)	The process of ensuring that a floating point number is as accurate as possible whilst allowing the greatest possible range.
NOT	Reverses a logical or Boolean statement so that true becomes false and false becomes true.
Object	Name given to all the data and the processes that will be used with it in an object-oriented language.
Object code	Machine code program that has been converted from either assembly language or a high-level language.
Object-oriented database (OODB)	Object-based database that can be used to store data such as sound and graphics.
Object-oriented language	Program based on the concept that all the data and the processes that will be carried out on it are kept together.
Octal	Number base 8.
Odd parity	See parity bit. The parity bit is set either to a zero or a one to ensure that the total number of ones in the code is odd.
Online banking	Setting up and maintaining accounts with a bank via the Internet.
Online service provider	A business that provides services on the Internet. Most ISPs are online service providers.
Online shopping	The purchase of products and services via the Internet.
Open database connectivity (ODBC)	A protocol that allows different database programs (such as Microsoft Access and Lotus Approach) to access the same database.
Operand	Numbers following the operation code in low-level programming that are interpreted either as addresses or data depending on the operation code they follow.
Operating system	Software used to control the actual operation of the computer itself providing an interface between the hardware, software and user.
Operating system software	A suite of software tools designed to set-up and maintain a computer allowing other application software to run.
Operation code	A command in a low-level programming language. The CPU looks the operation code up in an instruction set to see what to do with the operands that follow the code.
Optical character recognition (OCR)	A method of scanning written or typed text on a document and converting it into word-processed format.
Optical fibre	A type of insulated cable containing glass or plastic strands where data is transmitted as light rather than electricity.
Optical mark reader (OMR)	A device used to scan marks made on a page, for example, multiple choice exams.

OR	Logical operation that returns a value of 'true' if any of the inputs are true.
Output devices	Any piece of hardware used to get data from the computer to the outside world.
Overflow	Error caused by too much data being pushed on to a stack or queue, or the result of an arithmetic operation being too long for the register that stores it.
Packet	A portion of a data file – usually one part of a series of packets that, when re-assembled, make up a whole file.
Packet switching	A technique for transmitting data around networks where the data is split up into small units, transmitted separately and re-assembled at the other end.
Paging	Process of loading and executing just part of a large program in RAM. The rest of the program is loaded into RAM as and when it is needed.
Palmtop	A hand-held computer usually with a reduced set of features compared with a PC.
Paradigm	The way in which a programming language is organised.
Parallel processing	Process of using more than one CPU in a computer.
Parallel transmission	The process of sending data several bits at a time using a number of conductors (wires or pcb tracks).
Parameter	Mechanism for sending data to a procedure or function.
Parent node	Part of a binary tree that stores data and has branches down to other data stores called child nodes.
Parity bit	An additional bit added to a sequence of bits when transmitted. The extra bit is set either to a zero or a one depending on the number of ones in the code. It is used as a check to see if the byte has been transmitted correctly.
Partition	A section of a hard disk that the operating system 'sees' as another hard disk unit.
Pathname	Indicates the location of a file in a hierarchical structure – it shows the drive and folders that need to be accessed to reach the file.
Peer-to-peer network	A connection of computers where each workstation shares resources with the other – no one workstation is the server.
Peripheral	An input, output or storage device.
Personal computer (PC)	A stand-alone computer containing its own processing and storage capabilities.
Personal digital assistant (PDA)	Successor of the palmtop containing features associated with personal organisation, for example, diary, e-mail and a notepad.

Pixel	A picture element – the smallest graphical unit that can be represented.
Pointer	A variable used to indicate a particular element in a list or array.
Polymorphism	Where two (or more) objects share a common class in object-oriented programming.
Pop	The process of adding a data item to a stack.
Portable	A program that can be used with more than one type of CPU.
Presence check	A validation check that ensures data is entered into a field – sometimes known as a 'required field'.
Primary key	The attribute (field) that uniquely identifies each record within a table in a relational database.
Primary storage	Another term for immediate access store.
Print server	Server, or part of one, dedicated to controlling the print jobs being sent to a networked printer.
Private key	Part of a public/private encryption system. The receiver uses their private key to decrypt messages encrypted using a public key.
Problem-oriented language	Programming language designed to solve a particular type of problem.
Procedural language	Programming language based on a set of 'must do' commands. Same as an imperative language.
Procedure	A self-contained unit of code that carries out one or more related tasks.
Processor	Another term for a microprocessor or chip.
Program counter (PC)	Register that stores the address of the next instruction to be taken from main memory by the CPU.
Program/data independence	The concept that a database and the programs that are used to access it are independent of each other – altering the way the data is stored will not affect any of the programs that access the data via a DBMS.
Programming construct	Common commands that form the basis of any computer program using any language.
Protocol	A set of rules that ensure that data is transmitted between devices correctly.
Prototype	A cut down version of a system that can carry out all the major functions but lacks minor routines. Created to check the solution is going to work.
Pseudo-code	Sequence of instructions written in plain language that shows the flow of a program. Will need to be converted into a suitable computer language to implement it.

Public key	Part of a public/private encryption system. All senders get the public key but only the receiver has the decoder – the private key. Sender uses the public key to encrypt the data they are sending.
Push	The process of taking a data item from a stack.
Query by example (QBE)	A method of extracting data from a relational database.
Queue	A dynamic data structure that operates as a FIFO
Random access	Data can be retrieved in any order from any part of the storage medium.
Random access memory (RAM)	High speed storage used to run programs and temporarily store user's work.
Range check	A validation check ensuring data entry is between a lower and an upper limit.
Read only memory (ROM)	Storage on a microchip typically used to hold set-up instructions for the computer. Cannot be altered by the user.
Real	Collective name for all numbers – positive, negative, whole or decimal. Usually stored as a floating point number.
Real-time	An operating system where the computer must respond within a set time limit.
Record	Collection of fields about one thing or person in a file.
Recursion	Process of calling a procedure from within itself when programming.
Re-entrant code	Program designed to allow simultaneous use by two or more users.
Register	A very small section of temporary storage that is part of the CPU. Stores data or control instructions during the 'fetch-decode-execute' cycle.
Regulation of Investigatory Powers Act 2000	Defines the powers available to the police and other government agencies in relation to surveillance of telecommunications, and access to computer systems and data.
Relational database	Storing the contents of a database in a number of related tables.
Relationship	The connection that links two tables in a relational database.
Remote learning	Pupils and students interact from different geographical locations using different telecommunications technology.
Resolution	The clarity of an image either on the printed page or on the screen.

Resource management	Section of an operating system that controls resources such as processor time and memory.
Reverse engineering	The process of converting a program that is in machine code back into assembly language.
RGB	Red, green and blue – the three primary colours used to create all other colours in terms of light.
Ring network	One workstation is connected to the next which is connected to the next and so on. One of the workstations may be a file server.
Ripple sort	Another term for a bubble sort.
Root node	Starting point on a binary tree.
Router	Acts as a bridge between networks and also directs transmissions around different parts of the network.
Scheduling	An operation carried out by the operating system that decides the order in which to carry out tasks.
Search engine	A piece of software that lists web sites and web pages based on text enquiries input by the user.
Secondary key	A field that is not necessarily unique but can be used for searching in a relational database.
Security	Steps taken to ensure that computer systems and data are only accessed by authorised users.
Segment	Large LANs may be broken into smaller units to improve performance – each unit is a segment.
Selection	Program structure that bases a decision on a comparison, for example, an 'if' statement.
Sequential file	A collection of data/records that has been sorted in some logical way, for example, by a primary key.
Serial access	Data is retrieved by working through one item after another.
Serial file	Collection of data/records in, no particular order.
Serial transmission	The process of sending data one bit at a time.
Shift	Process of moving all the bits in a byte in a register, either left or right.
Socket	A virtual port that is created using software and enables a computer to be connected and recognised on a network.
Software	Any program or application run on a computer.
Software house	A company that creates software for other organisations.
Software suite	A number of programs sold together, for example, a word processor, spreadsheet, database and presentation package.
Sound sampling	The process of recording amplitude from an analogue wave at regular time intervals in order to re-create it in digital form.

Sound synthesis	The process of digitally re-creating analogue sound waves.
Source code	The code that is to be translated by an assembler, compiler or interpreter into object code which can be executed.
Speech recognition	Where the human voice is used to operate an application.
Spooling	Process of sending a file to a print server so that it can be sent on to a printer.
Stack	A dynamic data structure that operates as a LIFO.
Stack pointer	Pointer that indicates whereabouts in the stack the next item is to be popped/pushed.
Stand-alone computer	A computer that is not connected to a network.
Star network	Workstations have an individual cable that connects them to the file server.
Static data structure	Data structure that holds a set amount of data, even if some of the data is zero or empty.
Status register	Keeps track of various functions of the computer such as if the result of the last calculation was positive or negative.
Storage device	Any piece of hardware used to store data.
Stored program concept	The idea of storing a program in memory as a series of instructions that can be fetched, decoded and executed.
Structure charts	Diagrammatic way of representing a system as a sequence of subsystems, and each of those subsystems as a number of systems and so on.
Structured programming	Concept of breaking a program up into logical units.
Structured query language (SQL)	A language used for extracting data from a relational database.
Subroutines	Collective name given to routines/functions/procedures that make up a program.
Supercomputer	A computer with large amounts of processing and storage power designed to carry out specific complex tasks, for example, weather forecasting.
Synchronous data transmission	Sending data from one device to another where the clocks in both devices have been synchronised.
Syntax	The rules of a language.
System software	Programs designed to set up and manage the hardware and applications software and provide an interface with the user.
Systems flowchart	Graphical representation of a system showing a logical flow using symbols.

System life cycle	All the processes that a system goes through from the original problem to the evaluation. This then creates new problems and so the cycle starts all over again.
Technical documentation	Documentation that shows a user how to change the features and values used by a program.
Telnet	Software and protocols that allow remote access to a network.
Test data	Data put into a system where the expected outcome is already known.
The Copyright Designs and Patents Act (1988)	Sets out rules that prevent people copying from others – specific reference is made to software.
Threading	The path being followed by one user through a re-entrant code program.
Time division multiplexing (TDM)	A technique that allows separate transmissions to take place down the same cable at the same time by giving each user a time slice.
Time slicing	Method used by a CPU to allocate time to jobs in a multiprogramming operating system.
Top-down	System of taking a problem and breaking it down into smaller problems, then taking each of these smaller problems and breaking them down and so on until the problems become manageable.
Trace table	Table used to record the values held by variables as a programmer dry runs a program.
Trading partner	The sender or receiver of EDI.
Transaction file	File of records that will be merged with a master file or details of all the transactions that have been carried out on a direct access file. Used as a backup.
Transaction set	The contents of an EDI exchange.
Transistor	An electronic device that manipulates pulses interpreted as zeros and ones.
Transmission control protocol internet protocol (TCP/IP)	The set of rules that govern the addressing of computers on the Internet and the transmission of data across it.
Traverse	Process of working across a binary tree in order to extract the contents in some way – can be pre-, in- or post-.
Twisted pair	A type of cable used in telephone communications and for connecting computers and devices within a LAN.
Twos complement	A method of representing negative numbers in binary form.
Type check	A validation check that ensures that data entered is the correct type, for example, text or numeric.

Unicode	An alternative to ASCII as a method of representing the keyboard characters of many different countries in binary form.
Uniform resource locator (URL)	The way in which a resource on the Internet is addressed. It includes the protocol, domain name, and the name of the file, for example, http://www.awebsite.co.uk/index.htm.
Unit testing	Testing each individual unit before the units are put together.
Universal serial bus (USB)	A common connection method for external devices.
Unsigned integer	A positive whole number.
Usenet	An area of the Internet where users enter newsgroups, and post and read messages on a wide variety of topics.
User documentation	Documentation designed to allow an unfamiliar user to use a program.
Utility program	A program that carries out a specific housekeeping task on the computer.
Validation	Techniques used to ensure that data is input into a computer system in accordance with predefined rules.
Value added network (VAN)	A WAN owned by a company that then allows other organisations to use their WAN. It will contain additional features such as multiple mail boxes.
Variable	A value that can change during the execution of a program.
Variable field length	A field where the size of the data being stored dictates how much memory is put aside for that particular item.
Vector graphics	A method of representing graphics based on geometric proportions.
Vectored interrupt mechanism	Process used to locate the interrupt service routine required when an interrupt occurs.
Verification	Techniques used to ensure that data input from an external source is input exactly the same as it appears in the source document.
Video conferencing	Connecting remote computers using software and a video camera that allows all parties to see and talk to each other.
Virtual memory	Process of allocating a section of secondary storage (typically the hard disk) to act as part of the main memory.
Virus	Program written with the express intention of causing inconvenience or damage to a computer system.
Visual verification	Data entered into a computer system is manually checked against the source document.

Voice recognition	Where the human voice is used to operate an application.
Volumetrics	Details of the volume of data a system can be expected to cope with in a specific time period.
Web browser	A piece of software that enables users to view the contents of the WWW.
Web cam	A digital video camera.
Web hosting	Businesses that allow users to store web sites on their servers so that others can access them via the Internet.
White box testing	Testing every aspect of a routine/program in an effort to make sure it will not crash under any circumstances.
Wide area network (WAN)	A connection of computers over a large geographical distance.
Windows, icon, mouse, pointer (WIMP)	Describes the component parts of a GUI.
Word	A number of bytes joined together.
Word length	The length of a word measured in bits.
World Wide Web (WWW)	The collective term for all of the content available over the Internet.

Index